M000206032

Budgeting
for Public
Managers

Budgeting
for Public
Managers

John W. Swain and B.J. Reed

M.E.Sharpe
Armonk, New York
London, England

Library of Congress Cataloging-in-Publication Data

Swain, John W., 1948–
   Budgeting for public managers / by John W. Swain and B.J. Reed
     p. cm.
   Includes bibliographical references and index.
   ISBN 978-0-7656-2524-3 (cloth : alk. paper)—ISBN 978-0-7656-2050-7 (pbk : alk. paper)
   1. Budget—United States. 2. Finance, Public—United States. I. Reed, B.J. II. Title.

HJ2051.S93 2010
352.4′80973—dc22   2009023958

Printed in the United States of America

IBT (c)   10   9   8   7   6   5   4   3   2   1
EB (p)   10   9   8   7   6   5   4   3   2   1

Contents

Preface and Acknowledgments

Books reflect their authors' aspirations. We wrote this book with the singular purpose of helping Master of Public Administration (MPA) students understand public budgeting from a management perspective. Other texts in the field emphasize and focus on budget policies, federal budgeting, politics, reforms, policy elites, and other concerns where public managers' participation is peripheral. We believe that MPA students are best served by being presented with materials that relate to their current or future positions as public managers and to matters that do or will concern them. Our specific goals include the following:

- placing public budgeting into the larger context of public organizations;
- explaining historical developments in public budgeting, including reform efforts;
- presenting the revenue side of public budgets;
- describing the many possible aspects of annual budget processes;
- discussing how budgetary politics relates to public managers;
- detailing various ways of organizing and processing budget information;
- offering insight into the use of analysis in public budgeting;
- making public budgeting operating techniques intelligible; and
- illuminating economic insights into public budgeting.

We also aspire to cover all forms of public organizations, including federal, state, and local governments and nonprofit organizations; to write as clearly, concisely, and accessibly as possible; and to be topically comprehensive and practically oriented. We believe that our readers can better understand course materials that acknowledge the existence and relevance of all kinds of governments or nonprofit organizations. We believe that clear, concise, and accessible writing, although difficult and time-consuming, increases comprehension and facilitates using class time for discussing material instead of deciphering a textbook. We believe that public budgeting weaves so many different concerns into one process that students are poorly served when a public budgeting text is not topically comprehensive. Finally, we believe that MPA students as actual or potential public managers are interested in practice and that a public budgeting text oriented toward practice will serve them well. We certainly hope you find that our aspirations have been met.

We would like to thank especially those who helped in the preparation of this text. We thank Melanie Kiper at the University of Nebraska at Omaha; Sheryl Gallaher, Phyllis Anderson, and Cindy Matthias at Governors State University in University Park, Illinois; and Kathy Swain for their assistance. We thank the anonymous reviewers who gave their time to review the book proposal and parts of the manuscript. Finally, we thank our spouses, Kathy Swain and Chris Reed, for putting up with us while we worked on this text.

Budgeting
for Public
Managers

1

Introduction

Public Budgeting for Public Managers

A Practical Approach to Public Budgeting

This book differs from most other public budgeting texts by not focusing primarily on budgetary politics, budgeting reform, or federal budgeting. It focuses on how public budgeting relates to what public managers do. Here, a public manager is a person who exercises discretion in supervising the work of a public organization. By contrast, an executive is an elected or appointed official who engages in policy-making, as do board members and legislators. Managers at the upper levels of public organizations, often referred to as administrators, supervise other managers and interact more with policy-makers.

Public Budgeting Defined

Public budgeting means the acquisition and use of resources by public organizations. Acquisition of resources means finding and obtaining useful things, mostly money. For the most part, public organizations in the United States find resources in the private sector; they obtain these resources as taxes, fees, or gifts. Use of resources refers to how resources are spent to achieve public purposes. Resources can be spent on contracts to provide services, to provide direct funding to individuals and organizations, or to purchase input factors, such as labor, capital improvements, supplies, and equipment. The use of resources also refers to the purposes, ends, and functions of public organizations, such as education, public health, criminal justice, art appreciation, and safe travel. Public organizations pursue myriad purposes, ends, and functions that define their meaning. For example, the Scleroderma Foundation concerns itself with research, education, and support related to a chronic connective tissue disease.

Public managers acquire access to resources so that they can spend them by gaining policy-makers' approval of budget proposals. Policy-makers determine generally how resources are used by what they formally approve and by their informal guidance, and managers specifically determine how resources are used by their decisions responding to particular situations.

The Two Sides of Budgeting

Acquired resources are called revenues, and resources being used are called expenditures. Generally, public organizations deal with revenues and expenditures separately, which contrasts with how they are handled in the private sector.

Private sector revenues and expenditures relate closely and clearly. Expenditures are directly associated with production of a good or service for sale. The sale of products generates revenue. As a result, private sector enterprises expend most of their resources on the products and services that are most directly related to the production of revenues.

Expenditure and revenue decisions in the private sector are relatively simple. Revenues are determined by the number of units of a good or service that are sold and their selling prices. Expenditures are the resources purchased to produce products: for example, labor, capital, equipment, and land. The difference between revenues and expenditures is profit or loss. A number of factors complicate this simplistic description, but the basic points are accurate.

For the public sector, the relationship between revenues and expenditures is often neither close nor clear. Public organizations' revenues and expenditures mostly operate separately. Governments obtain revenues largely from taxes that are imposed on individuals and business. Specific tax revenues have little relationship to specific expenditures. For example, when federal officials evaluate how much to spend on national defense, the debate centers around external threats to national security, previous expenditures, and anticipated costs. When federal officials look for resources to support defense and other expenditures, they focus on how much revenue to gather to support total expenditures. Those revenue sources have little to do with the production of national defense products and services.

In the private sector, the price mechanism determines what products are produced. In the public sector, policy-makers mostly decide the kinds and levels of revenues and expenditures separately. Policy-makers express those decisions in budget documents. Governmental fees for such things as toll roads and entrance to national parks most closely mirror private sector price mechanisms. However, even where fee-for-service operations exist in public organizations, the fees often reflect only a portion of the actual expenditures for particular services.

The Public Budgeting Process

The public budgeting process can be divided into four general stages that occur sequentially: preparation, submission and approval, implementation, and reviews and reports. The four stages constitute a cycle from a beginning to an end with the stages following each other during distinct time periods, although some activities from each of the stages may overlap into following stages. Each cycle is named for the time period of its implementation, which is usually one year in length: for example, Fiscal Year 2015. Each budget cycle always overlaps at least two other budget cycles that are at different stages. For example, the implementation stage of one budget cycle always overlaps the reviews and reports stage of the previous budget cycle and the preparation stage of the succeeding budget cycle. Sometimes public managers work with three or four different budget cycles at the same time. Figure 1.1 shows a fairly typical pattern of overlapping budget cycles. Notice that the implementation stages follow each other.

The preparation stage formally starts when someone begins working to produce a budget for an upcoming fiscal year. Usually, a central office or central official creates and communicates a calendar of budgeting events, budget instructions, and perhaps preliminary revenue and expenditure estimates for the upcoming fiscal period to others in an organization. The instructions require managers to produce estimates of expenditures, usually in some specific degree of detail. Sometimes managers also estimate the likely results of the expenditures or revenues related to their operations.

Managers' budget proposals are mostly words and numbers indicating the costs of providing services. Administrators, executives, or both review those budget proposals and decide whether they approve each proposal. Unapproved proposals are revised. Eventually, a top-level executive or administrator produces a comprehensive budget proposal for a public organization. Comprehensive budget proposals usually contain estimates of revenues and expenditures, perhaps along with a general policy statement. Although some authors, policy-makers, and public managers emphasize managers' expenditure-estimating role in budgeting, managers remain active throughout the budget process.

The submission and approval stage starts when a comprehensive budget proposal is submitted to a policy-making body. This stage centers on policy-makers. They examine the comprehensive proposal and gather related information from formal and informal contacts with managers and other interested parties. Policy-makers usually discuss budget proposals in one or more meetings and may make changes in a proposal before formally approving it. The time and effort required for approval of a comprehensive budget proposal vary widely

Figure 1.1   **Overlapping Annual Budget Cycles**

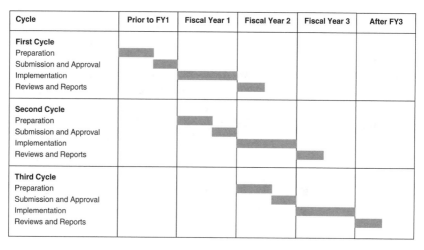

Cycle	Prior to FY1	Fiscal Year 1	Fiscal Year 2	Fiscal Year 3	After FY3
First Cycle Preparation Submission and Approval Implementation Reviews and Reports					
Second Cycle Preparation Submission and Approval Implementation Reviews and Reports					
Third Cycle Preparation Submission and Approval Implementation Reviews and Reports					

Note: FY = Fiscal Year.

among public organizations. Managers often adapt their budget proposals to this stage because gaining approval is required to make a budget proposal an expenditure reality. Changes in a comprehensive proposed budget are usually relatively minor compared to its overall size. This stage ends when policy-makers finish approving a comprehensive budget proposal.

The implementation stage starts when one or more central officials undertake actions to put an approved budget into effect. Managers, start your budgets! A key first step is communicating expenditure authority and any revenue-raising instructions. Some central official or office communicates expenditure authority to the highest level of managers in the operating units, perhaps with restrictions, and they in turn communicate expenditure authority down the organizational hierarchy, probably with restrictions. Although most revenue is collected from ongoing revenue programs, some budget approvals include revenue-raising instructions that a central official communicates to the appropriate places, which might be a central revenue-collecting entity or particular operating units that collect revenues. Then, managers supervise collecting revenue, making expenditures, and recording information on both. Although many authors, policy-makers, and public managers seem to believe that this stage is merely mechanical or clerical as managers follow the great ideas set forth for them by policy officials or high-level administrators, managers at all levels influence high-level administrators and policy officials into forming their great ideas, and public managers may ignore their organizational superiors to some degree in implementing budgets. Managers have a much greater range or degree of discretion in this stage than is generally understood. Otherwise, why are there so many public managers? If budget implementation were mechanical, robots could implement budgets. This stage ends when the collecting and spending stops.

The reviews and reports stage involves various people looking at a budget year to see what can be learned, and producing required and perhaps optional reports in connection with or independent of reviews. Parties internal and external to an organization conduct reviews. External reviews usually involve someone outside an organization conducting a review in a highly formal fashion to answer one or more specific questions in a written report. Internal reviews involve people within an organization or organizational subunit conducting reviews of a budget year in an informal fashion to answer the general question of what can be learned by looking at that budget year or specific questions; many such reviews are not reported on in any official fashion. Additionally, public organizations also generate reports, frequently required or expected, that are completely independent of reviews or that are intended to be the basis of reviews. Reviews and reports of past budgets may provide useful guidance for later ones. Examples of reviews include external financial audits conducted by accountants who examine annual financial reports from accounting systems to determine if accounting rules were followed and if financial statements reflect the financial condition of the organization, and informal reviews of a budget year by public managers concerning their own area of responsibility. Annual reports intended as a means of informing the public of the valuable public services provided by a public organization may be essentially free from an internal review process, but they may be the basis for reviews by others using the information provided.

Multiple Budget Documents

People often refer to "the budget" of a particular public organization as if that term referred to one specific document. The proper use of the term "budget" refers to the acquisition and use of resources generally and to a wide array of documents created and used in the various stages of the public budgeting process; no one document is "the budget." Knowing about the wide variety of different budget documents helps in understanding budgeting activities. Here, some common budget documents are described. The specific details of many of these documents vary greatly depending on their audiences.

During the preparation stage, central offices or officials produce documents meant to inform and guide others, and operating units prepare more detailed documents. A budget calendar shows a schedule of activities, often with deadlines and responsibilities. A call or call letter instructs managers how to prepare and present proposed budgets. A manager of an operating unit creates an expenditure proposal and perhaps a revenue estimate for revenues collected by that unit. Managers incorporate operating unit expenditure proposals and any revenue estimates into ever more comprehensive proposals that eventually become a final proposal. Meanwhile, a central office or official makes calculations for one or more documents showing estimates of general revenues, and operating managers may produce one or more revenue estimate documents relative to their operations; revenue estimate documents become incorporated into a comprehensive budget proposal.

During the approval process, an organization's policy-makers may work on one or many forms of budget proposals, either portions of a comprehensive proposal or competing alternatives. Also, policy-makers' staff may prepare documents that provide information or analysis. Policy-makers record their budget decisions in one or more approved budget documents.

During implementation, each organizational unit relies on at least one document derived from an approved budget document that indicates how resources can be collected and spent. Each organizational unit usually gets monthly or quarterly expenditure reports, and those concerned with the collection of revenues get monthly or quarterly revenue reports.

During the reviews and reports stage, managers produce financial reports, auditors produce audit reports, and managers responsible for reviews may produce other reports. In any case, memorandums and letters may flow before or after the reviews and reports.

Finally, some public organizations use separate capital budget documents for projects and equipment similar to other budget documents because capital items are considered particularly important. "Capital" here refers to long-lasting, expensive facilities and equipment. Such documents may be used in a regular budget process or a separate capital budgeting process. When public organizations deal with capital items separately during regular budget processes, they may use specialized capital item documents for proposing, submitting and approving, implementing, and reviewing and reporting. For example, expenditures on capital items over certain amounts may require separate justification documents. A separate capital budgeting process uses the same sorts of documents as the regular budget process, but only for capital items.

Multiple Participants

Many people and organizations engage in public budgeting processes, usually in typical roles. Here, "role" refers to expected actions or behaviors much like those of characters in plays. The role that a person or an organization plays in the process depends on organizational position or the relationship with a public organization. Typical roles can be thought of as internal, external, or both. Internal roles include those played by policy-makers, chief executive, chief administrator, central officials, managers, staff, union representatives, and employees. External roles include those played by interest groups, constituents, suppliers, and clientele. Courts, unions, and individuals with two different positions can take overlapping roles. Sometimes, it might seem as if a scorecard is necessary to keep track of all the players in the various roles.

Differences Among Federal, State, Local, and Nonprofit Budgeting

Although this book generally focuses on public budgeting similarities, some differences are consistent and significant. Nonprofit organizations differ from governments, and governments at the federal, state, and local level differ consistently from one another.

Nonprofit organizations, which number in the hundreds of thousands, both resemble and differ from governments. Nonprofit organizations resemble governments in serving public purposes, a requirement for governments affording them nonprofit status. Nonprofit organizations differ from governments in that they lack the power of taxation and focus more narrowly. The foci of nonprofit organizations include religion, ethnicity, geographic location, subject matters, professions, issues, and particular services. Nonprofit budgeting situations and practices relate to their foci and their need to obtain nontax revenues.

Nonprofit budgeting is generally characterized by small size, responsiveness to economic conditions, diverse compositions of revenues and expenditures, and relatively simple budgeting arrangements. Most nonprofit organizations are relatively small because they appeal only to a small portion of American society; even small local governments are larger than most nonprofit organizations because most nonprofit organizations are based on a geographic locality and some other attribute: for example, local churches or the Friends of the Flossmoor Library. Nonprofit organizations respond to the specific economic conditions of their revenue sources. Like private organizations, nonprofit organizations have to sell someone on their services in order to gain the revenues that make their expenditures possible.

The composition of revenues and expenditures for nonprofit organizations may seem surprising. Most nonprofit revenues are fees for services rather than donations. Grants, which are essentially service contracts in many cases, and donations generate an approximately equal amount of revenue for nonprofit organizations. Of course, some organizations rely exclusively on fees, grants, or donations. Nonprofit organizations mostly spend on input factors to provide services, such as education and health services, which generate fees. Even donations can be seen as linked to the expected performance of particular activities, such as religious services by churches and lobbying efforts by advocacy organizations. Levels of expenditures relate directly to revenue levels.

Nonprofit organization budgeting is simpler than governmental budgeting because of fewer constraints and more directness in dealing with changing situations. Nonprofit organizations do not follow the many budget-related laws that constrain governments, including difficult-to-change annual budgets. Nonprofit organizations adjust their budgets as conditions change.

Budgeting in the federal government is unique because of its size, its frequent large deficits, its composition of revenues and expenditures, and the degree of technical complexity involved. The U.S. government is the largest financial entity in the world; it frequently spends significantly more than it collects. Both its size and the frequent large deficits are made possible by its being the national government for the world's largest economy.

The composition of the revenues and expenditures of federal budgets involves things that are familiar and unfamiliar. Income taxes are familiar; they make up 70 to 80 percent of federal revenues. Other revenues serve particular purposes (postal fees), represent a historical tradition (taxes on liquor), or resulted from a particularly good opportunity to collect revenues (telephone tax, a tax on the rich passed in 1898 to pay for the Spanish-American War).

Most federal expenditures differ from those of other public organizations, common understandings of expenditures, and tradition. For most public organizations, in the minds of most people and historically, budgeted expenditures pay for goods and services that are used in providing public services to improve citizens' situations. Now, most federal expenditures are for programs and policies designed to shape behavior by transferring money, although many programs and policies operate based on purchasing things, with defense being the largest example. Examples of transfer programs include Social Security, aid to state and local governments (mostly grants), Medicare, Medicaid, and agricultural price support payments. Additionally, two other kinds of federal "expenditures" do not appear the same way as expenditures in budgets or in public perceptions: revenue expenditures and credit support. Both have the same kind of impacts as behavior-focused expenditures. Revenue expenditures, mostly tax-related, are revenues that would be owed but that are not collected because a person or an entity shows some behavior or status. For example, the deduction from the federal personal income tax for home mortgage interest expenses effectively means that the federal government is paying people to buy homes by not collecting tax monies. The federal government expends much more on that particular tax provision for private housing than it does for public housing. Credit support refers to a variety of arrangements by which the federal government makes, subsidizes, guarantees, or otherwise facilitates loans. Borrowers who receive federal credit support obtain loans that they would not otherwise be able to get, obtain loans at a lower rate than borrowers without federal credit support, or both. The federal government provides credit support for student loans, deposits in financial institutions, small business loans, home loans, and most recently automobile companies and financial institutions under the Troubled Asset Relief Program (TARP). Sometimes the federal government ends up having to pay for loan losses. The collapse of the savings and loan industry in the 1980s cost the federal government approximately $125 billion by 1999, according to the Federal Deposit Insurance Corporation. The Congressional Budget Office estimates that the value of federal government subsidies in the TARP program at approximately $159 billion, including $50 billion for home foreclosure mitigation; see "The Troubled Asset Relief Program: Reports on Transaction Through June 17, 2009."

Federal budgeting is highly technical because of its uniqueness, associated tangential requirements, and responsibilities. Federal budgeting terminology is unique; learning federal budgeting more closely resembles learning a foreign language than anything else, even for people familiar with budgeting. The federal government provides a two-day introductory workshop for employees on the basics of federal budgeting. Federal managers have to fulfill many tangential requirements that are formally related to budget proposals: for example, reports on information technology, motor vehicle fleets, and energy efficiency management. The federal government deals with a wide variety of complex substantive areas, such as environmental regulation, medical care, and various research programs. Also, it deals with hard-to-predict situations that involve singular events, such as war and major economic events, and actions beyond the federal government's immediate control, such as the national economy and the number of people taking advantage of a particular transfer program or a revenue expenditure provision.

State budgeting is characterized by large size, responsiveness to economic conditions, particular compositions of revenues and expenditures, and a significant degree of complexity. State budgets are large, in the range of the largest businesses and foreign governments. Because of constitutional or statutory requirements, states do not routinely run large deficits; they respond to economic conditions and maintain budgets that are mostly balanced.

States use familiar compositions of revenues and expenditures. They rely on a variety of revenue streams, mostly income and consumption taxes, federal aid, and fees. States spend resources primarily for traditional services within the realm of police powers; that is, actions for the sake of public welfare, health, safety, and morals. The largest areas for state expenditures include legal systems, health care, corrections, welfare, education, and transportation. States transfer much less of their budgets than the federal government.

State budgeting is complex because of state responsibilities. However, states differ from the federal government in respect to having smaller budgets for relatively routine programs over which they have greater formal control.

Local government budgeting, which displays much diversity, differs from state and federal government budgeting. The more than 80,000 local governments vary greatly among themselves in respect to responsibilities and size, as well as specific revenues and expenditures. The responsibilities and financial size of local governments depend on the kind of government and the size of their population and territory. One key difference is what a government is created to do. When created under the authority of states, a local government is one of five basic kinds given specific responsibilities under state laws, revenues sources, and budget requirements. Municipalities—cities and villages—are most visible. They provide urban services to population concentrations. Counties exercise powers delegated by states for specific territories. Townships range from essentially municipal operations to subdivisions of counties with one or a few significant responsibilities. School districts provide educational services. Special districts provide a wide range of services, such as recreation, street lighting, irrigation, and transportation. Very few district governments deliver more than one type of service. Local governments provide day-to-day services and facilities needed by their communities, including public safety, public works, public health, and public education.

Local government budgeting differs from state and federal budgeting in respect to size, responsiveness to economic conditions, composition of revenues and expenditures, and complexity. Because of narrower responsibilities and smaller territories and population, local budgets tend to be much smaller in size than state budgets, excepting the largest local units of government, such as Los Angeles County and New York City. Local budgets respond to economic conditions because of limited resources and limited borrowing authority.

The composition of local revenues and expenditures is determined by each state government. Local governments, often referred to as subdivisions of states, generally exercise only expressly delegated powers, including revenue collection powers. States create revenue systems for themselves and their local governments, which generally result in states having better revenue sources. States assign revenue sources to the different local governments in highly defined terms; for example, what revenues can be collected on and the procedures that must be followed. Local revenues come primarily from state and federal aid, property taxes, and fees. Some local governments rely on one primary revenue source, and others use a wide variety. Local governments spend primarily on input factors to provide services.

Local government budgets generally display less complexity than other governmental budgets because they are smaller, cover fewer services, and involve fewer people. Some small local governments may budget only because of state requirements.

Perspectives

People differ in the perspectives that they take on budgeting. Perspectives on budgeting reflect what people see or expect in budgeting and what they hope to accomplish through it. Three themes and five values are associated with budgeting perspectives. Different perspectives can be associated with different behaviors, including ways of speaking about budgeting. The themes and values may be seen as competing with one another in their groups as individuals generally express one dominant theme and one dominant value.

The three themes are control, management, and planning. People express the control theme in being concerned about the details of expenditures. People displaying this theme tend to see accountability in terms of spending behavior and to monitor expenditures in terms of what is purchased (were the correct number of specific pieces of equipment or specific kinds of supplies purchased as indicated in the budget?). Local elected officials most commonly express this budgeting theme.

People express the management theme by being concerned with achieving well-executed programs and policies through the selection of appropriate means. People displaying this theme tend to see accountability in terms of managerial performance (were the available resources managed well to achieve results?) and in terms of the relationship between money spent on purchases and resulting outputs (were streets swept or people counseled?). Public managers and public administration students tend to express this theme.

People express the planning theme through their concern for linking activities to long-term goals. People displaying this theme tend to see accountability in terms of reaching long-term goals (did the services performed achieve the desired outcome?).

The five values are economy, efficiency, effectiveness, responsiveness, and social equity. The economy value, often associated with the theme of control, refers to minimizing expenditures. The value of efficiency, often associated with the theme of management, involves maximizing outputs for a given level of spending. The value of effectiveness, often associated with the theme of planning, emphasizes achieving desired outcomes. The value of responsiveness refers to public organizations doing what their constituents want them to do; people with this value want to see budget priorities reflecting constituents' preferences. The value of social equity refers to the desire of some to use budgets as a means of making social conditions fair, often by redistributing wealth from the more affluent to the less affluent. What theme(s) and value(s) do you prefer?

Topical Outline

The following eight chapters cover the key substantive areas of budgeting. The material in each of the chapters overlaps and intertwines with information from other chapters and has been organized here for the sake of presenting the material in a logical order.

Chapter 2, "Historical Development of Public Budgeting," presents a sequential account of developments in budgeting. The focus is on historical developments in regard to budgeting practices rather than merely nifty ideas. The key historical trends have been shifting political dynamics and the increasing use of new technologies, particularly ones for manipulating information.

Chapter 3, "Sources, Characteristics, and Structures of Public Revenue," covers different perspectives on public organizations acquiring resources, criteria used to evaluate revenue sources, managers' revenue activities, revenue sources, and overall revenue structures. Revenues supply the resources to produce programming and should be a concern for that reason.

Chapter 4, "Public Budgeting Processes: Annual, Episodic, and Standing Policies," explains the common steps in budget processes in detail. The chapter shows who does what, to whom, and when, illuminating the whole temporal sequence of budgeting events. Public managers participate in those events and are affected by their outcomes.

Chapter 5, "Politics Within Public Budgeting," outlines the possibilities of action and reaction by public managers, the different political roles of political actors in the budgetary process, and common political strategies generally available to public managers. Politics is essential to budgeting. Managers need to concern themselves with budgetary politics. This chapter also contrasts the traditional and the reform perspectives on budgeting politics, which differ on public managers' proper political role.

Chapter 6, "Organizing Concepts for Expenditure Budgets: Formats and Approaches," goes into general conceptualizations of budgeting formats and approaches and the practical details of producing an expenditure budget proposal by providing examples of formats for five major budgeting approaches and specifying how the approaches work. For example, the line item budget format results from using the line-item budgeting approach. The formats have similarities and differences as the approaches are designed for the same and different purposes. The chapter emphasizes what is actually done rather than fancy academic or reform theories about how using a particular approach results in budgeting beautification.

Chapter 7, "Analysis in Public Budgeting," illustrates various methods used in public budgeting with an emphasis on kinds of analysis that practicing managers can realistically expect to do themselves. Although elaborate research projects may be called analysis, the only kinds of analysis that are regularly used by public managers are the kinds that they can do themselves or get done by others relatively easily. The chapter lays out four basic conceptual models and provides practical examples to illustrate their use.

Chapter 8, "Routine Operating Techniques in Public Budgeting," which are ways of doing things, introduces budget-related activities. Those techniques include accounting, forecasting, handling resources, purchasing, dealing with personnel costs, auditing, dealing with risks, and capital budgeting. The chapter emphasizes what the techniques are used for and the basics of using them. For example, public organizations use accounting to keep track of budget information in specific categories. The most important accounting categories for managers are how much they can spend, have spent, and still have available to spend.

Chapter 9, "Economic Explanations in Public Budgeting," discusses the economic roles carried out by public organizations; the economists' view of public budgeting, which usefully describes budget consequences; and the federal government's role in managing the national economy.

Because we see this text as a starting point for learning about public budgeting and closely associated topics, we offer a section at the end of each chapter labeled "Additional Reading and Resources." These readings and resources provide more content related to specific chapters. We divide them into readings in print and Internet-based resources. Generally, the readings provide more depth, and the Internet resources provide more current information. These readings and resources are briefly annotated to indicate what they have to offer. We recommend these readings and resources. The readings especially have informed our understanding of public budgeting, and the Internet resources are reliable and trustworthy sources of current information.

Additional Reading and Resources

Print

Textbooks commonly used in public budgeting courses include:

Finkler, Steven A. *Financial Management for Public, Health, and Nonprofit Organizations.* 3rd ed. Upper Saddle River, NJ: Prentice Hall, 2009.

Lee, Robert D., Jr., Ronald W. Johnson, and Philip G. Joyce. *Public Budgeting Systems.* 8th ed. Sudbury, MA: Jones and Bartlett, 2008.

Lynch, Thomas D., and Robert W. Smith. *Public Budgeting in America.* 5th ed. Upper Saddle River, NJ: Prentice Hall, 2003.

A collection of classic articles on public budgeting:

Rubin, Irene. *Public Budgeting: Policy, Process, and Politics.* Armonk, NY: M.E. Sharpe, 2008.

A journal that discusses current issues in the area of budgeting, published by the Association for Budgeting and Financial Management Section of the American Society for Public Administration and the American Association for Budgeting and Program Analysis:

Public Budgeting & Finance.

Internet

U.S. Government
The U.S. government's official web portal for federal, state, U.S. territories and outlying areas, local, and tribal government websites, many of which display links to budgets or search facilities that can be used to find budget-related information, is at www.usa.gov.

The City of San Diego: Annual Budget
The budget site for San Diego, California, is www.sandiego.gov/fm/annual/.

Church Budgets
Budgets for some churches can be found on the Internet. An annual budget can be found on the home page of the Episcopal Diocese of West Tennessee at www.episwtn.org/diocesan_convention.html.

National Association of State Budget Officers
The National Association of State Budget Officers website provides a variety of information, including links to state budget offices, at www.nasbo.org and www.nasbo.org/directoryPublicDirectory.php.

National Governors Association
The National Governors Association provides budget-related information on its website. The easiest way to access budget information at the website is to use one of the two search boxes found on the home page, one general and one focused on best practices at www.nga.org.

National Conference of State Legislatures
The National Conference of State Legislatures website provides a wealth of information from a legislative perspective. The home page includes a search box, and the site contains many documents and pages explicitly related to budgeting and the latest fiscal (budget) information in the states: www.ncsl. org/index.htm and www.ncsl.org/programs/fiscal/fskllink.htm.

U.S. Government Budget Offices
The president's budget office, the U.S. Office of Management and Budget, is at www.whitehouse.gov/omb/.

Congressional budget-related offices—the Congressional Budget Office (CBO)—are at www.cbo.gov, and the U.S. Government Accountability Office (GAO) is at www.gao.gov. The CBO deals more with proposals, including issue analysis; the GAO provides reports and testimony in many different areas. An example of a CBO report is The Troubled Asset Relief Program: Reports on Transaction Through June 17, 2009, at www.cbo.gov/ftpdocs/100xx/doc10056/06-29-TARP.pdf.

U.S. Government Printing Office
Searchable databases of U.S. government publications, including current legislation, are at the U.S. Government Printing Office Access Home Page at www.gpoaccess.gov.

2

Historical Development of Public Budgeting

The study of budgeting history provides an opportunity to see how present-day budget practices came into existence. Present-day practices make more sense when one understands the historical circumstances from which they arose.

The linguistic path taken by the English verb "budget" from the French noun "bougette" exemplifies historical changes. "Bougette" originally referred to a pouch or bag used to hold coins when the French-speaking Normans ruled England and later to the pouch carrying documents from an English monarch requesting money from Parliament. Later still, the term referred to requesting documents themselves. Now, budgeting refers to activities concerning the resource acquisition and utilization decisions denoted in budget documents.

Public budgeting has changed over time due to gradual shifts and explicit reforms. The significance of gradual shifts may be recognizable only after periods of time, but advocates argue for the advantages of reforms. Changes may be classified as political or technical depending on whether they are oriented toward politics or techniques. Political reforms affect the distribution of political power, the budgeting process, and the results of budget decision-making. Political reforms occur with changes in who has political power, the sequence of budgeting decisions, and shifts in the composition of revenues and expenditures (who, how, and what). Technical reforms involve new ways of gathering and processing information. Examples include accounting for revenues and expenditures, calculating whether expenditures exceed revenues, and forecasting revenues.

The Beginning Period

Public budgeting emerged after thousands of years of rulers making decisions about collecting and using resources. Rulers were constrained by the extreme scarcity of resources and their ability to secure compliance from their subjects. Revenues initially included labor, land, products of the land and sea, and scarce goods. The development of money allowed rulers to collect money or to convert other goods into money, and to borrow. Expenditures were used for the support of ruling households, war, public works, religious and cultural institutions, and food in time of famine. Recurring revenue and expenditure decisions became customary in many places.

Public budgeting developed from England's unique political history. Various Germanic tribes conquered parts of England beginning in the fifth century as the Roman Empire receded. The Normans, a Germanic tribe (Norsemen from the "northlands") living in the Normandy portion of present-day France for about a century, concluded successful invasions by conquering all of England in 1066.

Germanic tribes were defined by kinship or family relationships; organized by their warriors' personal loyalty to specific leaders, some of whom were elected; and guided by customs and traditions. During the fifth- and sixth-century invasions, each tribe was able to control only a small territory in England because of the tribes' mode of organization and numbers. Tribal warriors were essentially free, landholding men who participated in governance by collectively providing advice and consent to leaders. Leaders who lost the support of tribal warriors commonly lost their leadership position. Leaders held large tracts of land from which they were expected to support their personal and leadership activities. Other landholders owed military service to their tribes and their leaders during times of war. Gradually, kings descended from the Germanic invaders conquered each other's territories until one English kingdom emerged.

The Norman kings introduced a secular nobility based on large-scale landholding (initially land holdings were distributed within their political-military hierarchy). Landholders were obliged to provide military manpower according to the amount of land that they held. Norman kings remained dependent on the warrior class, especially the large landholders who acquired subordinate followers by distributing land to others. Christianity came to England during the Roman period and during the period of invasions by Germanic tribes, and Norman kings distributed land to the Roman Catholic Church and had Normans appointed to English leadership positions within the church, thereby creating a spiritual nobility with military obligations. Large landholders, including the spiritual nobility, essentially ruled their own territories subject to limitations imposed by kings.

English kings made decisions and issued decrees. However, they consulted with an assembly of great or wise men on far-reaching decisions and most likely considered the effects of their decisions on their followers.

The Germanic kings did not use taxes. They relied on "ordinary" revenues. "Ordinary" revenues came from royally owned land that was sold or used to produce goods, feudal obligations, and royal prerogatives. Feudal obligations included labor, supplies, food, and lodging. Royal prerogatives that generated revenues included coining and, occasionally, debasing money; the sale of offices, honors, monopolies, and town charters; resources from the wealth of the church; the collection of penalties; and the control of land ownership in cases where ownership shifted or was disputed. Monarchs concerned themselves with the transfer of land ownership because land was the basis of military service and wealth. Additionally, kings could borrow or accept gifts. When rulers asked for loans or gifts, those being asked might suffer a variety of harms, including loss of property, exile, imprisonment, or death, whether they made a loan or gift or not. At best, a loan might be repaid.

Taxation appears in Norman-ruled England in the ninth century. English kings collected money from landholders to pay tribute to Germanic tribes residing in Scandinavia, which continued on and off until the twelfth century. Those collections were considered consensual rather than representing a right of kings to impose taxes. Under the Germanic English kings, such taxes were considered "extraordinary" revenues that were used for special occasions (weddings, funerals, coronations, and especially wars). Beginning in 1159, English kings moved toward monetary taxes when they established "scutage"; they allowed landholders obliged to provide military service to discharge that service by paying money instead, and the monarchs then paid that money to soldiers.

Some Norman kings spent more than they could afford using ordinary revenues and raised other revenues by forcing loans and gifts, selling justice (taking bribes to decide legal cases or bringing people to trial in order to confiscate their property), interfering in land control situations, and levying new taxes without following the custom of consulting with their subjects. Their subjects, objecting to the new revenue practices, sometimes engaged in armed conflict. In 1215, a group of barons supported by many church and town officials met with King John in Runnymede, where both sides signed the Magna Carta.

The Magna Carta explicitly prohibited many objectionable revenue-related practices and required that all new revenues be approved by a council of barons. Modern public budgeting evolved from the requirement that English monarchs gain approval from another entity for new revenues. The council of barons eventually evolved into the English Parliament, which represented citizens more generally. The requirement that Parliament approve new revenues led to its power to approve expenditures.

Both modern budgeting and a modern representative government using public policy processes based on laws evolved from the Magna Carta. Public budgeting replaced ad hoc, autocratic, and personal financial decision-making by absolute rulers. The English innovated in the areas of politics, revenues, expenditures, techniques, and institutions. Although those innovations are historically intertwined, they are discussed here separately for the sake of brevity.

Politically, the English made their Parliament increasingly representative and therefore more democratic as they added elected representatives in the House of Commons, increased the power of that House, and widened who could vote for a representative in that House. The English monarch's kingdom eventually became the English nation, which joined with Scotland to become Great Britain in 1707. Parliament used its power over approval of new revenues to gain the power to approve expenditures and to make monarchs propose and justify revenues and expenditures for approval every year. Gradually, officials chosen by Parliament ("the government") supplanted the monarch's role in public affairs as governing replaced ruling. The resources of the monarch and those of the nation became separated so that the government controlled the nation's resources.

Although revenues continued to be personal, customary, and/or consensual after the Magna Carta was signed, the English moved toward employing revenues that were more consensual than personal or customary. Parliament specifically regulated revenues (e.g., the tax on the wool trade in 1275). It increasingly specified the purposes for revenues (e.g., taxes for war with Scotland in 1348 and 1353). Although Parliament levied some permanent taxes on specific products, it did not impose permanent taxes on land, personal property, or income until 1660. Then Parliament began to replace some of the monarch's "ordinary revenue" with annual stipends of fixed value (e.g., 700,000 pounds). In exchange for the stipend, the monarch gave up the right of the monarchy to collect some portion of their "ordinary" revenue. By 1760, monarchs no longer had any "ordinary" revenue, and Parliament levied all British revenue measures.

In the area of expenditures, Parliament moved from approving expenditures for special occasions, such as war, by approving new revenues to approving expenditures in general terms to approving expenditures in specific terms for all aspects of government annually. Initially, the approval of revenues sufficed for the monarch to make expenditures. Then, Parliament specified the expenditure purposes of revenues, usually war. In 1376, some members of Parliament publicly accused royal officials of fraud and corruption in spending revenues. Parliament then began occasionally putting conditions on appropriations; in 1390, some appropriations were for prosecuting the current hostilities and some for future hostilities. England's Hundred Years' War with France (1337–1453) led to annual meetings of Parliament for annual approval of revenues for the purpose of war and greater Parliamentary interest in how monarchs handled resources. In the 1600s, Parliament took greater control over expenditures, met annually to make appropriations, and prohibited using appropriations for any purposes other than the stated ones. The Restoration of 1660 was a key event in English budgeting history following the Puritan Revolution. The English monarchy, the Parliament, and the Church of England were restored to power following a civil war that was initially between Parliament and King Charles I and then between Parliament and its victorious army that resulted in the hanging of the king and the establishment of a religious-based republic under Oliver Cromwell. The restored Parliament, with monarchial support, increased taxation as noted above in order to appropriate annually for a standing army, because both Parliament and the monarch had reasons to fear a permanently funded army, and began the practice of appropriating money to pay for the salaries of people who worked for the monarch, referred to under the name "The Civil List." In 1760, Parliament took control of all governmental expenditures. After the signing of the Magna Carta to 1760, when Parliament was concerned about the handling of resources and in a position to do something about that concern, it increasingly tended to examine the actions of the monarch and the government more closely, require more information, and provide appropriations under stricter rules.

English rulers and governments imported and developed a wide variety of techniques (i.e., ways of accomplishing results) and institutions (i.e., organized patterns of human activity) to implement techniques. For example, the political technique of approval of new revenues used by the political institution called Parliament has been noted. The Normans brought the practice of accounting carefully for revenues in public forums. English monarchs established the practice of having their money held at one place for the sake of convenience in paying for resources. Parliament required monarchs to report on revenues and expenditures and examined and criticized those reports. The English borrowed money based on the example of the Dutch by having Parliament commit the nation to repaying loans from national resources; by doing so, the English nation paid much less to borrow than monarchs, who had historically been bad credit risks. Beginning in the early 1600s, the English started using the idea of one pot of money to account for the collection and spending of public monies, which they called the General Fund. Parliament later required that the revenue and expenditure records associated with that one pot of money be kept in one place and still later required that information to be published annually. The English developed separate institutions to handle public monies and to oversee various budgetary and financial functions. The sheriffs and Exchequer collected revenue, the Treasury held money, auditors reviewed payments made, and the Bank of England borrowed and repaid money. Public budgeting developed over a long period in England and was then transmitted to English colonies. Other countries, such as France and Austria, only started developing budgetary practices in the mid-eighteenth century.

The Colonial, Revolutionary, and Founding Periods

English colonists established several geographically dispersed, religiously diverse, and commercially oriented North American outposts in the seventeenth century. The colonies exercised self-government while England engaged in revolutions and European-focused wars. Without hereditary nobility, property-owning colonists elected their own leading citizens to colonial legislatures.

The colonies followed English budgeting practices. Colonial governors whose power came from the English monarch and government took the role of the English monarch and then the English government in proposing and administering revenues and expenditures. The colonial legislatures approved or disapproved revenues and expenditures and dominated the governors, who lacked sufficient political support in the colonies or England to avoid being dominated. Legislatures thwarted governors, especially unpopular ones, by refusing to approve revenues or the pay of governors and their officials and by specifying their approval of expenditures in great detail (what, when, and by whom). English inattention was particularly exemplified by Parliament passing but not enforcing taxes on colonial imports (customs duties). The salaries of officials collecting customs duties often exceeded the amounts they collected.

The American colonies became the United States through a revolution and governmental experiments partially based on budgetary concerns. After the French and Indian War in North America ended in 1763, the British government decided that American colonies should provide more financial support for expenditures on military defense. The British increased customs duties and efforts to collect those duties. American colonists evaded those taxes and complained that their right to self-government was being abridged. When the thirteen American colonies joined together to revolt, they argued "No taxation without representation." Declaring their independence, the colonies became states and prosecuted the American Revolution as a coalition under the Second Continental Congress and then the Articles of Confederation.

Although their revolution succeeded, the former colonists were dissatisfied with their collective governmental and budgetary arrangements. Confederal revenue collection depended on voluntary state payments that states often withheld, making collective action difficult.

The U.S. Constitution, adopted in 1787, created a stronger government with the ability to tax. The provisions of the Constitution reflect both continuity and change in budgeting. Continuity is most visible in features related to self-government: elected representatives, legislative approval for revenues and expenditures, governmental officials handling revenues and expenditures, the power to incur debt, and public accounting of revenues and expenditures.

Change is particularly evident in the invention of federalism and a presidential system, both of which limited the new government. Federalism means two or more separate governments governing the same people. A presidential system means an independent executive that is stronger than other American executives, with that strength being used to counterbalance the power of the federal legislature and to implement policies.

The Nineteenth Century

Budgeting in the United States until the turn of the twentieth century showed more continuity than change. The basic features of budgeting that had evolved in England and the colonies persisted with a few notable developments. The trend toward greater democratization of voting rights continued, as did increased legislative dominance of American governments. Legislatures were expected to lead in developing public policy much more than executives. Legislatures got budgets requests, interacted with agency officials, decided budgets, and supervised budget implementation. Chief executives seldom acted in budgeting and then only in extreme situations because executives were not expected to involve themselves much with policy-making. Legislatures organized their own budgeting activities using their own internal rules and dealt with operating units using laws and oversight.

This period is notable for changes in views of the public sector, expansions of public organizations, a shift in emphasis among the three levels of government, and the emergence of nonprofit organizations.

Americans displayed radically changing views of how to operate government. From the colonial period until the early nineteenth century, Americans elected and appointed gentlemen as government officials. Jacksonian democracy (starting in the 1820s) was a political reaction against social elites: Americans began staffing government with common men, fostering wider participation in government by making more positions elective and by rotating governmental personnel much more frequently. Because Jacksonian democracy increased the difficulties of dealing with governments, political machines arose in many places for the sake of gaining control of governments. Political operatives traded governmental positions and policies as "favors" for political support (votes, money, and work) in order to gain and keep control of governments. Although some political machines operated reasonably honestly and effectively, some dishonest ones were phenomenally corrupt, and occasionally an unhappy job seeker would kill a public official; for example, President Garfield was shot by a disappointed office seeker, Charles Guiteau, in 1881. The Progressive Movement reacted against political machines by promoting efficiency and morality. It emphasized using government for social reform, employing experts to formulate and implement policy, and increasing the role of executives.

The public sector grew as nineteenth-century Americans reacted to the Industrial Revolution, great population growth, and increasing urbanization. Wars consumed resources and left debts and pensions for military veterans and their dependents. By the time of the Spanish-American War at the end of the nineteenth century, the United States had become an international military power. The United States expanded territorially through military efforts in Florida and Texas and the purchase of the vast territories of Louisiana and Alaska. U.S. governments increased spending on existing responsibilities, including poor relief and transportation facilities such as roads, railroads, canals, harbors, and dredged river channels. Governments acquired new spending responsibilities in the form of primary, secondary, and higher public education, as well as public health-related spending on water and sewer systems.

Budgetary expansions were uneven over time as governments reacted to wars, social and political movements, and technological developments. Wars limited the amount of resources available for other purposes. Social and political movements encouraged more spending. Social movements greatly affected spending on prisons, poor relief, and public education. The sequential shifts in political views coincided with increasing public budgets. Government by gentlemen was mostly oriented toward very limited government. Jacksonian democracy was more responsive to public desires: political machines traded in favors, and corrupt machine politicians enriched themselves. The Progressive Movement viewed government favorably and argued for expanded government services. Government activities also expanded and changed due to great changes in technology. Improved agricultural technologies made urbanization possible and increased services necessary. Governments spent on transportation facilities as steam engines powered ships and trains. The development of industrial steel allowed for the creation of new machines and structures.

The relative emphasis among the three levels of U.S. government shifted as they reacted to specific situations. Federal expenditures, debt, and revenues related mostly to wars (Revolutionary War, War of 1812, Civil War). States actively financed railroads, canals, other public facilities, and banks in the first half of the century. In an economic downturn that started in 1839, several states defaulted on infrastructure debt, and corrupt state practices came to light. Many states adopted constitutional provisions that curbed such debt. Following the Civil War, local governments rapidly increased spending on infrastructure, including clean water, sewers, bridges, roads, schools, police and fire stations, jails, museums, administrative buildings, and parks. By 1890, local governments spent, collected, and borrowed more than the federal and state governments combined.

Nonprofit organizations emerged when the federal and state governments recognized a separate legal status for nongovernmental public organizations. Previously governments had created, funded, and operated all public organizations, including official churches and colleges. Nonprofit organizations increased in numbers and finances especially after the Civil War.

The Twentieth Century

The public sector continued to expand in the twentieth century. That expansion was closely related to other changes and a number of budgetary reforms.

Budget-Related Changes

Budget-related changes in the twentieth century included extraordinary revenue growth, extraordinary growth in governmental and nonprofit spending, new forms of spending, continued shifts in emphasis among the three levels of government, and new relations among public organizations and between them and private parties. Revenue growth stemmed from a growing, money-based economy, revenue innovations, and changing spending priorities. The federal and state governments led the way using income and sales taxes, which became the two greatest sources of governmental revenues.

Public spending increases in the twentieth century related to changing situations, newer needs, generally increasing trust in government, and greater capacities to acquire resources. Military-related spending increased as the United States participated in World Wars I and II, a variety of other military conflicts, and a successful arms race that left it the leading military power in the world. Near the beginning of the twentieth century, state-organized military units pursued Pancho Villa in Mexico on horseback; near the beginning of the twenty-first century the U.S. military had bases around the world and worked on intercepting and destroying ballistic missiles from space. Spending on public works increased as the U.S. population concentrated in urban areas and as national road and air transportation systems were built and maintained. Poor relief was largely supplanted by income security programs that provide money or benefits (such as health care and housing) based on income levels, age, and employment status. Providing for people during hard economic times became more important because an urbanized population could not readily revert to subsistence farming. Educational spending increased as people on average spent many more years in schools.

Public interest in existing and new nonprofit concerns, increasing wealth, and governmental decisions contributed to nonprofit organizations also collecting and spending a great deal more money in the twentieth century.

Governments increased the scope of activities that qualified for nonprofit status and provided nonprofit organizations with a number of financial advantages, including exemptions from income, inheritance, estate, sales, and property taxes; reduced postal rates; grants; and payments for services.

Governments developed new forms of spending (indirect expenditures) to control behavior as a matter of public policy rather than using the traditional form of spending where revenues were used to buy resources to provide services (direct expenditures). These spending devices were revenue expenditures, grants and other transfer payments, credit support, price support, and income security programs. In many cases, these programs were "entitlements" that provide defined legal rights to collect money based on proof that certain conditions exist; for example, Medicare benefits require proof of age. These new forms of spending, which often featured unlimited funding commitments, were particularly prevalent at the federal level and to a lesser extent at the state level.

The shifts in emphasis among levels of government took place relatively early in the century from local governments to state governments and then to the federal government. Initially, local governments dominated financially and continued to expand financially. State finances expanded more than twice as rapidly to build roads, to provide higher education, to support local education, and to operate services that formerly had been handled by local governments (health, welfare, public safety, and corrections). Federal finances expanded early in the century to encompass serious commitments in a variety of service areas: aid to agriculture, conservation of natural resources, regulatory activities, public health and other social services, and public works projects, including rivers, harbors, and the Panama Canal. Wars consumed much federal spending, but the federal government became the financially dominant level of government in response to the Great Depression, which stopped the growth of local finances and made the financial positions of the federal and state governments relatively stronger. The federal government reacted to state and local financial weakness with intergovernmental transfers and engaged in wide-ranging social welfare spending.

Relationships among public organizations and between public organizations and private organizations changed in the twentieth century. The finances of the three levels of government became intertwined as officials at the three levels saw themselves engaging in cooperative federalism. Cooperative federalism involved the various governments working together to solve problems and provide services. The federal government provided grant monies to state and local governments, and state governments provided grant monies to local governments. In the latter half of the twentieth century, grants typically constituted 20 percent of state revenues and 33 percent of local revenues. The federal and state governments both provided lesser amounts of grant funding to nonprofit organizations. Nonprofit organizations relying on governmental funding, of course, had to comply with governmental regulations to maintain that funding.

The relations between governments and private parties changed in various ways. The affairs of private parties became intertwined with government policy-making.

Government relations with private parties expanded through increases in direct expenditures, the widespread use of indirect expenditures, and various regulatory programs. Increases in direct expenditures by governments mean more services, more employees, and more sales to governments.

Governments used indirect spending to encourage nonprofit organizations and private parties to engage in particular behaviors. Private parties often turned to governments for financial advantages. Various groups supported governmental spending from which they benefited. Medicare (for the old) and Medicaid (for the poor) also benefit the medical industry; food stamps for the poor also benefit agriculture; income tax exemptions for owner-occupied housing also benefit the real estate and construction industries; and student aid and tax advantages for higher education also benefit the higher education industry.

Federal and state regulatory programs imposed a variety of limitations on private parties. Examples include licensing various occupations, mandating automobile safety requirements, and maintaining prices for agricultural products. By the end of the twentieth century, private parties looked increasingly to governmental policy-making as a determinant of their well-being.

Budgetary Reforms

The twentieth century stands out as a time of great enthusiasm for budgetary reforms. Four general categories of reform are discussed here thematically for the sake of brevity: executive budgeting, formalities, new budgeting approaches, and management reforms.

Progressives reacted to the diffusion of accountability in nineteenth-century governments by proposing that executives be held responsible for charting courses of action and that they be given tools to lead, including executive budgets. Initially, "executive budget" meant that a chief executive formulated and proposed a budget for a government that often became the starting point for legislatures. The executive budget reform, initially adopted by state and local governments, created the current generalized expectation that executives propose budgets. For public organizations without a chief executive (such as local district governments, council-manager forms of governments, and nonprofit organizations), the budget-proposing role often is assigned to another elected or appointed official, such as a clerk or a chief administrative officer.

Executive budgeting contributed to the rising power of executives by providing them with staff, clearance power, a greater agency oversight role, and discretion in expenditure decisions. Budget staff increased executives' capacity as they previously had little staff support. Clearance power refers to agencies being required to gain executive approval (clearance) to present policy proposals to legislatures or policy-making bodies. Budget formulation and preparation led executives to review more closely what agencies actually did and to exercise control over spending decisions. As governments grew in size over time, legislatures delegated additional budget-related powers to executives and their staff agencies, including discretion over whether to make expenditures.

Executive budgeting increased the formalities in budgeting. As legislatures yielded budgeting powers to executives in standing laws, the legislatures also imposed requirements on how executive budget powers would be exercised and specified the required contents of budget proposals and reports. In turn, executives imposed formal rules on agencies. In addition to asserting legislative and executive powers, formalities contribute to budgets being comprehensive, comprehensible, and systematic.

Reformers introduced three new budgeting approaches in the twentieth century, generally under the banner of providing more information for improved decision-making. Here, the term "budgeting approach" refers to a general way of preparing a proposed expenditure budget. Budgeting approaches differ in the use of particular information, particularly categories of expenditures. The lump-sum and line-item budgeting approaches, which were used before the twentieth century, were illustrated earlier in this chapter. The lump-sum budgeting approach involves proposing expenditures as a total amount, a lump sum, for very general purposes or broad categories: for example, a certain amount for a war with Scotland or to pay the people working for the English monarch (the Civil List). The line-item approach involves proposing expenditures in terms of items to be purchased; sometimes that approach includes prices and quantities, as was done during colonial times. The three later budgeting approaches are results-oriented. Their names are performance, program, and zero-base budgeting. Zero-base budgeting is a particular version of "what-if" budgeting. Respectively, they organize proposed expenditure information by the work to be done, by the outcomes of expenditures, and by choices. Budgeting approaches are covered in greater depth in Chapter 6. Here, the three later approaches are discussed only as budget reforms.

The performance budgeting approach, which became prominent around

1950, involves organizing expenditure information by the work to be done. The idea can be traced at least to 1907 in a study of the New York City Health Department by the Bureau of Municipal Research (*Making a Municipal Budget*). The report of President Taft's Commission on Economy and Efficiency, 1910–1912, and the Budget and Accounting Act of 1921, which followed that commission's recommendations, refer to classes of work. In the late 1940s, some local governments organized expenditure budgets by tasks or activities. In 1949, the Commission on the Organization of the Executive Branch, appointed by President Truman and led by former president Herbert Hoover, recommended that the federal government use performance budgeting, which was defined as budgeting by activities, projects, and functions. Reformers argued for using this budgeting approach, which was used by various governments in various ways. For example, the U.S. Department of Defense used performance measures in its budgeting in 1970 with a focus on the work activities performed. From the 1990s through the first decade of the twenty-first century, interest in the concept of performance resurged, and the term "performance" has been applied frequently to budgeting in efforts launched at the federal, state, and local levels of government. However, in this resurgence, performance does not simply refer to work to be done; sometimes, it refers to outcomes, work done, or both.

The program budgeting approach, which was developed in the Office of the Secretary of the U.S. Department of Defense in the early 1960s for analysis of weapons system choices, involves organizing expenditure information by the outcomes, the desired results. Program budgeting burst onto the national scene in 1965 with great fanfare when President Johnson indicated that his administration would use that budgeting approach. Some state and local governments followed the federal example. Program budgeting basically follows a rational decision-making or a planning logic. For example, managers start by positing goals or purposes; then they prioritize the goals or purposes; then they choose means for pursuing those goals or purposes after evaluating the alternative means; and finally they forecast the various line items based on quantities and prices of expenditures. Program budgeting is associated with analysis, planning, and multiyear budgeting since some outcomes may not occur immediately.

The zero-base budgeting approach, which became prominent in 1975 when Governor Jimmy Carter of Georgia campaigned for the U.S. presidency by promising to bring it to the federal government, involves making choices in respect to expenditure priorities expressed as outputs or outcomes. Zero-base budgeting is a particular version of the budgeting approach that we call the "what-if" budgeting approach. "What-if" budgeting shows proposed choices for different levels of expenditure in some fashion. The label that we use to identify this budgeting approach arises from the following formulation given to people preparing budgets: *"What* would you do *if* you had to cut expenditures or could increase expenditures?"* What-if budgets suggest, if they do not explicitly state, the impact of changes in expenditure levels. Zero-base budgeting explicitly states the expected effects of various expenditure levels.

In the twentieth century, reformers introduced a multitude of budget-related management reforms that substantially changed the work of public managers and increased their numbers. Those reforms, which involve the acquisition and analysis of information for making decisions, emanated from areas that developed substantially in the twentieth century. Those reforms occurred in long-term decision-making processes and in short-term operational techniques. Specific areas include the following:

- formal planning
- forecasting
- capital budgeting
- quantitative analysis
- accounting
- auditing
- administering revenues and expenditures
- purchasing
- managing money (cash, investments, and debt)

Much of public managers' public budgeting work involves activities in these areas. Managers themselves or those they supervise gather and analyze data, produce information, and interact with technical specialists in these areas. Education and training in these areas is highly developed and prevalent. Reforms in these areas assist the public and policy-making officials in dealing with the joint problem of maintaining accountability of managers while still enabling them to exercise discretion in a time of large, complex public organizations by producing, analyzing, and presenting more information to political officials and the public. Chapters 7 and 8 discuss analytical and operational management reforms associated with budgeting.

Conclusion

Public budgeting has developed both politically and technically since 1215. The earliest developments were primarily political as a theoretically absolute monarchy was forced to allow others to approve revenues and then expenditures. Representative institutions eventually gained control over budgets. English public budgeting was transmitted with other political institutions to the American colonies, which adapted it to their own unique public situations. Over the course of American history, representative institutions have become more democratic, public budgets have expanded greatly, and executives have taken on a much larger role than earlier in the nation's history. Technical reforms occurred especially in the twentieth century as newer approaches were developed and tried and as a wide variety of budget-related, information-oriented management reforms became entrenched in public organizations.

Additional Reading and Resources

Print

A wide-ranging history of budget-related phenomena:
Webber, Carolyn, and Aaron Wildavsky. *A History of Taxation and Expenditure in the Western World.* New York: Simon & Schuster, 1986.

A Progressive Era investigation of how budgeting was done:
Bureau of Municipal Research. *Making a Municipal Budget: Functional Accounts and Operative Statistics for the Department of Health for Greater New York.* New York: Bureau of Municipal Research, 1907.

A comprehensive account of budget history in the United States:
Lewis, Carole W. "The Field of Public Budgeting and Financial Management, 1789–2004." In *Handbook of Public Administration*, ed. Jack W. Rabin, Bartley Hildreth, and Gerald Miller, 151–225. 3rd ed. Boca Raton, FL: CRC Press, 2006.

A municipally oriented budget history:
Rubin, Irene S. *Class, Tax, and Power: Municipal Budgeting in the U.S.* Chatham, NJ: Chatham House, 1998.

A discussion of the evolution of budgeting approaches in the United States:
Schick, Allen. "The Road to PPB." *Public Administration Review* 26 (December 1966): 243–258.

The first serious examination of budgeting at the federal level was initiated by President Taft:
Cleveland, Frederick Albert. *The Need for a National Budget: Message from the President of the United States, Transmitting Report of the Commission on Economy and Efficiency on the Subject of the Need for a National Budget.* Washington, DC: Government Printing Office, 1912; http://openlibrary.org/b/OL16319288M/Need_For_A_National_Budget.

Internet

U.S. Codes on Budget and Accounting

The original law organizing federal budgeting as we know it today is the Budget and Accounting Act of 1921, and the current configuration of federal budgeting can be found at the Office of Law Revision Counsel of the U.S. House of Representatives: http://gaounion.net/wp-content/uploads/2008/05/1921-budget-and-accounting-act.pdf or http://gaounion.net/?p=110; http://law2.house.gov/download/pls/31C11.txt and http://law2.house.gov/.

U.S. Census Bureau

The U.S. Bureau of the Census publishes historical data from the colonial to the current period. The best starting point for most general information is the clickable "previous editions" page for the current edition of the Statistical Abstract of the United States: www.census.gov/compendia/statab/past_years.html. The past editions may also be found by searching on "Bicentennial Edition: Historical Statistics of the United States, Colonial Times to 1970" and "Statistical Abstract of the United States."

The Congressional Budget Office

The Congressional Budget Office has recent (1968 and after) federal budget data at www.cbo.gov/budget/historical.shtml.

Internal Revenue Service

The U.S. Internal Revenue Service provides historical revenue statistics, including information on charitable and other nonprofit organizations, at www.irs.gov/taxstats/article/0,,id=188060,00.html.

Government Information Online—Ask a Librarian

The Government Printing Office website has a link to communicate with federal government librarians at http://govtinfo.org.

3

Sources, Characteristics, and Structures of Public Revenues

Revenue is often lost in the discussion of public budgeting. Most managers in public organizations do not give much thought to revenue; their focus is almost exclusively on expenditures. This is understandable because, for them, revenue is a given that they need not worry about since it is largely outside their control.

For upper-level executives, policy-makers, and elected officials, however, revenue is central to the budget process. This is also true for managers and administrators whose budgets and revenues, to a significant extent, are driven by producing products and services that generate dollars for their units or agencies.

Revenues flow from several sources. Most revenue collected by government comes from taxes, and most revenue collected by nonprofit organizations comes from enterprise activities. The U.S. Census Bureau reports that 92 percent of federal dollars come from taxes if you include Social Security payroll taxes in that mix. For states the comparable figure is 75 percent, and for local governments it is 62 percent.

Taxes are mostly structured along three major bases of measurement: income, consumption, and wealth. A variety of other taxes relate specifically to business activities. Income refers to all revenue derived from activities of individuals or corporations and ranges from salaries and wages to rents, royalties, and dividends from equities. Income manifests itself with individual and corporate income taxes as well as federal payroll taxes. Consumption is linked to sales and value-added taxes. Property taxes, primarily taxes on homes and businesses, are the bases for most wealth tax revenues. However, there are also taxes on inherited wealth and on the sale of investments such as stocks and bonds.

Most other dollars flow from enterprise activities. These revenues from "business-like" activities generate all of the revenue for some nonprofit organizations and can create as much as 30 or 40 percent that a local government raises from its own sources, which are called own-source revenues. These are often earmarked for specific purposes (e.g., roads, utilities, recreation). Enterprise activities are those where the cost of a service or product and the beneficiaries of those services or products can be identified. The beneficiaries also can be largely excluded from the certain benefits of those services or products. Those who use public municipal golf courses or those who go to concerts provided by a local nonprofit opera company can be charged a fee for use of those services and the benefits can be identified. Almost all governments and nonprofits have some form of revenue that is generated from such activities.

According to the U.S. Census Bureau, state and local governments also receive extensive intergovernmental revenue from the federal government. States receive approximately 28 percent of their general revenue in this manner, and local governments receive 36 percent from their state governments and 4 percent from the federal government. Most "other revenue" makes up a small portion of the overall dollars that governments and nonprofits depend on, including wide-ranging items such as donations, fines, dues, interest incomes, and rents.

Revenue generation is largely a mechanical process, but decisions about where those revenues come from are a function of the following:

- legal authority
- potential for stability, return, and/or growth
- alignment with strategic goals, including fairness and equity
- ease of collection
- political choices
- neutrality versus social and political purposes

In each case, the government's ability to tax individuals and organizations is tied to its legal authority to do so.

Several factors also go into determining how revenue is generated:

- the base from which revenue is measured
- exemptions or exclusions
- deductions from the base identified
- the rate calculated against the base
- the actual revenue owed
- any credits charged against the amount owed

We will explore each of the major revenue sources, functions for measurement, and factors tied to the calculation of revenue in the context of these functions and their linkage to the budgeting process.

Perspectives on Revenue

The old adage "Where you stand depends on where you sit" is certainly true in the case of revenue. Each perspective or prism is based on the needs at each level. For policy-makers or chief executives, revenues must be acceptable to external constituencies. Revenue sources that do not erode political support while providing autonomy to the organization may be the most attractive. Wealth taxes on real estate always cause political difficulties because they are highly visible and are often collected annually or semiannually, making them easy targets of discontent. Sales taxes, on the other hand, which are collected at the point of sale and often hidden in the actual cost of the item being purchased, raise less political resistance as a result, except for large-ticket items.

As noted, managers and first-line supervisors often do not focus on revenue sources in the budget process. They are primarily focused on expenditures instead. Managers are not responsible for revenue except if they are writing grants or collecting fees. In those cases, they are going to pay attention to what they plan to collect from those sources because their expenditure levels often hinge on those grants and fees. Otherwise, they are primarily focused on staying within the expenditure levels dictated by the budget itself.

Employees are even further removed from the revenue aspects of budgeting. Other than perhaps those directly connected with collection of revenue, employees may know little about what revenue is collected, how it is collected, or its overall impact on their operations. Employees are focused on carrying out activities within the constraints of the budget and look to managers and supervisors to frame what limits exist to accomplish their tasks.

Citizens, constituents, and clients are directly affected by the revenue decisions of the budget process because they are paying those revenues into the governmental or nonprofit organization as taxes, fees, or services. Still, perspectives are very different. Citizens or residents of a governmental organization pay taxes whether they want to or not. Citizens affect how much they pay and for what type of tax through their elected representatives; however, they have little direct control. When taxes become highly visible, increase dramatically, or become an increased burden, taxpayers will express their displeasure to policy-makers and, in some cases, advocate for the removal of those policy leaders. Consumers of goods and services often have a say as to whether they purchase that good or service from a particular governmental or nonprofit agency (e.g., greens fees at a municipal golf course or medical services from a nonprofit hospital). In that case, those consumers will pick and choose based on factors such as price, convenience, and quality.

Other external stakeholders' views on revenues often focus on the alignment of their interests with those of the governmental or nonprofit agency with which they are linked. Donors will determine their revenue support based on how well the agency or organization meets their philanthropic goals. Grantor agencies will determine how well the governmental or nonprofit organization applying for those grants meets their requirements or meets the needs the grant was designed to address. Those external stakeholders' purposes for use of the revenue may conflict with the goals and objectives of the organization receiving those funds.

Functions Associated With Revenue Generation

Legal Authority

Several elements go into evaluating the appropriateness and viability of different revenue sources being used by governments. First and foremost, the collection of revenue must be within the legal power of a government. This has been a significant issue throughout American history.

For the U.S. government, the Sixteenth Amendment to the Constitution was probably the single most important delegation of authority in the history of the United States. The amendment states: "The Congress shall have power to lay and collect taxes on incomes, from whatever source derived, without apportionment among the several States, and without regard to any census or enumeration." Prior to the passage of this amendment, the Supreme Court had ruled very narrowly concerning the government's right to tax individuals and corporations based on their income. Today, the federal government generates almost half its annual income from individual taxpayers and over $800 billion a year for the Social Security system.

States are also limited significantly by their constitutions and by statutes. Local governments, being creatures of the states, have the most restrictions on their ability to levy taxes and rates. Similarly, local taxing jurisdictions, such as local sanitary improvement districts, are often limited to one source of revenue, which is usually collected by another entity such as a county or state and then passed through to those jurisdictions.

Potential for Stability, Return, and/or Growth

Certain revenue sources have greater potential for producing large returns than others. Revenue from building permits, licenses, and fees, for example, may generate large sums in communities undergoing rapid growth but have little impact in regions with stable or declining construction. Similarly, communities with large retail business areas would find sales taxes quite beneficial while bedroom communities would see little value in them.

Revenue generated by taxes is required to be paid by the government imposing the tax. The term "involuntary extraction of resources" has a nice ring to it if you are government. Still, most taxes are benchmarked against some event happening that has revenue implications: for example, houses being built, income being generated, sales of goods and services taking place, and appreciation of property occurring. These "events" often are referred to as the "revenue base."

If bases do not remain and grow in a significant way, then governments cannot meet their expenditure demands unless they raise rates charged against their bases. Governments are interested not only in growing revenue bases (and therefore maintaining or lowering the rate), but also in maintaining some stability of revenue sources. Wild fluctuations in bases over time can cause significant problems in predicting revenue from one budget cycle to the next. Except at the national level, governments must ensure that the budget be "in balance," meaning that expenditures do not exceed revenues. Lack of predictability in revenue requires those governments to build large contingencies into their budgets or restrict expenditures significantly until revenue has actually been collected. Stability and predictability allow those governments to anticipate and structure their budgets more efficiently.

Alignment With Strategic Goals, Including Fairness and Equity

An obvious strategic goal of the revenue collection process of government is to raise enough resources to support programs and services. Many people think that is the only reason a particular revenue structure is chosen. In many cases, however, revenue structures are chosen to serve other purposes. For example, governments may place a tax or fee on a particular good or service because they wish to manage its consumption. Fees for parks or taxes on gasoline earmarked for road improvements are attempts to align at least some of the costs of those services with the revenue needed to support them. Government may also wish to ensure that those most able to pay incur the heaviest burden in terms of taxes that support programs and services. This is referred to as "progressivity" or "ability to pay." Individual income taxes are considered the best means to achieve such a strategic goal because as a citizen's income increases, the ability to pay an increasing percentage of revenue generated from that income also increases. So, for example, current federal tax rates range from 10 percent to 35 percent. Depending on marriage and household status, individuals will pay progressively more of their income in taxes as that

Table 3.1

2007 Federal Income Tax: Schedule Z for Head of Household

If taxable income is over	But not over	The tax is
$0	$11,200	10% of the amount over $0
$11,200	$42,650	$1,120.00 plus 15% of the amount over $11,200
$42,650	$110,100	$5,837.50 plus 25% of the amount over $42,650
$110,100	$178,350	$22,700.00 plus 28% of the amount over $110,100
$178,350	$349,700	$41,810.00 plus 33% of the amount over $178,350
$349,700	No limit	$98,355.50 plus 35% of the amount over $349,700

Source: Internal Revenue Service, U.S. Department of Treasury, www.irs.gov/formspubs/article/0,,id=164272,00.html.

income increases up to a set amount. (In 2007 it was $349,700 for a head of household, for example.) Above that amount, individual heads of household would pay no more than 35 percent of their income in taxes no matter how much income they generated. Of course, these percentages do not reflect the actual revenue owed, which links to various deductions, exclusions, and exemptions in taxable income. These reductions in the definition of "taxable" income often reduce the progressivity of the tax structure. These elements will be described later in this chapter. Table 3.1 shows the progressivity of federal individual income tax rates in 2007 for a head of household.

This goal of progressivity has a strong fairness component. However, a government may also have a goal to stimulate economic investment and encourage economic development and growth. In such instances, tax progressivity may be seen as negative. Here the goal would be to maintain a flat or neutral revenue or tax burden even as income or ability to pay increases. When a government makes the tax structure flatter, it reduces the actual percentage of tax liability that exists for individuals, thereby leaving more of their income to be used by those individuals for their own use, including spending and investing in ways that may stimulate economic growth. In other cases, taxes are neither progressive nor neutral but regressive. A regressive tax is one where the tax burden increases proportionally as the ability to pay decreases. A sales tax on food is an example of a regressive tax. All people need to purchase food no matter what their economic circumstances. Since those with lower incomes pay a larger proportion of their income on necessities such as food, they pay a higher proportion of their income in consumption taxes on food than higher-income individuals pay.

Other goals may be linked to the government's desire to change individual or organizational behavior in some way. Tax-exempt nonprofit or not-for-profit organizations were created in order to establish entities whose primary role would be to carry out activities that would meet some public purpose that government or the private sector could not achieve. Hospitals, human service agencies, recreation programs, and cultural and performing arts entities are all seen as valuable public purposes that, in theory, would not exist unless the federal government used the tax code to allow them exemption from corporate income taxes.

Ease of Collection

Governments often have to weigh their strategic goals relative to revenue generation, alignment of services provided to those who pay for those services, or the desire to achieve a socially beneficial outcome with the costs and complexities associated with collecting that revenue. In some cases, it is easy to track and collect revenue. For example, if someone goes to the store and buys a camera, a government can identify that a transaction took place, determine the financial value of that transaction, and determine what tax revenue will derive from that transaction based on the rate of taxation. Also, since governments use merchants as their agents to collect and remit the revenue, it is easy through use of technology to collect those revenues. Similarly, federal individual income taxes can be easy to collect when income is generated by salaried workers whose employers are required to withhold and send to the federal government the vast majority of tax revenues, serving as government agents to ensure that this occurs.

Other revenues are much more difficult to collect accurately. While salaried income taxes may be quite easy to collect, income from other sources—such as cash transactions or income from other transactions not easily tracked through technology or where the value of the transaction (base) on which the taxes are determined is ill defined—can greatly increase governmental costs. The most common example is taxation of property. While real estate is usually permanent and identifiable, its value for tax purposes is often hotly contested. The administrative cost to accurately assess a property's value is very high. Annual reassessments are often financially impossible to do, so cities and counties may not do such assessments for three, four, or five years, or they may do only a portion of all properties in any one year. The result is the likelihood that inaccuracies or disparities will occur between the actual value of that property and its assessed value for taxation purposes.

Wealth taxes are also very difficult to collect accurately because some wealth is easy to hide or misidentify. Although governments still levy taxes on personal property, such as household furniture and equipment, they may find it difficult to accurately identify and measure this property because it can be easily moved or is hard to assess. Even more difficult is property such as securities that may be purchased and sold without easily identifying when those transactions take place or the increased value of those securities. The easiest personal property items to identify are ones required to be registered (e.g., cars, boats, and planes). Some people evade taxes on these items by registering them in jurisdictions that do not tax such items or tax them at lower rates. Revenue agencies looking to increase compliance with such measures physically examine cars, boats, and planes to see if they are properly registered and taxed. For example, the Illinois Department of Revenue checks boats berthed in Chicago marinas for proper registration and tax payment.

Political Choices

Governments are led by elected officials who often make decisions based on factors beyond economic efficiency or effectiveness. Revenue collection represents one of the most challenging areas for elected officials, who balance constituency needs and demands, personal philosophy and views, and recommendations from administrative staff and other stakeholders in making decisions about which revenue sources to use to achieve the priorities developed in the budget. These tensions are continually reflected in the revenue budgets. As noted earlier, sales taxes on nondiscretionary purchases are considered regressive, yet they are politically attractive because often the cost of those taxes is hidden in the cost of the item being purchased. Consumers who buy a loaf of bread or a carton of eggs do not think about how much tax they are paying on the item and often generate limited resistance. The sales tax on automobiles and other large-ticket items, on the other hand, is more visible and more politically unacceptable than other sales taxes because of how it is collected. This is also true of individual income taxes paid by individuals who have their taxes withheld monthly or biweekly. On the other hand, property taxes are often politically unattractive because homeowners have to pay them once or twice a year, and this makes them very visible.

Sales taxes would be more progressive and more efficient if they were to include services as well as retail sales; however, many of those who provide services, such as lawyers, advertising companies, and accountants, strongly resist attempts to broaden the tax base. In the 1980s, Florida attempted to expand its sales tax to professional services. The outcry by private service companies was so severe that the Florida legislature later repealed the expansion to professional services. Because of the political resistance to expanding the base beyond retail sales, only New Mexico and Hawaii have a broad-based sales tax on services.

Neutrality Versus Social and Political Purposes

Policy-makers designing revenue sources often face a tension between the goal of keeping the collection of that revenue "neutral" in the sense that it does not cause unintended impacts and the desire to use revenue sources as a way to shape behavior that serves social or political purposes. If consciously designed, these are policy choices that elected officials, policy boards, and executives can use to serve public purposes to varying degrees while still raising needed resources for governmental and nonprofit organizations.

Neutrality may be the more difficult challenge. Almost every revenue source creates opportunity costs. Consumption taxes, if significant enough, can curb demand for products and services being consumed. Individual income taxes, once they become substantial, can lead taxpayers to attempt to shelter their income in order to avoid the impact of those taxes on their take-home revenue. High property taxes can lead corporations to move their business investment to other states and property owners to move to different subdivisions or even to purchase smaller homes. Fees paid to nonprofit agencies providing services can cause individual and corporate consumers to change where they obtain those services or the level of services they request. If neutrality is the goal, then organizations attempt to find revenue sources that are least likely to create negative or perverse impacts.

Revenue sources and the structure of those revenue collection processes are often used to encourage or discourage certain behaviors. The mortgage interest deduction is meant to encourage homeownership. Consumption taxes on liquor and tobacco are meant to create a disincentive to use those products (or at least this is one of the arguments for higher taxes on those products). Nonprofits that charge a sliding scale for certain services, such as health screenings, child care services, or access to cultural arts programming, want to encourage people with small economic resources to access those programs and services while hoping that those with large economic resources are willing to subsidize those services by paying higher fees. Use of the tax code, user fees, and other mechanisms can serve public purposes beyond revenue generation if designed strategically to do so.

Factors in Revenue Generation

Base From Which Revenue Is Measured

A revenue base is the empirical phenomenon or event upon which revenue is collected. People pay taxes on certain bases and charges on enterprise activities. Examples include income, sales, and wealth taxes and admission and metered utility usage charges.

Exemptions and Exclusions

In many cases, policy-makers decide not to use all possible elements in revenue bases to calculate revenues owed. These decisions result from policy decisions to encourage certain behavior by organizations or individuals. The policy-makers may also make such decisions simply to reduce the administrative or political cost associated with collecting certain taxes.

Certain employee benefits are exempt from income taxes because they are believed to encourage employers to provide those benefits as a societal good. Health care premiums are a good example of this type of exemption. Some critics argue that such benefits should be taxed, but others argue that to do so would place an unfair burden on people's ability to get health insurance coverage. Other examples of exemptions include property tax on real estate owned by religious or governmental agencies that is foregone by state and local governments.

In most cases, intangible goods are not included in the calculation of the property tax base. Intangible goods are such things as stocks and bonds. While there are very few public benefits to be gained from excluding such base elements, they have been largely eliminated because of the difficulty in tracking and measuring this form of property. The personnel and operating costs associated with such attempts have resulted in policy decisions not to include this component in property tax base calculations.

Deductions From the Base Identified

Almost all deductions that are taken from a particular tax base are to support certain behaviors or encourage other behaviors to change. State and federal income taxes are chock-full of such deductions. One of the largest, the mortgage interest deduction, encourages homeownership. Others, ranging from work-related expenses to charitable giving, are efforts to encourage and support certain actions by individuals and organizations. Community foundations and other nonprofit foundations have been established in large part to provide opportunities for individuals to take significant charitable deductions. A circuit breaker or homestead exemption is a deduction of some portion of the property tax base value for real estate property because of the age of the owner or a person's homeownership status. This is not really an exemption of the base but a deduction in the value of the base for tax purposes.

The Rate Calculated Against the Base

Once the revenue base has been defined through exemptions, exclusions, and deductions, a rate will be calculated against that base. This can be a flat or

Table 3.2

2007 Federal Income Tax: Schedule Y-2 for Married Filing Separately

If taxable income is over	But not over	The tax is
$0	$7,825	10% of the amount over $0
$7,825	$31,850	$782.50 plus 15% of the amount over $7,825
$31,850	$64,250	$4,386.25 plus 25% of the amount over $31,850
$64,250	$97,925	$12,486.25 plus 28% of the amount over $64,250
$97,925	$174,850	$21,915.25 plus 33% of the amount over $97,925
$174,850	No limit	$47,300.50 plus 35% of the amount over $174,850

Source: Internal Revenue Service, U.S. Department of Treasury, www.irs.gov/formspubs/article/0,,id=164272,00.html.

invariable amount or percentage (e.g., $10 or 1 percent), as in most consumption or sales taxes, or it can be on a sliding scale of amounts or percentages depending upon the value of the base itself. The federal individual income tax in 2007 had sliding scale rates of 10 percent to 35 percent on different portions of taxable income. Table 3.2 displays the federal individual tax rates in 2007 for someone married and filing separately. The first $7,825 of this person's income is taxed at 10 percent, the amount between $7,825 and $31,850 is taxed at 15 percent, and so forth. As a result, someone making $175,000 is not actually paying a 35 percent tax rate on all income but an adjusted tax rate based on tiers of income categories and the rate charged against that income tier.

The Actual Revenue Owed

Once the calculation of rates multiplied by the taxable base has occurred, the individual or organization has a known tax liability. In the case of a consumption tax on sales, this is relatively easy to calculate since the base has been defined (e.g., products included within the base and the retail value of those products) and a flat rate is applied to that base. In the case of a wealth tax on property, the challenge is identifying and valuing the base (e.g., real estate). Once that is completed, a flat rate is applied composed of the summing up of all the jurisdictions levying a property tax on each particular piece of property. Within states, property taxes vary primarily due to the tax levies by different governments. In the case of sales taxes, the burden for valuing the base lies with those who sell the products. In the case of property taxes, property identification, billing, and collection are primarily the responsibility of governments, although those who own the property are required to self-report property improvements and the value of those improvements.

The most challenging area for identifying revenue owed is income taxes. It is the responsibility of individual taxpayers and their employers to identify what income has been earned and what is exempted, excluded, or should be deducted from that earned income based on federal or state law and to then calculate individual tax liability based on the correct rate applied to that taxable income. Because of the complexity of various governmental tax codes and the variability by which income can be earned, self-reporting can be fraught with intentional and unintentional errors. It is then up to governmental revenue auditors to verify that the tax liability that has been presented is accurate and complete.

Credits Charged Against the Tax Liability

Tax liability can be adjusted also through the application of credits. Credits are dollar-for-dollar reductions in tax liability. These credits are most common on income taxes and include a range of items such as childcare expenses, energy expenses, and credits for low-income individuals.

Tax credits also exist on certain kinds of property tax. In New York State, for example, farmers may be eligible for a state income tax credit for school taxes they paid on working farmlands. In some states, the elderly may be eligible not only for property tax exemptions that affect the taxable value of their property but also for income tax credits on their property tax liability. Finally, sales tax credits may be offered by certain states and localities on purchases such as energy-efficient products (Rhode Island) or pollution control equipment (Nebraska).

Sources of Revenue

There are several categories of revenue. Some revenue occurs through the "involuntary extraction of resources," or what we all have come to know and love as taxes. Taxes can be levied by governmental jurisdictions. The federal government, as discussed earlier, has altered the U.S. Constitution to allow taxation of income and has the power to levy taxes on consumption and wealth as well. Similarly, state governments can levy taxes on a variety of bases (the object of the tax) as long as it is allowed by their constitutions and by statutes. States decide what revenues they will allow local governments to employ. As noted earlier, localities (cities, counties, school districts, and so forth) are creatures of the state and have no power beyond that granted by their state constitutions and state statutes. States place limits on the taxes localities can levy and on the rate at which those taxes can be applied.

Nontax revenue is also important to governments but particularly important to nonprofit agencies. Nontax revenue usually comes in the form of enterprise activities; specific fees can be charged for particular products and services provided by those governmental or nonprofit organizations.

Revenues of public organizations are described as "own-source" or "not own-source." If a governmental or nonprofit agency collects revenue directly, that revenue is referred to as own-source revenue. Taxes and enterprise activities generate own-source revenues. On the other hand, revenue provided by a third party to a governmental or nonprofit agency is referred to as not own-source. Intergovernmental transfers, grants, and donations are all examples of not own-source revenue.

Tax Structure

Income Taxes

Income tax, as the name implies, focuses on acquiring revenue for a government based on a percentage of income generated by individuals and businesses. Why are income taxes such an important structure within the federal and state revenue systems? Historically, taxes were based primarily on the measurable wealth of property because of the agrarian nature of society. With the rise of the Industrial Revolution, salaries and income derived from specialized work became more prominent. Although the government continued to tax the accumulation of wealth, the growth in income among a broad range of individuals became an increasingly attractive source of tax revenue. Still, income taxes did not become a major source of governmental revenue until the beginning of the twentieth century. A federal income tax, passed in 1894 but later ruled unconstitutional, was a key part of William Jennings Bryan's presidential campaign in 1896, but would take almost twenty years to be made part of the U.S. Constitution.

As individual incomes grew, so did federal and state reliance on the tax on income. According to the U.S. Department of the Treasury, in 1939 only about 9 million people paid federal individual income tax. The total collected in 1941 amounted to about $8.7 billion. By 1945, because of significant changes in the tax law, over 43 million persons were paying $45 billion in income tax. Today, according to Transactional Records Access Clearinghouse, the federal government collects almost $1.4 trillion in individual income taxes, $836 billion in payroll (social insurance) taxes, and almost $400 billion in corporate income taxes.

Income taxes collected by states and localities, although a much smaller proportion of their total taxes collected, have also grown significantly, according to the Tax Foundation; in 2006 over $244 billion had been collected by states in individual income taxes. Only seven states (Alaska, Florida, Nevada, South Dakota, Texas, Washington, and Wyoming) do not have state income taxes in some form. Per capita rates of income taxation range from $32 in Tennessee to over $1,600 in New York and Connecticut.

Consumption Taxes

Consumption taxes, as the name implies, are based on the economic value or units of production of what an individual or an institution consumes. The most common are taxes on transactions incorporating the value of retail goods at sale or taxes on units of a good sold, such as gallons of gasoline (sometimes referred to as an excise duty).

Other alternatives include the use of a value-added tax (VAT), which is common in Europe. The VAT works by calculating the "value added" to a product at each stage of the production process and then charging the cumulative value added to the consumer at the final sale. Essentially, a tax is levied at each stage in the chain of production and distribution, starting with basic raw materials; as "value" is "added" at each stage in the product's development, a tax is placed on the monetary measure of that value added until the final sale of that product or service.

Much attention has been focused on consumption taxes in recent years as a superior alternative to the taxes on income, particularly at the federal level. There have been attempts to create a national sales tax. The most visible such effort is called the FairTax. According to Americans for Fair Taxation, FairTax would "replace all federal income and payroll based taxes with an integrated approach including a progressive national retail sales tax, a prebate (an advance payment) to ensure no American pays federal taxes on spending up to the poverty level, dollar-for-dollar federal revenue neutrality, and, through companion legislation, the repeal of the 16th Amendment."

Gilbert Metcalf notes three major arguments in support of a consumption tax. First, it is relatively simple because it can be measured accurately. The federal individual income tax, with its extremely complicated set of exemptions, exclusions, deductions, multiple rates, and credits, is inaccurate because measuring actual income is almost impossible. Second, because the consumption tax applies only to individuals who actually consume goods and services, it will generate increased savings and investment. The federal individual income tax, on the other hand, punishes those who save and invest and rewards those who spend. Finally, the consumption tax is considered superior to the income tax because it is fair and has horizontal equity, especially if the base is broad—it treats everyone the same way and it does not hide the impact of the tax by treating people in similar economic situations differently.

Still, there are weaknesses to such taxes. One is that such taxes can be regressive, especially when the item taxed is a staple required no matter what capacity the individual has to pay the tax. Sales taxes on food, clothing, prescription drugs, and other basic commodities have a disproportionate impact on low-income persons. Similarly, taxes on the purchase of gasoline can impact low-income families more than those with greater abilities to pay. Advocates argue, however, that the gasoline tax revenues dedicated to improving roads or infrastructure is inherently fair because taxes are collected only from those who "use" or "consume" the benefits of that investment. Still, there is no doubt that such revenue collection can skew against the ability to pay. If consumption taxes were applied to a wide range of professional services as well as retail items or if the taxes were applied only to discretionary purchases, the progressivity of these taxes would increase significantly.

A national sales tax might lessen "free rider" concerns; however, since current taxation of consumption largely occurs at the state and local level, considerable disparity remains. Individuals can cross city or state borders to avoid paying tax on large items or can purchase items on the Internet with little or no taxation; the ability of these consumers to avoid paying tax creates disparities and behaviors that undermine the perceived equity of the tax. Destination or use taxes do exist that require purchasers to pay the tax where they plan to use the product or service rather than where they purchase it, but these taxes are easily avoided and are very difficult to administer without strong cooperation from other jurisdictions.

Finally, consumption taxes can be closely tied to economic conditions. As economic conditions deteriorate, discretionary consumer spending declines and revenue generation can drop significantly. Interestingly, the more progressive the consumption tax is, the more likely it is to be impacted by economic conditions since individuals may choose not to buy a new car or other expensive item but rather keep their old vehicle or purchase a cheaper item instead.

Taxes on Individual Wealth

Along with poll or capitation taxes (a tax on individuals as individuals) and some excise taxes, taxes on individual wealth are among the oldest forms in the world, according to Tax World. In the United States, according to an article by Glen Fisher at the United States Economic History Service website, in the last part of the eighteenth century only four states had a tax on a totality of property (real and tangible personal property), but by the end of the nineteenth century over thirty states had all property taxed equally by value. Some of this tax structure stemmed from the effects of Jacksonian democracy and the view that those who have accumulated wealth should be subject to equal taxation.

During this time, taxes on wealth included not only real estate but also all wealth, both tangible and intangible. Tangible wealth referred to wealth that had a physical presence, such as land, improvements on land (e.g., buildings), and personal property (e.g., livestock and furniture). Intangible wealth included items that represented wealth (e.g., stocks and bonds). However, the administrative cost of tracking intangible wealth has led to the demise of taxation of intangible property. Today only Florida levies such a tax. The same has been true of personal property tax. Personal property that is licensed and can be identified (e.g., boats and cars) is still a source of significant revenue at the state and local level. However, personal property that can be easily hidden or moved is difficult to identify and assess, and therefore taxes on such property have become less common. In 2005–2006, state and local governments collected almost $360 billion in property taxes. This amount represented about 20 percent of all their own-source revenue.

Taxes on wealth are attractive to state and local jurisdictions because they tend to be a steady source of income that does not fluctuate nearly as much as income or consumption taxes, especially during ups and downs of the economy. Of course, this can be a detriment if economic growth occurs quickly and revenue flow from property taxes lags behind while demand for services (and expenditures) increases more quickly. Taxes on wealth also represent, in theory, a more equitable form of revenue collection because the base is tied to economic wealth and individuals' and corporations' ability to pay. Wealth taxes also have a grassroots element. While states set the parameters for how property tax bases are established and the range of rates that can be assessed, historically wealth taxes have been seen as a tax base that primarily resides at the local level; the control of property tax has been vested in elected officials at that level who set rates and determine how those revenues are allocated among competing needs.

Still, there are a number of difficulties with wealth taxes. First, as the tax base has narrowed through the elimination of intangible wealth (e.g., stocks, bonds) and wealth on personal property (e.g., furniture, appliances), the equity of the tax has declined as well. Focusing primarily on real estate (land and improvements) ignores significant wealth generated by high-income taxpayers who invest extensively in stocks, bonds, and other wealth instruments.

Second, accurately measuring wealth for real property is notoriously difficult to do over time because its value is a function of worth at the point of transaction or based on the income that derives from that property. Since most real estate is not bought or sold frequently, its value has to be based on other measures, such as the sale of comparable property. The difficulty of defining "comparable" property causes a great deal of disagreement and conflict between government and owners.

Third, the actual "incidence" of the tax may not be the owners of the property at all if they are renting that property to others or using it in business or commercial activities. In those cases, property owners can shift the cost of the tax to those renting that property or to those who deal with the business, such as consumers. When housing or commercial property is in high demand, such shifting is common. When there is an oversupply of housing and commercial property, as has been true in recent years, such shifting is less likely to occur because renters have more options and can pick comparable property to rent at lower cost. This also leads to lower revenue generation because of lower production and lower housing values.

Finally, wealth does not necessarily reflect income flow or liquidity and therefore can distort the ability to pay. This is particularly true of the elderly, whose primary wealth is tied up in housing ownership. For such individuals, total wealth may appear significant, but the actual flow of revenue is based on fixed income, such as Social Security and annuities linked to retirement savings. For these persons, the costs of property taxes may create a significant burden in the proportion of their actual annual income going to such a tax.

Enterprise Activities

State and local governments combined raise 20 percent of their total own-source revenues in 2005–2006 from enterprise activities, primarily from fees and charges for everything from highway tolls to greens fees to play golf. For local governments, that figure is approximately 26 percent. Those percentages have probably increased as pressure has increased to break out expenditures for identifiable individual beneficiaries. Similarly, many nonprofit agencies depend heavily on fees and charges for the services and programs they provide. A recent study by the Humphrey Institute published on the Minnesota Council on Nonprofits website found that about 20 percent of the revenue generated by nonprofits in Minnesota came from program services fees. Nationally among all reporting public charities, the number is 70 percent according to the *Nonprofit Almanac 2008* (p. 145). Fees and charges require that individuals and organizations can be identified and excluded from the benefits of the service or product. Because a public purpose is assumed if such fees are charged, the revenue generated may not represent the total cost of that service or product. Tuition at public universities is a good example. Tuition generally makes up less than half of the actual cost of such universities. Other revenue (e.g., state appropriations, grants, and donations) makes up the remainder. If tuition were raised to pay for the actual cost of higher education at these institutions, it would greatly reduce access to a large number of people who could not afford to attend college.

Grants and Donations

Externally funded grants and private donations can also make up a significant proportion of funding, particularly for nonprofit agencies and some public institutions such as universities. According to the *Nonprofit Almanac 2008* (p. 145), public charities derive more than 20 percent of their revenues from private contributions and grants. If universities and hospitals are excluded, this number goes up to 40 percent. For higher education institutions, grants and contracts as of 2004–2005 provided almost 20 percent of all operating revenue, according to Public Agenda, a nonprofit group devoted to facilitating public policy discussions. State and local governments also depend heavily on grants or other forms of intergovernmental revenue from the federal government. Intergovernmental revenue totaled just below 17 percent of their revenues in 2005–2006 according to the U.S. Census Bureau. It is difficult to determine what type of philanthropy flows to such governments, but it is certainly less than 2 percent of the overall revenue flow of state and local governments.

The challenge for both governments and nonprofit organizations is to build sustainability into funding from sources that may be sporadic and short-term in nature. For state and local governments, much intergovernmental revenue may be fairly consistent over time (e.g., Medicaid and community development block grants), while other such revenue may be available only upon competitive solicitation and may last only a short period of time. Most grant dollars to nonprofit agencies are competitively sought and may last only a few years or are subject to "sustainability" requirements by funders who do not wish to become permanent supporters of the agencies' activities. The same is likely true of donors who wish to support the projects and activities of an agency, but not its "administrative operations" and who do not wish to be seen as permanent sources of revenue. Many nonprofit agencies work diligently to build unrestricted endowments that allow them to fund basic operations with the interest income generated from those endowments.

Overview of Revenue Among Governmental and Nonprofit Organizations

Clearly, governmental and nonprofit organizations vary dramatically in the structure of their revenue systems. The federal government has become increasingly dependent on income taxes, while states lean more heavily on both income and consumption taxes. This has left local governments as the primary collector of wealth taxes. Nonprofit organizations range dramatically in their revenue structure from "private-like" institutions in which fee-for-service revenue dominates to more "community-based" institutions that depend much more heavily on grants and donations to maintain their operations. No matter what the source of revenue, for budgeting purposes governmental and nonprofit agencies look for funding that (1) is stable and predictable, (2) increases to keep pace with rising expenditure demands, (3) is relatively easy to collect, and (4) meets reasonable thresholds of fairness and political acceptability. Since no one revenue source can meet all these criteria, most organizations search for a combination of revenue sources that will achieve these goals.

Conclusion

Revenues are often the forgotten part of the budget process within governments and nonprofit organizations because they are dealt with primarily at the policy level rather than the management level. However, budgets, particularly in public organizations, are often the only way in which revenues and expenditures are linked directly. In private organizations revenue is a function of producing goods and services for sale. In public organizations most revenue is totally separate from the production of goods and services. The budget provides that linkage.

Revenues come from myriad sources, each with their unique characteristics and impacts. Each revenue source has not only revenue implications, but also policy implications because revenues change behavior and achieve purposes and goals beyond simply creating funding to support governmental and nonprofit operations. Understanding the nature of these revenue sources will better inform the budgeting process and improve decision-making at both the policy and management levels.

Additional Reading and Resources

Print

Historical accounts of revenues:

Aronson, J. Richard, and John L. Hilley. *Financing State and Local Government.* 4th ed. Washington, DC: Brookings Institution Press, 1986.

Pechman, Joseph A. *Federal Taxation.* 5th ed. Washington, DC: Brookings Institution Press, 1987.

Webber, Carolyn, and Aaron Wildavsky. *A History of Taxation and Expenditure in the Western World.* New York: Simon & Schuster, 1986.

Economists have been the most prolific authors on revenue. Their knowledge can be found in public finance–oriented texts:

Fisher, Ronald. *State and Local Public Finance.* 3rd ed. Cincinnati: South-Western College Publishing, 2006.

Hyman, David N. *Public Finance: A Contemporary Application of Theory to Policy with Economic Applications.* 5th ed. Cincinnati: South-Western College Publishing, 2004.

Rosen, Harvey. *Public Finance.* 8th ed. New York: McGraw Hill/Irwin, 2008.

Stiglitz, Joseph E. *Economics of the Public Sector.* 3rd ed. New York: W.W. Norton, 2000.

The most comprehensive overview of financial characteristics of nonprofit agencies ever compiled nationally:

Metcalf, Gilbert E. "Consumption Taxation," in *The Encyclopedia of Taxation and Tax Policy,* ed. Joseph J. Cordes, Robert D. Ebel, and Jane G. Gravelle. Washington, DC: Urban Institute Press, 1999. The article is also available at The Urban Institute website at www.urban.org/publications/1000522.html and www.urban.org/uploadedpdf/1000522.pdf.

Wing, Kennard T., Thomas H. Pollak, and Amy Blackwood. *Nonprofit Almanac 2008.* Washington, DC: Urban Institute Press, 2008.

A special journal issue devoted to revenue:

"Raising Revenues," ed. John W. Swain, *International Journal of Public Administration* 22 (11 & 12) (1999); includes John W. Swain and Margaret A. Purcell, "Multiple Perspectives on the Meaning of Revenue," 1535–1560.

A discussion of a particular revenue decision for the state of Texas:

Swain, John W., and E. Bernadette McKinney. "State Lotteries: Explaining Their Popularity." *International Journal of Public Administration* 16 (7) (1993): 1015–1033.

Internet

A number of organizations provide historical overviews of public revenue sources, structure, and operations:

U.S. Census Bureau

The U.S. Census Bureau offers wide-ranging data on state and local finances for all revenue sources, for example, "State and Local Finances by Level of Government, 2005–2006," at www.census.gov/govs/www/estimate.

U.S. Office of Management and Budget
The U.S. Office of Management and Budget analyzes federal FY2008 revenues in comparison with revenues in earlier years at www.whitehouse.gov/omb/budget/fy2008/pdf/hist.pdf.

U.S. Department of Treasury
The U.S. Department of Treasury provides a clear, concise history of the U.S. tax system at www.ustreas.gov/education/fact-sheets/taxes/ustax.shtml.

Tax World
Tax World provides a short, concise overview of taxation throughout history at www.taxworld.org/History/TaxHistory.htm.

The United States Economic History Service
Glen Fisher provides an excellent history of property taxation at http://eh.net/encyclopedia/article/fisher.property.tax.history.us.

Transactional Records Access Clearinghouse
The Transactional Records Access Clearinghouse has all federal income tax collections between 1910 and 2008 at http://trac.syr.edu/tracirs/highlights/current/incomeTax1910_pres.html.

National Bureau of Economic Research
The search function at the website for the National Bureau of Economic Research will supply further information on almost any aspect of revenues at www.nber.org.

Federation of Tax Administrators
The Federation of Tax Administrators website contains revenue information and links to revenue agencies at www.taxadmin.org.

Streamlined Sales Tax
An ongoing multistate project to improve sales taxes is at www.streamlined-salestax.org.

Illinois General Assembly's Legislative Research Unit
The Illinois Legislative Research Unit's Tax Handbook for Legislators is at www.ilga.gov/commission/lru/lru_home.html.

Internal Revenue Service
The U.S. Internal Revenue Service generally, and tax statistics specifically, can be found at www.irs.gov and www.irs.gov/taxstats/index.html.

Catalog of Federal Domestic Assistance
A listing of federal grant programs is on the Catalog of Federal Domestic Assistance website at www.cfda.gov.

Joint Committee on Taxation
The Joint Committee on Taxation of the U.S. Congress publishes a variety of reports on taxation, including tax expenditures, assessments of presidential tax proposals, and explanations of passed legislation at www.jct.gov/publications.html.

Urban Institute
The Urban Institute publishes a variety of public policy research. Documents on revenues are in the Economy and Taxes Issues section of their website at www.urban.org/economy/index.cfm.

Tax Foundation
The Tax Foundation makes research and data on taxes available on its website, www.taxfoundation.org, including a listing of state individual income tax collections per capita for Fiscal Year 2007 at www.taxfoundation.org/taxdata/show/282.html.

Americans for Fair Taxation
Americans for Fair Taxation advocates for a national sales/consumption tax to replace federal income and payroll taxes at www.fairtax.org. Readers should judge the arguments on their merits.

Public Agenda
Public Agenda, a nonprofit group devoted to facilitating public policy discussions, offers a variety of information and views on revenues, including, for example, a graph on revenues for higher education at www.publicagenda.org and www.publicagenda.org/charts/higher-education-revenue-sources.

Minnesota Council on Nonprofits
The Minnesota Council on Nonprofits publishes a survey conducted by the Humphrey Institute of the University of Minnesota that covers revenues of Minnesota nonprofit organizations in 2005 at www.mncn.org/images/NPERQuarterlyReport2.pdf.

4

Public Budgeting Processes

Annual, Episodic, and Standing Policies

The budgeting process refers to the sequence of activities by public organizations in making revenue and expenditure decisions. Although usage tends to favor "the budget process," a close inspection of budgeting activities reveals three similar but distinct processes. First, this chapter focuses on formal budgeting processes that produce annual budgets. Many public organizations create and operate a formal budgeting process for fiscal year budgets. Governments enshrine formal budget processes in laws and nonprofits in formal policies; state governments require formal processes of themselves and their local governments; some nonprofit fund-raising organizations, such as United Way, require them of funded nonprofit organizations.

Second, many public organizations, especially small ones, have not adopted a formal budget process and instead make revenue and expenditure decisions on a relatively informal basis when relevant issues arise. In other words, they budget on an ad hoc basis. These organizations undertake preparation, approval, and implementation of revenue and expenditure decisions within relatively short time periods. When a public organization only budgets informally, we surmise that its leadership does not see sufficient reasons to budget formally.

Third, some revenue and expenditure decisions are made outside of an ongoing process by standing policy decisions that remain in force unless and until they are changed. Such standing policies impact how much revenues and expenditures are predetermined and how much are decided on annually. Although standing policies may be changed within or relative to formal or informal budget processes, they tend to stand for extended periods of time.

Organizations may use two or even all three of these processes as events unfold. For example, a formally budgeting government may have to budget on an ad hoc basis for an unexpected major event, such as a natural disaster; an ad hoc budgeting nonprofit organization may budget formally for a major planned event or program; and any public organization can make standing revenue and expenditure decisions, although the most noteworthy standing revenue and expenditure budget policies are governmental.

Constrained Revenues and Expenditures

Standing revenue and expenditure decisions differ from nonstanding decisions in how they are treated during a formal budget process. Standing policies are assumed to continue standing. The primary preparation activities for standing policies are forecasting revenue and expenditure amounts.

The formal budget process involves making decisions. Continuity of prior decisions is one of its most remarkable attributes. With few exceptions, public organizations collect and spend money very similarly from year to year. Still, public organizations do make changes from year to year, and those changes do matter. Overall, small changes in budgets cumulate, and public organizations change over time. Specific changes matter greatly to public managers as the activities for which they are responsible change.

Standing policies constraining revenues and expenditures may be enshrined in charters or in more changeable policy statements. For example, the Illinois Constitution of 1970 requires that the state pay employee pensions. Many laws specifically authorize revenues and mandate activities that require expenditures. Various terms characterize these sorts of revenues and expenditures and their opposites: mandatory, restricted, and uncontrollable versus discretionary, unrestricted, and controllable. These standing policy decisions are changeable, with lesser or greater difficulty, even if they are not changed regularly.

For the present purpose of discussing the formal budget process, a brief general description of the workings of standing policies suffices. For a fuller discussion of standing revenue and expenditure policies see Appendix on page 85. For the most part, revenue policies are standing policies that are not seriously considered in the formal budget process. Some revenues have additional constraints on them that direct how they are spent. All revenues not otherwise constrained are available for expenditure decisions. Some expenditure decisions are constrained. After constrained expenditures are forecast and subtracted from the amount available for expenditures, the remainder of the expenditure amount available can be decided on in the formal budget process. Resources on hand, saving, and borrowing also can affect the amount of unconstrained expenditures. Table 4.1 summarizes the relationships between constrained and unconstrained revenues and expenditures in the formal budget process.

Diversity of the Formal Process

The formal public budget process remains constant in respect to its basic features across public organizations while many details vary. The basic similarities are the four stages in the process and annual appropriations. Differences

Table 4.1

Forecasts of Constrained and Unconstrained Revenues and Expenditures

Total revenues   − constrained revenues   = unconstrained revenues
Unconstrained revenues − constrained expenditures = unconstrained expenditures

in details stem from variations in size, complexity, and formality of public organizations and from some organizations choosing particular budgeting details. In many cases, particular features of a public organization's budget process can be traced to the choices of one person, a few people, or specific historical events.

Large organizations tend to deal with many resources, many different subject matters, and a lot of territory. They also tend to have many people participating in budget activities, many levels in their organizations, great formality, and a high degree of specialization. Accordingly, large organizations' budget processes tend to be long because their budgets have many details and have to be dealt with by many people in different places in the sense of geographic location, organizational level, or technical specialization. Large organizations, particularly governments, tend to use staff devoted to budgeting matters, often in separate organizational units. At the federal level, for example, the Office of Management and Budget serves the president, the Congressional Budget Office and the General Accountability Office (formerly the General Accounting Office) serve Congress, the departments have inspectors general, and agencies have their own budget specialists, including the job titles of budget technician, budget officer, and budget analyst. The federal budget process for each fiscal year starts approximately one and a half years before that fiscal year is scheduled to begin.

Governments differ from nonprofit organizations in respect to legal requirements. Nonprofit organizations operate relatively free of legal restrictions in budgeting. They may find restrictions in maintaining their nonprofit status; in complying with legal limitations on nonprofit organizations; and in grants, contracts, or other funding mechanisms with other organizations (this is particularly true for umbrella fund-raising agencies, such as United Way). Other than those kinds of restrictions, nonprofit organizations are free to budget as they please. In contrast, even the smallest government finds itself subject to a wide variety of specific legal requirements affecting budgeting. The federal and state governments subject themselves to many budget laws.

The use of biennial budgeting is one much-talked-about process variation. Although most public organizations budget annually, some states and local governments employ a biennial budget process in which they prepare and approve two fiscal years of revenues and expenditures together. This procedure allows those governments to spend less time on preparing and approving budget proposals and more time on other activities.

The Budget Cycle

The budget process represents a time-oriented perspective on budgeting activities from a beginning to an end. Here, we examine the budget cycle in isolation from overlapping budget cycles shown in Chapter 1. The budget process is a recurring, cyclical sequence of repeated events. In that sequence, participants produce information and decisions and take action in regard to the revenues and expenditures of public organizations. Here, the procedural aspects of the process are emphasized rather than the political aspects, which are emphasized in Chapter 5. In discussing the procedural aspects, we describe and explain who does what to whom and when.

Each budget cycle is identified by the fiscal year or years with which it deals. A fiscal year is identified by the calendar year within which it ends. The budget cycle serves as an organizing concept to distinguish the activities of one cycle from all others and to place associated information and activities into an intelligible context. As budgeting became more formalized, budgets became regularized for definite annual periods that had to be identifiable for political, legal, and practical reasons. Further budget information and activities were identified relative to the annual periods. Public organizations have added many budgeting requirements over the years.

Budget cycles center on the year of implementation. The preparation and the submission and approval stages precede implementation, and the reviews and reports stage succeeds it. Each stage of the budget process has characteristic requirements and activities. We examine the myriad details associated with the budget preparation, submission and approval, implementation, and reviews and reports stages.

Preparation

Public managers experience the most involvement with budgeting activities during the preparation and the implementation stages of the process. They recognize budget preparation as being distinct from the rest of their regular, ongoing work. In the preparation stage, they shape budgets that policy-makers approve.

Budget preparation, also called formulation or planning, can be considered in terms of six sets of activities, listed below, that are only loosely grouped together:

- acting prior to preparing a budget
- making budget calls
- deciding about proposals
- preparing proposals and related documents
- reviewing proposals
- finalizing an overall budget proposal

These activities are frequently interspersed with one another in practice.

Before public managers become involved in budget preparation activities, they engage in their ongoing responsibilities. In the course of that work, they become aware of problems and opportunities relative to those responsibilities. They recognize and deal with information relevant to their work. Public managers become aware of information from many possible sources, including ones away from their work sites such as news outlets or their own imaginations. For example, maintenance public managers may have imagined robotic vacuum cleaners, floor washers, and lawn mowers, or they may become aware of them in advertisements. Public managers gather information. They assess needs and conduct analysis, most often informally. They sort and store information on actual and potential opportunities and problems that they may wish to pursue further. In some fashion, if only subconsciously, they choose which ones they wish to consider in the context of budgeting. They analyze informally and, perhaps, even conduct formal analysis. In some cases, they may begin budget preparation work, such as gathering information for expenditure forecasts prior to the formal budget process.

Central officials, who include members of policy-making bodies, executives, administrators, and their staffs, prepare for the budget process by gathering and disseminating policy-related information and preparing material related to the budget call, which is discussed below. General policies, general policy discussions, public statements, formal plans, and financial information set the stage for budget preparation. Central officials or bodies issue budget calls. A central official or body may produce one or more revenue forecasts prior to the call, which guide what goes into a budget call.

Initial forecasts of general revenues may occur prior to budget calls or afterward when public managers prepare budget proposals. General revenues mean major revenues collected by central offices or units, such as a state department of revenue. Some specific organizational units may forecast minor revenues associated with their operations that they collect and may hold themselves separate from a central treasury. Central officials forecast major revenues, usually by revenue measure.

A budget call in its simplest sense is a signal for operating units to begin preparing fiscal year proposals for funding. A budget call may be as informal as an oral instruction, "time to start budgeting," or as formal as a manual with appendixes, legal citations, and directions for obtaining more information. In addition to signaling "begin preparing budget proposals," budget calls may include guidance on the budget process, policy, and technical requirements. Some organizations have general manuals on budget preparation that budget calls reference. Where multiple organization levels exist, administrators may add additional guidance to a general budget call.

Process guidance ranges from a simple indication of when and where to submit budget proposals to a very complete explanation of what is done when and by whom in the process. Budget calendars are a particularly common manifestation of process guidance. At the very least, budget calendars show dates on which or the time periods within which participants are supposed to fulfill major budget-related responsibilities.

Budget calendars portray key aspects of the budget cycle by dates or time periods. Legal requirements tend to get the most attention, but the calendars frequently show other activities and the particular officials or organizational units associated with those activities. Sometimes legal citations also are given. The dates typically include either deadlines for the completion of certain activities or a period within which certain activities occur. In either case, the ending points garner the most attention. Some periods are indeterminate. The beginning point in constructing a budget calendar is identifying the beginning and ending points of the implementation time period and then all other relevant legal, policy, and administratively imposed requirements, which all bear some time relationship to the implementation period. Before the implementation period, people in a budget cycle look forward toward implementation; afterward, they look backward toward implementation. Although the two examples given here do not do so, many calendars also indicate key activities during a fiscal year, the ending point, and key activities after the fiscal year ends.

Table 4.2 shows a budget calendar for the state of West Virginia prepared by the State Budget Office. It starts with a budget call and ends with the beginning of the implementation period on July 1, which is when most states start their fiscal years. The term "Expenditure Schedule Guidelines" refers to an apportionment process, which controls when expenditures can be made during the fiscal year, and the term "Revenue Cabinet Secretary" refers to the department head over the State Budget Office who represents the governor.

Table 4.3 shows a detailed budget calendar for Texas counties displayed on the state comptroller web page. This calendar focuses on activities up to the start of the fiscal year. It emphasizes revenue-related activity in eleven of the twenty-six steps. That emphasis arises from the assessment process, the annual setting of property tax rates, and a state limitation on property tax increases. Starting in the 1970s, many states imposed tax and expenditure

Table 4.2

The Budget Process Calendar for the State of West Virginia

Issue Appropriations Request Guidelines	July
Agencies submit requests	September
State Budget Office reviews requests	September
State Budget Office Hearings with State Agencies	September–October
Official Revenue Estimates completed	November
Final Budget Recommendations	December[a]
Governor presents Proposed Budget to Legislature	January[a]
Legislative Budget Hearings with State Agencies	January–March[a]
Senate Finance Bill and House Finance Bill	[a]
Legislature passes budget	March[a]
Governor approves/vetoes	March[a]
Issue Expenditure Schedule Guidelines	April
Agencies submit Expenditure Schedules	May
State Budget Office reviews schedules	May–June
Revenue Cabinet Secretary approves	June
Schedules entered into WV Financial Information Management System	June

Appropriations are ready for agencies to process payments when new Fiscal Year begins July 1.

Source: West Virginia, State Budget Office, www.wvbudget.gov/charts/BudProcText .htm.

[a]Following a gubernatorial election, these six steps in the budget process are delayed by one month.

limitations on their local governments. Activities relative to that limitation appear particularly in August and September. The limitation requires detailed restrictions that are expressed in the activity for August 7 in the calendar. Other state-imposed requirements on the expenditure side of the budget include the provisions for public inspection of a proposed budget, a public hearing on a proposed budget, the adoption period, and the filing requirement. Also, this calendar promotes the role of a budget officer, which may not always represent how Texas counties actually operate.

Top-level policy officials provide policy guidance orally or in writing and directly or indirectly. Written policy guidelines may appear in a budget call, be discussed in meetings, or both. For example, the president's Office of Management and Budget does consult with and provide policy guidance to federal agencies prior to their preparation of appropriations requests for that fiscal year. Formal public speeches may have budget priorities as an explicit or implicit topic. Even when policy officials do not explicitly indicate that they are addressing budget policy, their statements on policy matters may be inferred to reflect budgetary concerns. Policy-makers communicate their opinions and preferences in respect to changes that they would like to see in budget proposals. In budgets calls, policy guidance is likely to be thematic rather than detailed. Financial themes might include cutbacks, extreme frugality, or making wise investments for the future. More substantive themes include emphasizing e-technology, education, helping the less fortunate, and economic development. Some other policy themes include innovation, war on drugs, war on poverty, and improving energy policy. Although policy guidance is general, the intent is to encourage budget preparers to offer specific proposals. Policy guidance indicates what policy-makers think or say that they want in general terms; later they have to figure out whether actual proposals are what they really want. Whether budget guidance has been followed appropriately is a matter of judgment that can only be answered with certainty by policy-maker approval of budget proposals. Budget policy guidance lies somewhere between suggestions and commands: following the guidance may or may not bring rewards, and not following the guidance does not produce much chance of punishment.

The technical requirements found in budget calls can be extremely extensive, especially for large governments that deal with many complexities. The technical requirements also could be called information requirements. The required information ranges from material clearly central to a budget proposal to information that is supporting or peripheral to information that may appear to be window dressing. The heart of any set of technical requirements concerns the proposed expenditures. Other requirements may be meant to help explain the proposed expenditure forecasts, especially for certain kinds of expenditures; guard against efforts to manipulate budget situations; and demonstrate that certain matters are important. The technical requirements typically concern the categorization or organization of appropriation request information, the time periods, the procedures used to make the expenditure forecasts, and other required information.

The categorization or organization of information in appropriation requests varies tremendously because many relevant categories exist. In many cases, budget offices provide forms that reflect required appropriation request information categories. The most basic organizing concepts are organizational unit, object of expenditure, account, and fund. Additional common organizing concepts include function, activity, project, program, goal, source of funding, and new or continuing expenditures. Less common organizing concepts include authority, obligation, outlay, own-source revenues, resources currently available, and character. Some public organizations use other organizing concepts.

Public organizations, especially governments, appropriate by organizational unit. Public managers supervise organizational units; budget responsibilities

Table 4.3

Sample Budget Policy Statement for Texas Counties
County of Good Public Servants

Date	Action	Official
January 1	Assessment date	Chief appraiser
January	Prepare preliminary revenue estimates (revenue estimating is really a year-round process)	Budget officer
February	Establish budget policy	Governing body
	Establish budget calendar with governing body	Budget officer Governing body
	Develop budget format and outline of contents	Budget officer
	Begin preparing statistical and other supplementary information	Budget officer
March 1	Communicate budget policy and budget calendar to department heads and all employees	Budget officer
	Distribute departmental request forms	Budget officer
March/April	Help departments complete request forms	Budget officer
May 15	Chief appraiser submits estimate of total appraised value to appraisal review board for review and determination of protests	Chief appraiser
May	Revise revenue estimates	Budget officer with department heads
	Prepare preliminary budget	Budget officer with department heads
	Revise departmental estimates and/or develop spending alternatives for governing body's consideration	Budget officer
June	Governing body reviews budget	Governing body
July	Departmental hearings	Budget officer with department heads
July 25	Deliver certified appraisal roll to tax assessor	Chief appraiser

August 1	1. Deliver the appraisal roll to the court showing	Tax assessor
	• Total appraised, assessed, and taxable values	
	• Total appraised, assessed, and taxable values for new property	
	2. Certify a collection rate for the current year	
August 7	Calculate, publish, and present to the court	Person designated by the court
	1. Effective tax rate, rollback rate, and calculation methods	
	2. Estimated amount of unencumbered interest and sinking, and maintenance and operations balances	
	3. Schedule of debt obligations	
	4. Projected sales and use tax to reduce property tax	
	5. Amount of increase (decrease) based on effective tax rate	
	6. Information on transferred departments or functions	
	7. Information on tax effect of transferred departments or functions	
August	Complete proposed budget	Governing body
	File proposed budget with county clerk and make it available for public inspection at least 15 days prior to public budget hearing	Budget officer
	Decide whether it is necessary to increase taxes by more than 3 percent over the effective tax rate	Governing body
August/September	Hold public hearings for tax increase; if necessary vote on tax increase	Governing body
	Hold public hearing on budget	Governing body
	Adopt budget	Governing body
	Levy taxes before September 30, or the 60th day after the date the certified appraisal roll is received. (If not, the tax rate for the county for that tax year is the lower of the effective tax rate calculated for that tax year or the tax rate adopted by the county for the preceding tax year.)	Governing body
	File copy of adopted budget with county clerk and county auditor (if required)	County clerk

Source: Susan Combs, Texas Comptroller of Public Accounts, *Budgeting Handbook for Texas Counties*, October 2001, Chapter 5, www.texasahead.org/lga/budgetco/.

indicate the managerial status of a position. "Object of expenditure" refers to different kinds of items purchased or services obtained. Major object categories include personnel, supplies, equipment, contracts, and capital expenditures. These major categories may be subdivided extensively. Public organizations budget and track revenues and expenditures within funds and accounts. Organizational units and objects are represented in accounts and funds; for example, in the General Fund, the Public Works Department may have a heavy equipment account within which the department would request funding for the purchase of a dump truck.

The additional common categories represent different types of concepts. The terms "function," "activity," "project," "program," and "goal" (which also can be expressed as "output," "outcome," "performance," or "service efforts and accomplishments") often represent budgeting approach or format ideas, which are discussed further in Chapter 6. "Program" may also refer to a set of activities, sometimes in reference to the underlying legal authority or general policy. "Source of funding" refers to how the money supporting particular expenditures is being obtained; associating revenues and expenditures provides a basis for decision-making on those expenditures. During periods of revenue shortfalls or expenditure overruns, expenditures from general revenue sources tend to be reduced before those supported by user fees or grant revenues. The categories of "continuing" or "new" expenditures assist policy-makers in identifying departures from previous approved budgets because they tend to focus more on new proposed expenditures than continuing ones.

The less common of the concepts listed tend to express financial information that assists budget reviewers in gaining a finely tuned or precise appreciation of resource requirements and that tends to impede budgetary gamesmanship. "Authority" refers to any source of expenditure authority, but when the term authority comes up in budgeting, the concern is generally for expenditure authority besides annual appropriations. Authority to spend may originate in many different ways. Specific kinds of authority, besides annual appropriations, encompass appropriations for a multiyear period or without any specified time limit; authority to enter into contracts or debt, which is usually expended on later; or access to nonappropriated monies from gifts, grants, or own-source revenues. "Authority" is very interesting to those preparing and reviewing budgets, as it constitutes a capacity for action outside the annual formal budgetary policy process. Occasionally, agencies accumulate and use authority in ways that central policy-makers find inappropriate. A $300 million federal office building appeared in the Washington, DC, area in the 1990s without any official blessing above the agency level—the agency was in the Department of Defense and worked with the Central Intelligence Agency. The resulting investigations of this budgetary trick revealed that the

National Reconnaissance Office had accumulated more than one billion dollars in authority because it saved expenditure authority by putting off buying some capital equipment because the capital equipment that the expenditure authority was for lasted longer than expected.

"Obligation" refers to the act of committing expenditure authority. In all but the federal realm, obligation means legal obligation that may not be rescinded by one party to a transaction; in the federal realm, obligation usually means a commitment that may be rescinded unless a legal obligation is incurred. In the federal realm, obligations may be "deobligated" by federal officials. Federal contracts for goods and services frequently have a provision allowing the federal government to terminate the agreement at its convenience. Outlay often follows obligation and refers to payments actually changing hands. Organizational units may be asked to forecast how much of their appropriation and other authority will become obligated and outlaid during the upcoming fiscal year. Own-source revenues are revenues that do not go to a general treasury; for example, revenues from student fees, some grants, and business activities remain in the hands of public university officials. "Resources currently available" are all manner of resources that an organization might use to operate; a large inventory of equipment or supplies might mean that an organization does not need as much money appropriated. "Character" refers to the time category in which expenditures are expected to be beneficial relative to the fiscal year (past, present, or future).

The time periods are fiscal years, typically one to four fiscal years. A budget proposal always contains information for the proposed fiscal year; for biennial budgets, two fiscal years are proposed at one time.

Information for the currently implemented fiscal year can be handled in three different ways. Each of the three methods creates advantages and disadvantages for making budget decisions. First, budget proposals may show the current fiscal year in terms of the approved budget. Second, the current fiscal year may show expenditures to a particular point in time in the current year (year-to-date). Third, the current year may be shown as a combination of actual expenditures for the year-to-date and projected expenditures for the rest of the current fiscal year. Sometimes, the first way of showing the current year expenditures is combined with the second or third way. Finally, expenditures for the immediately past fiscal year are frequently included. Sometimes, two or three past years are displayed. The use of multiple historical years allows policy-makers to see continuity and change in budget proposals.

The advantages and disadvantages of the three methods of obtaining current year information relate to the efforts necessary to develop the figures and their accuracy. The first method is the easiest because the figures are readily available from the current year budget, but those figures are likely to be less accurate than figures developed using the other two methods as they do not take any current year information into account beyond the previously approved budget figures. The second method is next easiest because the current year expenditures to any point in time are usually easily obtainable from an accounting system; however, the fractional portion of a current year covered by those figures means that their accuracy for annual budgeting purposes depends on the people using those numbers knowing the normal pattern of expenditures and what portion of that pattern is not represented in the partial year figures. For example, any expenditures that vary greatly by season, such as energy usage for heating or cooling, or by specific events may range from being barely represented to being completely represented within partial year figures. The third method involves the most work and produces figures that are most likely to be accurate.

Budget calls may require specific procedures or values for forecasting. Specific values may include salary increases, general limits on increasing prices, a rate at which personnel slots will be unfilled, and rates for mileage or per diem travel reimbursements.

Budget calls and supporting documents indicate limits. Technical limits are more like process limits than policy limits because of their clarity. Technical limits may be anything that can be limited, especially numeric items: amounts of money, rates of change, and number of new proposals, pages, or topics.

The other required information takes different forms and varies by organizations. Some forms are tables, lists, memorandums, and general or detailed reports. The variety of content includes revenue forecasts, kinds of objects of expenditures, plans, justifications, policy authority, and prior results. The requirements for information on objects of expenditure include personnel, debt, capital expenditure, information technology, training, travel, and grants. Personnel information, often in the form of a staffing table, is the most common requirement. A staffing table shows authorized positions by pay levels or by specific person. Personnel information is required because personnel expenditures are typically the largest expenditure for public organizations with paid personnel.

Revenue forecasts are required for minor revenues collected by operating units because those revenues may offset operating units' expenditures. Also, operating units may have a greater ability to forecast those revenues accurately than do central officials.

Plans show how appropriations requests fit in a long-term perspective for the organizational unit. They also might constrain how an operating unit may explain in the future what it has done, is doing, and will do since their written form makes them relatively accessible.

Justifications, which consist of arguments and supporting evidence, indicate why expenditures are appropriate. Public managers frequently present arguments based on the ideas of higher demands or needs, prior commitments, legal obligations, pressing problems, future savings, new technology, and better results. Justifications may be required generally or specifically for capital items or other objects of expenditure, items over a specific dollar amount, or something new, such as programs or locations.

Policy authority, legal authority for governments, may appear pro forma as an information requirement. However, with such a requirement, someone in an organizational unit has to find and report the authority for a funded activity at least once.

Prior results reporting may be a simple narrative without specific requirements or a highly detailed report constrained by previous reports or other requirements. Some public organizations using a budget format based on results deploy elaborate reporting systems. One example is the federal Government Performance and Results Act of 1993, which requires relating strategic plans, annual performance plans, and annual program performance reports. This law instructs agencies to provide their Program Assessment Rating Tool assessments, which are annual program performance reports, when they are available.

Other required information may fit within the categories noted above; for example, the federal motor vehicle fleet report and agency information technology investment portfolio report obviously focus on capital expenditures. In contrast, the federal budgeting requirement to consider privacy and information technology investment in the context of preparing an appropriation request is an additional and different requirement, although one also established in a separate law.

When budget calls arrive in the hands of public managers, they begin making initial decisions about what to propose and how to go about making forecasts. In the ordinary course of events, the pertinent question is what to change from last year's proposed budget. Generally, public managers decide on changes rather than make a fundamental evaluation of how they conduct their organizational mission. This public manager perspective could be described as expressing a bias toward continuity or inertia. Budget practitioners, on the whole, appear to favor an incremental approach to changes, and budget reformers favor a more rational approach. Here, we focus on how participants in the budget process behave. Reform perspectives garner more attention in later chapters. In the nonordinary course of events, some situations do require fundamental evaluations of operations, whether resulting from changes in operating environments or policy guidelines.

Public managers' decisions on budget changes stem from budget calls, further guidance provided by policy-makers, and their own prior decisions.

The guidance in a budget call signals only the beginning points for operating units to figure out changes. Although many themes may appear to be less than promising, history provides many examples of operating units responding proactively by asking themselves, "What can we propose that fits with that theme?" An outstanding example of responding to a theme can be found in the National Defense Student Loan Program (1958), which followed the example of the National Interstate and Defense Highway System (1956). National defense was an overarching concern at that time. Similarly, the theme of holding costs down can be met with proposals for saving money by investing in labor-saving devices. Further guidance by policy-makers, such as administrators, can be as general as budget calls or very specific. Public managers' decisions on budget proposals reflect their knowledge of particular situations and prior commitments that they may have made. Some of their knowledge is derived from the current fiscal year.

Budget changes may be categorized as involving costs, operations, environment, or policy. Costs may change because of changes in prices or quantities. Price changes are particularly common. When costs change, usually increasing, public managers have to choose whether to propose higher expenditures, lower quantities of an object, or reductions somewhere else in a budget proposal. Operational changes occur as public managers choose the best available operational methods or ways of performing their tasks. Environmental changes may affect how services (demand-responsive services particularly) are rendered: for instance, more or less snow. Policies may change at any level from the operating units up to the top policy-making level in an organization. Those policy changes can affect budgets by starting new programming, stopping existing programming, making adjustments in programming, or changing budget requirements.

After public managers of operating units make initial change decisions, they forecast expenditures and perhaps minor revenues. Most public managers have two important biases in making changes. First, they prefer to increase appropriations requests so as to have more resources available to operate. Second, they prefer to avoid needless or pointless changes so as to minimize the work involved in preparing appropriations requests.

Expenditure forecasting may start with last year's budget proposal or decisions on programming plans. When operating units expect to buy about the same amounts of the same objects of expenditure as the previous year based on price changes, budget preparers only have to decide on price changes to use in calculating forecasts for expenditures. For example, if something is expected to increase in price by 3 percent, then the projected or estimated amount for that item would be increased by 3 percent. If changes in amounts also are expected, then looking at the programming plans helps determine where to start for expenditure forecasting. If the programming is directed—that is, a definite stated level of services or accomplishments—then the starting point is a work plan for those services or the projected accomplishments. A work plan is a general description of how resources will be used to provide the service: for example, hiring personnel to keep a public facility open. From a work plan, public managers can go into the details of how much of various resources are required to implement the work plan. Then, public managers forecast prices of those resources to calculate proposed expenditures (quantity x price). If the programming is demand-responsive and therefore unpredictable, operating units forecast a level of demand and determine how to deal with unexpectedly high levels of demand. In some cases, services may simply be capped at a certain level. In other cases, operating units may make plans for variable levels of response or shifts in resources from lower- to higher-priority programming, or propose other means of coping with high levels of demand.

Expenditure forecasting may vary based on whether forecasts deal with new or existing situations and predictable or unpredictable ones. Existing and predictable situations may be forecast more precisely than new or unpredictable ones. Greater uncertainty inclines forecasters toward forecasting expenditures on the high side.

Expenditures may be categorized in various ways for the sake of forecasting. Some expenditures may be "fixed" or "overhead" and others "variable" or "operating." Fixed and overhead expenditures do not vary according to levels of programming operations. Management positions, building rent, and capital expenditures typically are fixed or overhead expenditures. Variable and operating expenditures change according to levels of programming operations. Supplies, operating personnel positions, service contracts, and equipment typically are variable or operating costs.

Expenditure forecasting is crucial to operating public managers as they are implicitly promising that if they are given approval for their budget proposals they can provide services with the money provided. If they are incorrect on the levels of demand, the quantities of purchases, or the prices, then they have to figure out how to respond to actual situations with that approved budget. They may face problems, especially if their forecasts are on the low side. They can hope that forecasting errors counterbalance one another. They can cope by prioritizing their responsibilities. They can ask for more money.

Specific forecast values can be very complicated due to a high number of components to those values. For example, forecasting personnel expenditures can involve different kinds of personnel, various kinds of payments to personnel, various payments to others for fringe benefits for personnel, payment of a number of associated taxes, and a variety of related factors, such as longevity pay increases and vacancies in positions.

Expenditure forecasts at base involve prices and quantities of purchases and other expenditures. The prices of many purchases are determined in marketplaces. Some prices or payments are determined by policy choices: for example, raises for personnel. Some quantities depend on anticipated service demands that frequently vary, although not necessarily predictably, such as the number of school-age children.

Budget proposals represent a sum of their parts. Changes in certain aspects might require other changes. Price increases might lead to increases in expenditures, reduced use of an input factor, or perhaps a change in operational methods. Other changes from price increases may be offsetting price or quantity decreases for other expenditures.

After initially preparing appropriations proposals (appropriation requests and other required information), public managers finally decide on expenditure forecasts and other details of budget proposals and then submit them to the next higher level in their organization. If the policy-making body is the next higher organizational level, then the submission and approval stage begins. Public managers may experience only the upward submission of a budget proposal or one or more upward submissions followed by one or more downward request(s) for revisions.

People at the next higher levels and beyond review budget proposals, perhaps consult with the public managers responsible for the budget proposals, and make decisions on budget proposals. The word "review" literally means "to look at again," which also is suggested by the words "examine," "study," and "analyze." People in different positions review at different stages in the budget process. During the preparation stage, the reviewers are administrators and executives who receive budget proposals from others, and perhaps their staff or staff agencies review budget proposals before deciding what to pass forward. Staff may make recommendations, but the policy-makers are responsible for the formal decisions. During the submission and approval stage, members of policy-making bodies and their staff or staff agencies review budget proposals before deciding what to approve. During the implementation stage, public managers and policy-makers review the budget situation to see if their budgets are on course as approved. During the reviews and reports stage, implemented budgets are reviewed to determine what can be learned from them.

Here, the general process of reviewing is discussed without regard to the different stages or different actors involved. When people review, even though they might say or think that they are taking an unbiased looked at something, they tend to ask questions that reflect particular mind-sets. For example, accountants tend to ask or to address accounting questions, planners tend to ask or address planning questions, and politicians tend to ask or address political questions. People tend to use preconceived notions to frame their inquiries and to focus their attention. Technical specialists of various kinds tend to focus on technical questions such as the guidelines for forecasting revenues and expenditures, completeness in terms of all requirements being met, and technical correctness in the sense of the numbers adding up correctly and the technical requirements being fulfilled properly in a timely fashion and operationally reasonable in the sense of appearing arguably economical, efficient, and effective. Technically oriented review in many cases focuses on compliance, a pass-fail perspective rather than a comparative perspective between alternative uses of resources. Policy-oriented review focuses on the policy guidance in budget calls and policy preferences favored by the reviewers. Policy guidance in budget calls and policy preferences of reviewers tend to be relatively harder to discern and more prone to move relative to current events than technical review. Policy-oriented review tends to take a comparative perspective in that budget proposals provide choices among which policy-makers can choose. Staff personnel tend to do technical review, under policy-maker guidance, and policy-makers tend to review for policy issues.

The highest priority in review goes to new and changed aspects of budget proposals. Previously approved aspects of budget proposals tend to draw much less attention. Previously approved aspects of budget proposals tend to draw only cursory technical review and no policy review, unless an organization is considering cutbacks, dealing with problems or controversies, or someone is proposing serious changes related to a specific area. Policy-makers tend to focus on policies rather than details.

Reviewers may deal with budget proposals primarily on paper or primarily by discussion with budget proposers. Review interactions may be private or public. Although the interactions between organizational levels in dealing with budget proposals may be called "consulting" or "discussing," the communication flow might involve a one-way flow of things to change as well as an exchange of information and ideas both ways.

Those reviewing budget proposals have three obvious choices for resolving budget proposals situations: accept, reject, and revise (which is usually some blend of accepted and rejected portions). Each higher level uses all three options in varying degrees for portions or details of a budget proposal. Reviewers at each level generally accept most of the content of budget proposals, reject some new proposals and some specific forecast expenditures, and revise some figures to produce an acceptable proposed budget. Continued operation of organizational units requires eventual acceptance of a budget proposal in some form. Revisions may be made by the reviewing level or by whoever submits the proposal. People at higher levels give those who make budget proposals revision guidance that ranges from very specific to very general. The people at higher levels can take responsibility for revisions or force choices onto those who make budget proposals. Still, those at the higher levels bear the ultimate responsibility for budget proposals from their organizational domain because they control what is submitted to the next higher organizational level or the final decisions on a budget.

Both technical and policy-oriented reviews are likely to lead to revising appropriation requests downward. Public managers tend to ask for more appropriations than policy public managers will approve. They ask for more monies for currently purchased objects of expenditure with and without increased levels of activities. They ask for new objects of expenditure. They propose new activities. The reviewers' work may be seen as analogous to trimming bushes, especially in the preparation process, with public managers' budget proposals as the bushes. Those reviewing "snip, snip, snip" at prices, quantities, objects, assumptions, forecast values, and new projects and programs in budget proposals, with or without consulting the public managers who initially prepared the budget proposals. In effect, reviewers see budgets as puzzles with variable pieces that need to be adjusted, usually trimmed, to meet their own and others' concerns. A change in one piece often requires change in one or more other pieces.

Budget preparation concludes when executives or administrators complete budget proposals preparatory to submitting them to legislatures or policy boards. In some cases, multiple elected executives' proposals may be incorporated into one comprehensive proposal. Comprehensive public budget proposals include a transmittal document, appropriations requests, revenue forecasts, and perhaps a policy message. They may also include narrative explanations and supplemental information of various kinds.

Submission and Approval

Submission and approval of proposed budgets form an important part of public organizations' policy processes because policy-makers enable an organization to carry out particular responsibilities. Much of the activity in the policy-making process is political in character, as discussed in Chapter 5. In addition to political activities, the activities include submission, review, and approval.

Submission may be a very momentous occasion or a very low-key event. High-profile speeches by executives, such as the president's nationally televised State of the Union address and governors' televised State of the State addresses, punctuate some governmental budget submissions. Submission's import comes from its starting the formal policy process for approval of public organizations' budgets. That process requires at least a minimum of a formal majority vote by attending members of legislatures or policy boards. Submission usually starts with a comprehensive budget proposal.

After submission, policy-making board members and their staff or staff agencies review budget proposals and have opportunities to raise questions about those proposals.

The public policy process generally involves one policy-making body. The federal and all but one state governments use two legislative bodies. Governments may have zero, one, or multiple executives. In many cases, chief administrators in organizations without executives take over many of the responsibilities of an executive in executive budgeting without formal executive powers. Nonprofit organizations do not usually have executives with formal powers and independence from policy boards.

All policy-making bodies operate under general rules, which may be drawn from their charters or constitutions, standing laws or policies, and sets of procedural rules. Additional special rules may apply to budgetary matters. Special rules may apply in regard to special meetings, limits, majorities for approval, procedures, and veto powers. Special meetings may be required for public hearings or for voting on proposals.

States limit their own and their local governments' budgets in constitutions and laws. Examples of such limits include balanced budgets, debt (the number of years that debt may be owed and the amount of debt as a percentage of a government's property tax base), and various tax and expenditure limitations focused on rates of increases allowed.

Majorities required for approval are higher for some kinds of revenues and expenditures than others (the federal personal income tax was authorized by a constitutional amendment). In some cases, the majorities include a majority of the public voting in a referendum election on budget-related matters. A referendum may be required to pass or amend a state constitution, a local government charter, or a nonprofit organization's bylaws; to approve some local government revenue measures or debt issues; or to exceed a tax or expenditure limitation.

Special procedural rules may involve public notice, public hearings, number of readings (meeting sessions, in effect), deadlines, amending, discussion time, and matching total increases and total decreases in a budget proposal. Some rules specify how many specific proposals a budget may be divided into for consideration.

Policy-making rules are designed generally to facilitate deliberative discussion and expeditious decisions. Special rules concerning budgets make them public information, facilitate their resolution because they are necessary for funding operations, and limit revenue collections, borrowing, and expenditures. For example, proponents of special vetoes argue that those vetoes contribute to limiting expenditures, revenues, and debt. Some of the procedural rules involve committees and subcommittees.

Hearings may be public hearings or committee hearings. Public hearings are opportunities for members of the public to address legislators or policy board members about publicly available proposed budgets. These hearings operate under informal procedural rules similar to committee rules, which are discussed below.

Committees serve policy-making bodies by creating specialized subdivisions of a body so that a whole body can cover more material operating as committees than it can as a whole. In addition to the smaller number of members of committees, committees use much less constricting procedures since they do not take final actions. Some policy-making bodies operate as a committee of the whole when they are just discussing proposals. An important caveat is that committees can cover more material only if members of the various committees stay sufficiently close to the overall body's views of their specialized jurisdictions and if other members let committee decisions stand unless they are objectionable. Both of those concerns are addressed by a committee norm of reciprocity: go along with other committees and they will go along with you. Without reciprocal forbearance, policy-making processes would become seriously bogged down by a full body going over the exact same material covered by its committees. What is true of committees also is true of subcommittees used by larger legislative bodies. Where committees and subcommittees exist, most review by legislators or policy board members tends to take place within those confines. Policy-making bodies also may dedicate staff members to serving committees and subcommittees.

Committee hearings provide opportunities for committee members to take testimony from and to question administrators, executive officials, outside parties, and perhaps fellow policy-makers. Many who testify make opening statements. Committee members use committee hearings as an opportunity to gain a more detailed understanding of portions of budget proposals, as well as to express their own views on budget proposals.

When budgets are introduced into policy-making bodies, they may be submitted as a whole or broken up into pieces. The U.S. Congress deals with the federal budget as a whole for some purposes (overall revenue and spending targets) and on some occasions (continuing resolutions, discussed below), but the appropriations ordinarily are dealt with in thirteen separate pieces of legislation called bills. When broken up, each part of the submitted budget is treated as a separate proposal for purposes of approval. Despite all the possible procedural peculiarities, the general process is introduction to some body that reviews and approves some form of the budget proposal(s). The approval route runs (as procedurally required) from subcommittee to committee, from committee to floor (meaning full body), and from one body to another body where two bodies exist. When a policy process engages two policy-making bodies, approval requires their complete agreement. The two bodies' differences might be resolved by a joint or conference committee before being approved by each body. After approval by policy-making bodies, budgets can be implemented, unless the policy process includes an executive with approval or veto power (as in some governments). Some executives participate in the policy process through approval or veto power. In those cases, executives can deal with budget proposals by approving, not acting, or vetoing. If an executive approves, the policy is finalized. If an executive vetoes a budget proposal, the legislature can override a veto to finalize the policy. If the executive does not act (by "putting the proposal in a pocket"), the policy may be approved or pocket vetoed, as described below. The veto possibilities are roughly simple veto, pocket veto, partial vetoes (including reduction and line item vetoes), and amendatory veto.

Simple veto refers to a veto of a whole proposal. The pocket veto means that an executive does not approve a proposal. The results of pocket vetoes depend on whether a legislature is in session, typically for a specific time period. If a legislature is in session, the proposal may become finalized without executive approval or through a legislative veto override. If the legislature is not in session, the proposal is rejected. A pocket veto when a legislature is not in session will delay policy approval until the legislature is back in session; however, because budgets have to be passed eventually, executives with that power do not commonly use the pocket veto for major budget proposals. Partial vetoes allow governors to veto part of a budget proposal without vetoing the whole proposal. Within the category of partial vetoes, reduction and line item vetoes allow governors to reduce or eliminate specific amounts in a budget. In some cases, line item vetoes have been used to rewrite proposals by striking out specific words. Finally, the amendatory veto allows a governor to revise a proposal that can become law with majority votes, be overridden, or be ignored. In most cases, the major exception being the pocket veto, the executive returns the proposal with a veto message to the legislature, which has the option of acting.

In American governments, vetoes can be negated or overridden by legislative actions. Overrides of executive vetoes may be by simple or extraordinary majority votes of legislative bodies, both where there are two. The extraordinary majorities are typically three-fifths, two-thirds, or three-fourths.

Line item vetoes appear much beloved by proponents, who praise them as budget slimming. However, the sad reality is that executives can use line-item vetoes to increase or decrease budgets. As an executive power, a line-item veto simply gives executives another power to use to secure their preferences.

Sometimes policy-makers cannot successfully conclude a policy process to provide an approved budget proposal for any part of an organization before implementation is supposed to begin. In some cases, the lack of approval is inconsequential. In other cases, the stalemate continues and nothing can be done until the policy-makers resolve the stalemate; or they may approve one or more temporary resolutions of the situation; or the organization may operate under policies not requiring an approved budget proposal.

If an approved budget is not required to operate, some local governments routinely operate without an approved budget for a portion of their fiscal year. In those cases, the deadline for budget approval falls after the beginning of the implementation period. In a budget stalemate, an organization may lack authority to spend and have to suspend all operations. In situations using temporary resolutions (often called continuing resolutions), the policy-makers agree on time periods and level of appropriations. The time periods are often weeks, the details relatively few, and the expenditure authority usually approximates the status quo level from the previous budget. In situations not requiring an approved budget, governments have policies that allow officials to determine whether particular activities are "essential" and to make expenditures for essential activities. Expenditures for "unessential" or "nonemergency" employees and activities are stopped until the stalemate is resolved; usually, unessential employees get paid vacations as their pay is retroactively authorized. Finally, in some situations, executives, administrators, and public managers, knowing that they lack any valid authority to spend, continue to spend and to operate their organizations as if they did have spending authority because of their understanding of the necessity of the situation. In some cases, employees work even when their pay is not available for a time. Such a choice by public managers should be a last resort as such situations are fraught with the possibility of extremely negative repercussions involving job retention and criminal charges.

Stalemates are temporary in most cases. The final resolution for each proposal is an approved budget for the remainder of the fiscal year. Because budgets have to pass eventually for public organizations to operate, occasions arise when executives and legislative bodies use budget passage to extract concessions from the other side. In Connecticut in 1992, Governor Lowell Weicker used a budget impasse to force the legislature to pass the state's first income tax as an alternative to the state ceasing operations.

Implementation

Budget implementation, sometimes called execution, usually follows budget approval; however, partial implementation of a fiscal year might occur before the approval occurs. When a fiscal year begins without an approved budget, public organizations act on some other basis than the authority of an approved budget, as discussed earlier. Also, some implementation activities may precede and follow a fiscal year, as will be noted below. For present purposes, implementation can be grouped into four sets of activities: communicating, doing work, making changes, and engaging in financial routines. It should be noted that public managers are very much involved with budget decision-making during the implementation process and that implementation is not mechanical.

Policy-makers approve budgets in terms that range from very general to relatively general to relatively specific. Table 4.4 provides a very general example from a 2008–2009 budget proposal introduced in the California General Assembly. The U.S. Congress similarly appropriates billions of dollars in single sentences. In relatively general appropriations, we find general categories of objects of expenditure, such as personnel, equipment, supplies, and contracts, or major subdivisions of such categories. Relatively specific terms may refer to specific projects, specific objects of expenditure, and specific organizational positions. When the appropriations are less than relatively specific, the expectation may be that the persons being granted the expenditure authority conform to the pattern of expenditures in proposals, in committee reports, or from past practices.

Communicating occurs after a budget is approved and frequently before a fiscal year begins. An executive or an administrative official in a central office or agency prepares and distributes communiqués to persons in the top positions in various organizational units that indicate what expenditure authority has been granted to those organizational units in what categories. In some cases, a central organization oversees a process of apportionment where restrictions are placed on how much expenditure authority is available in what categories for what time periods. Apportionment frequently involves requests and approvals that leaves operating units with less expenditure authority than was granted by the policy-making board as well as time and category restrictions. When expenditure authority is granted in very or relatively general terms, operating units may allocate that authority into object of expenditure categories or subcategories. Finally, allotment refers to communicating expenditure authority downward in a hierarchy. Persons in higher positions tell persons in lower positions how much money they have for expenditures.

As public managers use expenditure authority for doing the work of their organizational units, they gather information, analyze it, and make decisions about deploying resources. In doing so, they act as agents for the public or the groups served by their organization and exercise discretion as they order priorities under conditions of uncertainty and scarce resources. Public

Table 4.4

Excerpt From Proposed 2008–2009 State of California Budget

1110-001-0108—For support of Acupuncture Board, payable from
   the Acupuncture Fund   2,514,000
Schedule
(1) 56-Acupuncture Board   2,537,000
(2) Reimbursements   −23,000
Provisions
1. The amount appropriated in this item may include revenues derived from the
assessment of fines and penalties imposed as specified in Section 13332.18 of the
Government Code.

Source: Page 75 of AB 1770 as introduced into the California State Assembly (house)
on January 10, 2008, by Assembly Budget Chair John Laird, www.assembly.ca.gov/acs/
acsframeset2text.htm. An updated version can be found at www.documents.dgs.ca.gov/
osp/GovernorsBudget/pdf/fbudsum_0809.pdf, p. 106.

managers typically have more discretion over deploying resources than over
what resources they have available. For example, personnel and supply appropriations are limited in amounts and may be highly detailed; however, public
managers decide exactly when, where, and how which of those resources are
deployed, unless they are otherwise restricted.

When public managers see a need for making budgetary changes during
a fiscal year, they have varying degrees of authority to act in how resources
are arrayed in expenditure categories. In some cases, executives, administrators, and public managers may have authority to move some expenditure
authority from one category to another. The authority ranges from none to
fairly broad grants of authority. Many local government legislatures choose
not to delegate this authority. Some public organizations provide a limited
amount of such authority, perhaps limited to specific categories or within
certain amounts by dollar amount or percentage. Some public organizations
provide fairly broad authority in this area. The broadest possible authority is
to authorize expenditures without any kind of policy approval, which the U.S.
Congress did in the Feed and Forage Act of 1861, which currently remains
on the books. The Coast Guard and the Department of Defense or individual
officers acting on that legal basis can purchase clothing, subsistence, forage,
fuel, quarters, transportation, or medical and hospital supplies for use within
the current fiscal year. The Feed and Forage Act is one of many laws granting
discretion to federal officials in handling expenditure authority. Generally,
large organizations find it useful to grant their public managers considerable
flexibility in dealing with the myriad details that they face. Generally, aside
from unexpected expenditures outside of appropriated resources, the two types

of common discretionary authority are transfer and reprogramming authority. Transfer authority is the ability to move appropriations from one category of objects of expenditure to another (e.g., between personnel and supplies). Reprogramming authority is the ability to use appropriations differently than initially anticipated or approved within the same object of expenditure category (e.g., a different kind of supply expenditure). Whoever makes the rules on making changes defines the categories, any limits, and communication requirements. If public managers make budget changes during a fiscal year, they communicate what they change to others.

Many budget changes during a fiscal year require policy board approval. In addition to transfers and reprogramming decisions in many cases, policy-makers might choose to increase or to decrease expenditure authority. Decreases sometimes are referred to using the verbs "rescind" or "prorate" or the nouns "recession" and "proration." Increasing expenditure generally requires policy board approval, either as a budget amendment or an additional appropriation, sometimes referred to as a supplemental appropriation. Decreasing expenditure authority may be done by a budget amendment or by provisions previously established in a standing policy by which expenditures are rescinded on a fixed basis (across-the-board percentages by organizational units) or on the basis of an executive's discretionary authority to direct cuts in organizations' budgets. In addition, some executives choose not to expend appropriations in particular categories for technical or policy reasons, which is called "impounding." Impounding is not controversial when it occurs for technical reasons, such as when a need no longer exists. The classic example of technical impoundment is President Jefferson's decision not to spend money on the war with the Barbary pirates after the war ended. Impounding is controversial when the reasons are policy-oriented. Then, legislators tend to disapprove, as was the case when Congress passed the Congressional Budget and Impoundment Control Act in 1974, over President Nixon's veto, in reaction to his impoundments. He said that Congress was spending too much money for the economic well-being of the country and that they were spending money on programs that President Nixon thought were the wrong priorities; in effect, he claimed the power to disapprove budget decisions made by Congress. Now, presidents have to ask for and obtain permission from Congress to rescind appropriations—permission that they have not been generally successful in obtaining. In many cases, public managers decide not to expend all the appropriations in particular categories because of concerns over later spending needs and because they are not able to make expenditures before the fiscal year ends. In most cases, expenditure authority lapses or expires at the end of a fiscal year.

Public managers juggle their decisions about making expenditures and using resources as they have to balance communicated budget authority against present needs and likely future needs within the fiscal year. When they reach the end of a fiscal year with spending authority available that they have saved to the end, they show little hesitation in finding useful ways of spending. Many critics castigate year-end spending with comments such as "fiscal year-end feeding frenzy." However, the critics fail to note that public managers were given budget authority by policy-makers and had not used it earlier. In many cases, such year-end spending results from the release of apportioned expenditure authority that had been withheld until the end of the fiscal year.

During implementation, public managers spend a great deal of time engaging in financial routines associated with budgets. They supervise the collection of revenues and the expenditure of resources. Actions related to expending resources include all the actions relative to paying personnel, deciding what to buy, and processing purchases. During implementation, public managers frequently consult their budgets as communicated to them and the various rules under which they are able to use those budgets. Public managers are responsible for accounting entries, created by virtue of the ever-present paperwork, to indicate orders, purchases, revenues, and expenditures. Those entries, in turn, become incorporated into accounting reports that provide public managers with information on how their annual budget implementation is going.

At the end of a fiscal year, remaining expenditure authority for that fiscal year may lapse or may be carried forward or carried over temporarily into the next fiscal year. Where expenditure authority lapses, someone has to make provisions for budgeting expenditure authority for items that are already on order or for other expenditure obligations incurred prior to the end of the fiscal year, such as payroll. Where unused expenditure authority is carried into the next fiscal year, the "carry" is only for expenditures approved for the previous year and not for anything else. Some organizations are experimenting with allowing organizational units that do not expend all their appropriations to retain some portion of them for future use.

Reviews and Reports

After a fiscal year ends, budgeting activities still continue in the form of reviews and reports. Reviews and reports may occur in relationship to one another or independently. For example, the most widely known review and report process concerns financial audits. Public organizations produce annual financial reports from their accounting systems; auditors review those reports and issue an audit report. People inside and outside public organizations review budget implementation in general or very specifically, informally or formally, and perhaps report review findings.

Reasons for reviews and reports vary. Reviews might afford opportunities for making better decisions in the future based on past experiences. Reviews and reports are used to fulfill legal or other imposed requirements while allowing operating units some discretion during a fiscal year and to maintain accountability of operating units by reminding them that they are supposed to be working for the public and using resources wisely. Reviews and reports may serve as public relations efforts.

Public managers review in order to do their jobs as well as possible, which includes anticipating possible budgetary changes and changes in budget proposals. They may ask themselves or have asked of them, "What was done?" "What lessons can be learned from your experiences in an implementation of a fiscal year?" "What went right?" "What went wrong?" and "What should be watched in the future?" Sometimes public managers may use various other categories for review, such as strengths, weaknesses, opportunities, and threats. Such reviews are informal. Sometimes small organizational units conduct multiple-person review sessions.

When public managers are required to make annual reports, they are likely to combine their reporting and reviewing efforts. However, they are unlikely to express all their thoughts in an annual report for various reasons. Such reports might require specific information, may be expected to be of modest length and detail, and might not be places where public managers want to display all their thinking. Annual reports may be stark statistical presentations of numbers or discuss challenges, accomplishments, services, and major events of a fiscal year and perhaps future plans; they may contain financial information. Just as budget proposals become incorporated into more inclusive proposals, some reports become the basis for reports submitted by people higher in an organization's hierarchy and eventually the basis for external reports. Required reports may be the basis for reviews of public managers' areas of responsibility by their organizational superiors. Many reports of a review character are not circulated beyond the administrative level of public organizations.

Outsiders may review and report to executives, administrators, policy boards, or the public informally or formally. Audits are the most common external formal review because most audits are required. "Audit" is just another name for a review. Accountants conduct most audits, and most audits are accounting-related audits rather than related to operating results. Accounting-related audits generally focus on questions concerning accounting rules, accuracy of information, and adherence to proper accounting and financial procedures. In addition, beginning in the last half of the twentieth century, external reviews increasingly turned to analysis or evaluation of organizational performance, efficiency, and effectiveness, which accountants term "service efforts and accomplishments." These sorts of efforts, whether called audit or something else, examine and report the performance of agencies in regard to results. Chapter 8 discusses audits in more detail.

For governments, external reviews relating to budgets include debt ratings and analysis for economic development activities. Debt rating agencies look at past and current budget information, especially audited annual financial reports where available, and other related information to assess the ability and propensity of public organizations to pay money to borrowers. They issue ratings that essentially report their assessments. As an outside party, such agencies often have greater credibility than persons associated with a public organization. Those engaged in economic activities, including home purchases and business activities, often review their expected or likely tax burdens within particular jurisdictions. Some economic development organizations provide overall economic development indexes.

Public organizations issue annual reports of various sorts. Annual financial reports, which are issued by most governments and governed by accounting rules, provide annual financial information in regard to what monies were collected, spent, borrowed, repaid, and the resulting financial situation of the public organization. Nonprofit organizations may have to file reports concerning revenues and expenditures with state officials; financially larger ones have to report to the U.S. Internal Revenue Service to maintain their nonprofit status relative to federal tax laws. Public organizations using results-oriented budgeting approaches may require annual results reports of some kind that relate to the claims made in budget proposals from their operating units, and they make those reports, or reports on reviews of those reports, public.

Conclusion

The formal budget process goes through four stages. The preparation stage, when public managers lay out proposed budget plans, is dominated by budget calls that guide the preparation of appropriation proposals and other documents. The submission and approval stage reflects the policy process with special rules for budgets and greater attention for budgets generally than most policy issues because of the importance of resources. The implementation stage, which includes the ordinary operations of organizations, requires many budget-related activities. The reviews and reports stage involves looking at budget implementation to see what can be learned for the future and involves making reports. Overall, the budget process is complicated, interactive, and cyclical.

The other two budget processes, informal and constrained revenues and expenditures, display different patterns of behavior. The informal process shows ad hoc responses to situations involving preparation, submission and approval, and implementation within relatively short time periods. Constrained revenues and expenditures, in contrast, are relatively permanent budget decisions that stand unless or until changed.

Appendix: Constrained Revenues and Expenditures

Certain revenues and expenditures are predetermined by prior policy decisions and not seriously considered in most budget processes. These constrained revenues and expenditures include most revenue measures, revenue expenditures, subvented revenues, earmarked revenues, revenues from business-like activities, formally restricted revenues, and revenues that come with fiduciary responsibilities. Most revenue measures are just assumed to continue as previously. Revenue measures with specific constraints affect how those resources are used. The resources that are constrained as a matter of expenditure policies include entitlements, debt, and other legal obligations. In few cases are these revenues or expenditures completely beyond policy-makers' control; instead, policy-makers decide not to control them during the budget process or believe that they cannot be controlled in that process.

Most revenue measures are based on standing policies that continue unless and until they are changed. During most budget processes, policy-makers do not even consider making changes in most revenue measures. Local property taxes are formally an exception because they are explicitly decided on in formal budget processes. Even for property taxes, the focus is on the amount of change—the bulk of property tax revenues remains the same from year to year. Concern for more revenue appears to be the most common reason for changing revenue measures during a budget process. When public organizations perceive a need for more revenues, they tend to make adjustments in existing revenue measures, introduce temporary revenue measures, or add new and ongoing revenue measures.

Revenue expenditures generally are invisible when not being directly discussed. Exemptions, deductions, credits, and special (reduced) rates result in reduced amounts of revenue collections.

Subvented revenues refer to specific revenue measures collected by a public organization that shares the proceeds voluntarily with other public organizations in a predetermined manner. Many states subvent a portion of their general retail sales, gasoline, or personal income taxes to local governments.

Earmarked revenues refer to revenues from some sources that public organizations dedicate to particular uses as a matter of policy. (The term "earmarked" refers to the practice of notching the ears of livestock to identify their ownership.) Revenues from some state lotteries are earmarked for educational spending. Earmarked expenditures, sometimes referred to as "earmarks," are specific projects that policy-makers designate within the formal budget process.

Some revenue providers specify how the resources that they provide may be used. Most grants, many gifts, and some subvented revenues carry such limitations. These limitations can be very general or highly specific.

Revenues for business-like activities, the buying and selling of goods and services, are frequently limited by policy or by external debt contracts that funded those activities as well as by the practical necessity of providing goods and services to collect the revenues. Utility revenues frequently have such debt-based requirements.

Public organizations collect monies for which they have a fiduciary responsibility, which means duties to others as a matter of law about how the monies are used. The monies may legally belong to other parties, like deposits and pension monies, which means that the other parties' interests must be protected, or may be limited only to the purposes for which the monies are used, such as scholarships or cemetery care.

Some revenue-related limitations only apply to general purposes or general areas of expenditure, and some are quite detailed in regard to specific amounts for specific events or specific purchases. Where such limitations are general, policy-makers or public managers can decide on specific details.

On the expenditure side of budgets, entitlements provide benefits under specific conditions to those who are entitled. If the conditions are met, then the public organization provides benefits to the beneficiaries. Those benefits may be payments, loans, or grants. Entitlements may be open-ended or closed-ended in the sense of an entitlement program having fixed limits on benefits paid. Those limits may be an annual total amount appropriated or a limit relative to recipients.

Public organizations make debt payments as a matter of course. Only in unusual circumstances do policy-makers deliberate on whether to do so.

Aside from debt, public organizations may have other legally binding obligations for expenditures. Lawsuit judgments or negotiated settlements, leases for buildings or equipment, service contracts, and credit, pension, deposit, or other guarantees of payments provide examples.

Policy-makers constrain revenues and expenditures for various reasons. First, constraints on general revenue policies arise from the recognition that those decisions have been made and that opening them up for revision will create unpredictable consequences.

Second, and similarly, some standing policies arise in situations where deciding not to collect or to spend in particular ways will create significant negative consequences. For example, not paying debt or other legal obligations or not using revenues to finance the services for which the revenues are paid have obvious negative consequences.

Third, in some cases policy-makers limit themselves from changing constrained revenues and expenditures because of a lack of public trust or political support by tying changes to something else or promising not to make changes. Some revenue measures, for example, are only acceptable with explicit constraints on how the revenues are used—say, for education. An interesting example of this phenomenon that went astray was the decision by federal policy-makers to use an automatic cost-of-living adjustment for old-age pensions to avoid the temptation of currying favor with older voters by increasing payments to them in the policy process. That decision, quite unintentionally, resulted in expenditure increases because the basis for the automatic increases (the Consumer Price Index for Urban Wage Earners and Clerical Workers) increased much more rapidly than expected. Previous to that decision, that basis changed less rapidly than general inflation rates; afterward, it increased more rapidly, and in effect, it granted an inflation bonus to Social Security recipients and increased funding difficulties for that program.

Fourth, some constraints represent an emphasis on fundamental values. For example, old-age pensions and veterans' benefits are highly valued. Although disputable in particular cases, many such claims appear reputable.

Finally, constraints on revenues and expenditures occur because of superior political power. People who believe that "their" causes or situation will benefit from constrained revenues or expenditures support those constraints. Because resources are limited, political power is a requisite for creating privileged revenues and expenditures. For example, according to Aaron Wildavsky in *The Politics of the Budgetary Process*, Representative Dan Flood of Pennsylvania secured disproportionate entitlement benefits for his district in the black lung disease program when he served on two House Appropriation subcommittees, Labor and Health, Education, and Welfare (chair) and Defense, meaning that he was a key policy-maker for approximately two-thirds of federal appropriations.

Constrained revenues and expenditures can contribute to making budgeting situations difficult when revenues lag, when constrained expenditures outpace revenues, and when new expenditure needs emerge. The difficulties involve hard budget decisions in the face of entrenched interests, which almost inevitably means political conflict. At the federal level, since the 1980s, constrained revenues and expenditures limited discretionary spending and contributed to persistent deficits and political conflict.

Additional Reading and Resources

Print

An earlier view of the budgeting process can be found in Chapters 4 and 10 to 14 of an early textbook:
  Burkhead, Jesse. *Government Budgeting*. New York: Wiley, 1956.

Internet

The City of Fayetteville, Arkansas—Budget Calendar
The city of Fayetteville, Arkansas, provides a budget calendar and quarterly management reports on the implementation of its annual budgets at www.accessfayetteville.org/government/budget/annual_budget_work_program/budget_calendar.cfm.

Laws About Budget Processes
Here are two ways to approach state and territorial laws about budget processes. The first is to access the state page at the usa.gov website and then proceed to an official home page for a territorial or state government to find its laws (often referred to as statutes and code) and even proposed laws (bills) and go from there. If the laws are not visible from a home page, they can be found on a legislature's home page at www.usa.gov/Agencies/State_and_Territories.shtml. The second is to use the following page at Cornell University Law School's Legal Information Institute, which contains links to state statutes at www.law.cornell.edu/statutes.html#state.

The National Association of State Budget Officers
The National Association of State Budget Officers website provides reports on "Budget Processes in the States" that contain a wide variety of budget-related information, the most current of which is listed at www.nasbo.org/Publications/PDFs/2008%20Budget%20Processes%20in%20the%20States.pdf.

The Federal Budget
The federal budget process is outlined in Circular A-11 from the Office of Management and Budget at www.whitehouse.gov/omb/circulars_a11_current_year_a11_toc.
  The Office of Management and Budget provides "A Glossary of Terms Used in the Federal Budget Process" (GAO-05–734SP Sept. 1, 2005), which contains appendixes on the federal budget process, appropriation categories,

and laws. That document can be viewed at and printed from www.gao.gov/new.items/d05734sp.pdf.

Budgeting-Related Federal Laws
Budgeting-related federal laws, which are collectively called the United States Code, can be found by searching on "budget" and other relevant terms at www.gpoaccess.gov/uscode/index.html.

5

Politics Within Public Budgeting

Budgetary politics concerns efforts to influence the outcome of decisions about how much money or resources are needed, where they come from, where they go, when, and how. Politics and budgeting relate to each other, especially in regard to budget decisions. Public managers relate to various kinds of politics when they make budget decisions. Participants in budgetary politics play various conventional roles. Budgetary politics presents threats to and opportunities for public managers' areas of responsibility. Public managers' actions have political import in budgeting, and they can exercise care in their choices of actions and reactions to favor their areas. Generally, public managers relate to budgetary politics by observing and choosing whether, when, and how to act relative to the politics of situations.

Budget decisions are ultimately political in the sense of being officially approved by the governing authorities of public organizations, even where politics and management do not ordinarily substantially overlap and even if managers do not want to participate in politics. Because budget decisions are political, managers are participating in politics when they make budget decisions. Managers simply do not get to choose whether to participate in budgetary politics. They may participate well or poorly. Their participation reflects greater or lesser political awareness and skill.

Politics often has been defined as the art of the possible. Public managers observe politics to discern what is possible in their area of responsibility. Politics guides and limits budget decisions. Budget decisions always are made in particular political contexts. For the most part, political actors determine political limits. However, public managers may be able to affect those limits at their margins. Still, public managers are not the most important or the most visible participants in budgetary politics.

Different Kinds of Politics

The different kinds of politics vary in scope, overall importance, relevance, arenas, and participants. The kinds of politics that concern public managers can be described as basic, partisan, policy, institutional, organizational, and personal politics. These kinds of politics do overlap. We will discuss each in turn here and then discuss how they relate to public managers making budget decisions.

Basic political principles, values, goals, and structural distribution of political power stand outside of ordinary budgetary politics. In extraordinary circumstances, when political basics are in flux, they may intrude or be thrust into budgetary politics. For example, during the 1980s and 1990s, political conflict between the two major political parties and between presidents and congresses reflected a basic disagreement about the proper scope and size of the federal government, leading to budget impasses. Inclusion of language in budget proposals and enactments concerning federal funding for abortion provides specific examples. Although the examples given here are primarily federal for the sake of relevance to all readers, similar examples can be cited for state and local governments and nonprofit organizations. Basic politics tends to be permanent and fundamental in character.

Partisan politics refers to politics concerning parts of a community or a group rather than a whole community or a whole group. Although all politics can be seen as partisan in the sense of being divisive when issues divide people, partisan politics here refers to ongoing divisions that produce recognized groupings, such as political parties and interest groups. Political divisions arise based on people's opinions, interests, beliefs, passions, and group identifications. Partisan politics generally aims at favoring or serving one side or one group at the expense of another side or group. The most obviously partisan politics includes political parties with which many people identify. Next in obviousness are interest groups based primarily on opinions, beliefs, and economic interests. Examples include the two major national political parties, people in geographic areas (snowbelt versus sunbelt coalitions in the U.S. Congress), gun enthusiasts (National Rifle Association), union members (United Auto Workers), and older people (American Association of Retired Persons). Divisions between people with different views in political communities and nonprofit organizational groups are very common. Jonathan Swift satirized the partisan politics of his day in *Gulliver's Travels* (1726) when he described two political groups who were divided over whether to break open a soft-boiled egg on the big or the little end of the egg. Partisan politics often appears similarly silly to those who are not involved, but partisan politics is often deadly serious to those who participate.

Politics involving political parties typically is oriented toward elections and the selection of officeholders. Political parties are designed to gain and exercise political power. In the United States, parties typically participate in electoral activities and organize governments. Other groupings, particularly organized interest groups, tend to focus on policy decisions. Parties and interest groups tend to favor or associate with each other; small business groups tend to align with the Republican Party, and labor unions and environmental groups tend to align with the Democratic Party.

Policy generally refers to official decisions by organizations. Policy politics includes formal budget decisions by governing officials and informal resource allocation decisions by public managers. Budgetary politics occurs generally within the context of policy politics.

Institutional politics refers to politics between institutional offices held by governing officials. Examples include conflicts and contests between executive and legislative branches, between two legislative houses, and between two or more executive officials.

Organizational politics refers to politics between different organizational units as they seek greater authority, influence, and funding within a larger entity (governments or nonprofit organizations). In a sense, all organizational units compete with one another for funding. In specific cases, related organizational units compete for advantages in particular areas; for example, all U.S. military services operate and compete for funds for their flying devices. Organizational politics often are connected to policy politics as specific organizations vie for policies that support their missions.

Personal politics focuses on advancing or retarding the advancement of the fortunes of particular individuals. Representations or actions make a person look good/smart/favorable or bad/stupid/unfavorable. Sometimes critics allege that certain politicians and administrators appear to be more concerned with looking good rather than doing good. Personal politics often is connected to partisan, institutional, and organizational politics because ambitious people acquire various positions to gain and exercise political power.

How Public Managers Relate to Different Kinds of Politics

Public managers relate to politics by observing and acting. They observe in order to be in a position to decide whether, when, and how to act relative to particular political situations that concern their areas of responsibility. Public managers generally engage in some kinds of political situations and avoid acting in other kinds of political situations. They primarily act relative to policy and organizational politics. Public managers find that acting in their official role works out badly for them in the other kinds of politics: basic, partisan, institutional, and personal politics. For a variety of reasons, these four kinds of politics contain many more chances for bad outcomes than good ones. These four kinds of politics generally produce winners and losers; public managers and agencies that participate in these kinds of politics therefore are perceived as taking a side, which may win or may lose. When public managers participate in these kinds of politics, in addition to the possibility of losing a

particular desired outcome, they may create enduring hard feelings in opposing participants, undercut their and their organization's creditability with all
political actors, cost particular managers their jobs, and reduce the capability
of agencies and the public to succeed in budgetary politics. Although there are
exceptions in places where public managers and agencies are expected to be
political actors, especially political appointees, most people generally view
public managers as appropriately taking a technically competent and politically neutral or nonpartisan role in public affairs. As private citizens, public
managers generally hold the same rights as other citizens, especially in regard
to voting and expressing personal political opinions. However, specific state
and federal laws, particularly the federal Hatch Act and similar state laws,
limit the political activities of governmental managers in two areas: activity
with or on the behalf of political parties and actions involving the use of their
official positions and other governmental resources for something other than
their official responsibilities.

In contrast, public managers are expected to participate in policy and
organizational politics related to their areas of responsibility. Expectations
arise because of their perceived technical competence in those areas and
because they are expected to take a favorable view of their responsibilities
and operating units.

To recap, public managers generally are not expected to participate in basic,
partisan, institutional, and personal politics. They are expected to participate
in policy and organizational politics that relate to their areas of responsibility.
Nevertheless, participants in budgetary politics, including public managers,
do observe basic, partisan, institutional, and personal politics because those
kinds of politics intrude on or play out in the realm of policy and organizational
politics that directly affects public organizations and their public managers'
area of responsibility. Knowledge about those kinds of politics helps managers
avoid stumbling into situations that they should avoid. Political situations to
avoid include advocating courses of action that are at odds with basic political principles, current institutional arrangements, a prevailing political party,
and particularly potent political actors. Public managers engage in political
situations involving budget and organizational politics, but without becoming
overtly partisan political actors.

Budgetary Politics

Budgetary politics is a particular kind of policy politics. The policy questions that budgetary politics addresses generally deal with amounts of
revenues or expenditures. The revenue question tends to be, How much
revenue from whom? The expenditure question tends to be, How much

expenditure for what? Inevitably, some situations combine the questions: How much revenue from whom, and how much expenditure for what? Revenues do have to come from some places in order to go to some other places as expenditures.

The politics arising in relationship to state financial aid to local schools provides a particularly fascinating area for observing the question of how revenues from particular revenue measures are used as state expenditures to provide revenues to schools so that the schools have money to expend without raising the revenue themselves from local revenue payers. The various potential revenue payers tend to be in favor of education funding coming from someone else, and schools currently benefiting from state aid prefer not to give up any of that aid regardless of how strongly their officials feel that other schools need more financial aid. As a result, states operate widely varying systems of financial aid for education.

The political activities associated with revenue decisions can be fairly described as policy and partisan politics in which public managers do not participate. The collection of resources from publics for collective activities has been a continual issue in human history. Those seeking resources justify their collection with various arguments, such as pleasing a god or gods, serving the common good, providing specific benefits, or taking because they can. The pattern of revenue politics tends to be initial establishments, modest revisions of basic and peripheral features, and upward adjustments in collections of specific revenue measures as ad hoc responses to specific situations, often involving a perceived need for resources to deal with specific problems, which may be presented in a crisis context (war, famine, and epidemics). Most of the time, revenues continue or remain as ongoing or standing policies that are minimally adjusted from time to time.

Under popular governments, governing officials choose revenue policies that they believe will produce sufficient revenues while still remaining relatively acceptable to the public, because deviating from public wishes results in those officials and their party losing their political positions and political power. In contrast, because nonprofit organizations do not have taxing power, they have to rely on voluntary exchanges for revenue, including payments for services, grants, gifts, and dues.

Because revenues and services, especially tax-funded ones, are not necessarily connected, revenue politics may be particularly intense and divisive, as school funding issues at the state level and national disputes over tax policies repeatedly demonstrate. Revenue politics can induce riots, political movements, and revolutions as groups seek resources held by other groups under the guise of serving the public good. Public managers, fortunately, have little to do with revenue politics.

Budgetary Politics and the Budget Cycle

Budgetary politics resembles budget processes in involving ad hoc, standing, or annual decisions (discussed in Chapter 4). Most budgetary politics discussions concern annual budget processes, as does most of the discussion here.

Ad hoc and standing budgetary politics differ from annual budgetary politics in that they tend to take place outside of an annual budget cycle in which multiple decisions are being made at approximately the same time. With fewer decision points at hand, ad hoc budgeting and standing budgeting politics focus more on one or a few issues at the same time. Fewer issues usually mean fewer major participants, less information to process, potentially more comprehensive analysis, and potentially more rational decisions. These kinds of situations can lead to more rational decisions if the decision-makers are rational or if they share the same values and views as the persons pronouncing whether the decisions are rational.

Ad hoc budgetary politics involves immediate, specific, discrete situations, such as deciding whether to repair or replace a roof damaged by a storm. The time horizons are short and participants few. These situations may occur in public organizations without public managers, at the level of policy boards, at the level of administrators in a hierarchy, at public managers' level of operations, and at more than one of these levels. In ad hoc situations, ordinary public managers tend to exercise discretion when not directed, to respond appropriately to directives for action or inaction, and to provide information. The political actions tend to be the selective provision of information and arguments as to what should be done. Still, the political activities associated with acquiring support for particular policy positions and dissipating opposition look very familiar to people who observe politics. Proponents of various positions offer information, arguments, and support for or opposition to those formally making ad hoc decisions. People generally express the view that their favored policy proposals are better for the public organization and its constituents. Critics may argue that favored policy proposals disproportionately benefit particular parties, groups, individuals, or ideological viewpoints or are excessively costly.

Standing budgetary politics generally involves broader policy concerns, longer-term time horizons, and more participants than ad hoc ones because standing policies generally involve significant resources and because public organizations with standing policies tend to be governments, which are generally larger and have more policy participants anyway. Formally recognized policy-makers decide on standing policies. Public managers, except for administrators, seldom participate in standing politics beyond providing information and analysis to the formal policy-makers. Whatever other goals expressed by those advancing standing policies, one clear goal is formally committing to conferring benefits or imposing burdens. Standing policies make future commitments that constrain future budget choices. For that reason, standing budget–related policies tend to draw significant opposition when they are proposed. Achieving or changing standing policies takes greater support for approval than ad hoc or annual budget decisions, also, because American political systems are structured so as to impede change. The policy process for standing budget policies resembles the general pattern of the policy process more closely than do ad hoc and annual budget decisions.

The general policy process pattern starts with one or more persons getting an idea for a policy; that is, a public organization should do something about this situation. Second, one or more persons convert policy ideas into one or more proposed policies. Third, policy entrepreneurs promote proposed policies. Fourth, proposed policies gain enough support to get onto policy agendas for consideration. Fifth, proposed policies gain enough support (often because of fortuitous circumstances) to gain approval in one or more places. Sixth, proposed policies gain enough support in all necessary places to become standing policies. The places where policies are approved include different institutions and parts of the same institution. Some of the places may be hierarchically related (court systems, organizations, or committees and subcommittees). General policy processes are awash in policy proposals: many, many policies are proposed; few get onto an agenda; fewer still gain approval in any one place; and very, very few actually are fully approved by gaining approval in all necessary places.

American policy-making systems, especially the state and federal ones, display fragmentation with multiple access points, widely dispersed political power, and fluidity of circumstances as events unfold and participants react to events. Gaining approval of policies often requires gaining approval in multiple places. An analogy for American policy-making is an obstacle course in which the obstacles move and course contestants purposely jostle one another. Exceptions occur where decision-making power is held in a few hands, such as in very small organizations, ones in which participation is low, ones in which one or a few people dominate, or where political machines operate.

Two Views of Annual Budgetary Politics

Annual budgetary politics differs from standing budget politics. With standing budget policies, the presumption is generally to leave settled policy alone. Public policy advocates find it difficult to get standing policies on policy agendas. In contrast, annual budget proposals formally become part of a public organization's policy agenda. Policy advocates, therefore, may find an annual budget proposal to be the most available path for putting a policy proposal on a policy agenda. At the same time, because of the breadth of annual budgets, policy makers effectively face a large number of related policy issues annually, which means that some policies get less attention than others.

Portrayals of annual budget politics tend to divide into two competing views held by disputing camps. The dispute concerns whether annual budget politics is or should be more rational and comprehensive on the one hand or contrarily less rational and less comprehensive (which is generally referred to in the budgeting literature as "incrementalism" because of the focus on incremental annual budget changes). In this chapter, the first view is considered a reform viewpoint; the second is called a traditional viewpoint; hereafter in this chapter, these two viewpoints are referred to using the terms "reform" and "traditional." The reform camp advocates that some budgeting is rational and comprehensive in the sense of following the rational decision-making model and that annual budgeting can and should be handled rationally. In contrast, the traditional camp suggests that annual budgetary politics is not, cannot, and should not be decided on by using the rational decision-making model. Simplified versions of the two views are presented here. Most authors on public budgeting take at least a qualified reform view; many are quite enthusiastic on the topic. Supporters of the reform view generally also support centralizing annual budget decision-making, usually through strengthening the executive's role; gathering more information as in using the later budget approaches of performance, program, and what-if budgeting; and using analysis. Supporters of the traditional view favor representative policy-making bodies for decision-making, not gathering more information than will be actually used, and doing analysis only when it will be used. Almost all public administration literature on public budgeting presents a reform view, which reflects the general reform perspective of public administration. Aaron Wildavsky pretty much established the traditional view with the publication of *The Politics of the Budgetary Process* in 1964, which went through four editions; he continued the basic arguments in *The New Politics of the Budgetary Process*, now in its fifth edition, with Naomi Caiden as coauthor.

The politics of annual budgeting as portrayed by the reform camp appears as rational decision-making. Those budgeting set goals, analyze, decide, and then plan accordingly. Rational budgeting politics, then, becomes the politics of goal setting, mostly by people in formal policy-making offices. After that, the decisions are more technical than political. The rationality displayed is ends-means rationality. Operating units and their public managers are expected to relate to those goals by providing information and analysis and not concern themselves with how politics affects their budgets or engage in politics from their official positions. Public managers in most cases are counted among the experts; they certainly see themselves that way.

The politics of annual budgeting as portrayed by the traditional camp appears as a decision process focusing on political support. All budget actors are perceived as being political actors seeking support. These political actors operate in complex political environments rife with uncertainty concerning how current actions relate to future outcomes. Budget actors observe their environment and decide whether, when, and how to act. In doing so, they focus their attention on particular aspects of their environments that they consider relevant. In effect, they screen out other phenomena. They identify relevant phenomena, weigh their importance, and then decide. Each actor pursues particular goals, purposes, ends, or concerns while participating in budget decisions. Because of limits on time, resources, and knowledge, political actors focus their attention on particular phenomena and limit their actions to ones that they believe have the greatest likelihood of affecting their goals. Because of the complexity of the subject matters and uncertainty of the future including the outcome of the budgeting process, political actors use a variety of devices to simplify their decision-making; Wildavsky calls these devices "aids to calculation." Some aids are generic to any kind of decision-making situation, such as a focus on things that will be changing. One aid, of major consequence for our discussion, is peculiar to annual budgetary politics: a system of perspectives and roles that divides the labor of making annual budget decisions. The various actors see the process differently, concern themselves with only a portion of available information, and act in a predictable fashion. Decisions made in such annual budget decision-making processes emerge as a result of political support and skill in analyzing political support and in role-playing.

Systems of Perspectives, Roles, Resources, and Decisions

Regardless of whether one advocates or accepts a reform, traditional, or blended view of annual budgetary politics, such situations can be seen as systems in which people in various offices and positions are connected to one another through their budgetary interactions. The offices and positions themselves primarily determine the various perspectives, roles, and resources that participants hold and the decisions that they make. Participants not only find specific perspectives, roles, resources, and decisions associated with particular situations; they also learn more specific interpretations of their perspectives and roles and about how to use the resources that are available to them to make decisions. One could say that the perspectives, roles, use of resources, and decisions are institutionalized into regular patterns of behavior that tend to endure absent a concerted effort to change them; even then, changing perspectives, roles, use of resources, and decisions is much harder than many people imagine.

Each particular annual budget political system differs in particulars. Some systems quite obviously display an overtly traditional character; the federal and many state governments are good examples. Some systems quite obviously exhibit a reform perspective; examples include council-manager municipal governments, some school and other district governments, and some nonprofit organizations. Participants learn the systems in which they find themselves operating. They learn by experiences, by examples of others, and by oral and written communications. The dominant forces in creating and enforcing the norms of annual budget political systems are the policy-makers and outsiders. Public managers operate within such systems without having much to do with creating them. Generally, at most, they can decide what they are personally willing to do. Others are likely to wish and to urge them to engage in political activity, perhaps more so than they desire. The only deterrents to such urgings are the possible legal and political consequences if those urgings are publicly revealed. On the other hand, public managers who operate contrary to the norms of the annual budget political system in which they find themselves operating may be facing the possibility of legal consequences, career stagnation or job loss, and lower levels of effectiveness in securing funding.

Perspectives refer to what people see from their offices and positions. Executives, legislators, and outsiders actually do see different things than public managers. All have perspectives that encompass their own situations and the people, offices, and positions with which they interact. In addition to their perspectives involving varying scopes and exposure to varying levels of detail, participants learn how to choose what to focus on and how to interpret what they observe. The perspectives include expectations as views of themselves and others in the process.

Roles here refer to characteristic patterns of behavior associated with offices and positions. Roles refer to representations or presentations that people make as they relate to others. Roles can be expressed in terms of jobs or work, sets of expressions or lines, relationships, or stereotypical behaviors. The concept of roles resembles the idea of a part or a character in fictional presentations, although the specific dialogue varies much more. Roles transcend particular individuals by virtue of their commonalities. Role content, which is expected by those playing the roles and by others in the process, relates to perspectives. Perspectives inform roles in that they provide explanations for why particular behaviors are directed to other participants. People learn perspectives and roles together when they begin in positions and offices, often from other participants with the same role or a related one. Although the particular people in particular offices and positions may change, the scripts that they express tend to endure over time.

Resources refer to formal and informal powers that can be used to influence the outcomes of an annual budgetary process. Clearly, various officials have the powers designated for their offices or employment positions. Outsiders, those not holding offices or employment positions in public organizations, have informal powers arising from their personal and organizational capacities to act for themselves or on the behalf of others. Outsiders may be able to influence someone holding an office or an employment position to act or to refrain from acting in a particular way. Generally speaking, more power means more capacity to affect budgetary politics.

Decisions refer to the typical choices that participants in the budgetary political process face and make. Those decisions are generally about how much to spend for what, but the decisions are nuanced in that usually participants do not arrive at their decisions in a completely isolated fashion. In other words, decisions they make may deviate from what they might like to decide in favor of what will work best in the budgetary political system in which they participate. Relationships define systems, and those relationships guide decision-making.

People within the operational and the policy-making realms of public organizations and those outside public organizations share some commonalities in perspectives, roles, resources, and decisions. Here, the emphasis is on the differences.

Public Managers' Perspectives, Roles, Resources, and Decisions

Public Managers' Perspectives

Public managers view themselves, their organizations, their organizational units, and their work as vitally important in serving the public, and they express those beliefs. They see their own motives as manifestly including altruistically "doing good," as well as earning a living and doing interesting work. Although some other participants and some authors may cynically dismiss that view and assert that they are predominantly self-interested, public managers' views are easily understandable from observing their education, training, career choices, and experience. Public managers typically choose their jobs because they believe in what they and their organizations do. Public managers tend to be cursed with the beliefs, first, that others just do not understand how important their activities are, and, second, that if others could just understand that vitally important truth, then public managers would obtain an appropriate level of funding (i.e., more funding) for carrying out their important, self-chosen tasks.

Public managers' perspectives on others include competitors, policy-makers, and outside supporters and opponents. Public managers' specific perspectives on the other roles vary by the level of the managers in a public organization, as well as by the size of their public organization. Being higher rather than lower in a public organization hierarchy typically means a broader perspective and a greater familiarity with policy-makers. Low-level public managers in small public organizations are in similar situations as high-level public managers in large public organizations in that both kinds of managers have a comprehensive awareness of the whole organization, its policy-makers, and its political environment. Public managers at lower levels, especially in large public organizations, possess limited exposure to competitors, policy-makers, and outside supporters and opponents.

Frontline managers, especially in large public organizations, tend to be most aware of their immediate organizational superiors and less aware of official policy-makers. Their immediate organizational superiors are generally the determinative or effective policy-makers in regard to funding their areas of responsibility, whether budget requests or budgeted resources. They have a narrow view of outside supporters because they deal with a limited scope of activities; they may be unaware or only vaguely aware of any outside opponents.

Public managers at higher levels tend to have broader perspectives, literally and figuratively. They tend to be more aware of other policy-making roles, including those outside of their own organization. Public managers above the frontline managers have the experience of getting requests for funding from their managerial subordinates that exceed their ability to support at higher levels or outside the organization. So they have the experience of having to say no to subordinate managers, as well as asking for more resources from those above them in the public managerial or administrative hierarchy or in the formal policy-making realm. These public managers take a more sympathetic view of formal policy-making officials who make budgetary choices from among an abundance of claims from public managers.

Public managers at higher levels tend to have more exposure to a variety of outside supporters (especially constituents and clientele), as well as to a variety of areas of responsibility under their supervision. Public managers at higher levels of public organizations possess greater awareness of specific institutional responsibilities, the various roles played by others in an annual budget process, and even detailed knowledge of official position responsibilities or powers and specific individuals.

Public managers at the apex of public organizations link those organizations with formal policy-makers. They have the broadest perspective within their organizations, as they are aware of the scope of the organization, its supporters, its opponents, and its relationship to formal policy-makers. They also have the most detailed information and perspectives on those in the formal policy-making realm and those outside their public organization.

Competitors are other public managers, organizational units, or organizations that seek funding and funding support from the same places to carry out similar activities. They often have the same or similar goals and may work with similar groups and technologies. Hospitals and universities compete with each other, as do their constituent units. Geographic subdivisions of public organizations provide other examples of competitors. Public managers representing other organizational units or other organizations within or outside a public organization are seen as being in a competitive position because there never seems to be enough funding for everyone. Public managers view competitors as claimants on resources that should be made available to their areas rather than those other areas.

Public managers view policy-makers as persons who hold power over their budgetary situation, generally conceived of as access to budgetary resources for their area, and who have to be won over to gain that access. Public managers form more specific perspectives on policy-makers by kind of position, by specific features of those positions, and by situations surrounding those positions. Public managers typically see four kinds of policy-making positions: those higher than they are within their organizational hierarchy, executives or executive surrogates, legislators or policy board members, and staff. The next higher public manager in a hierarchy is a potent policy position generally held by persons who are considered relatively permanent and who must be accommodated by subordinates. Public managers who fail to accommodate their organizational superiors experience negative consequences, budgetary and careerwise. Still, despite the imbalance of power in their relationships, higher-level public managers cooperate with subordinate public managers because they, in turn, need cooperation. Public managers' views of public managers beyond their immediate organizational superiors and other policy-makers are formed on much less information than is available for their immediate superiors. Public managers often analyze and interpret policy-makers based on perceived motives.

Public managers tend to see policy-makers' motives as politically rational, politically irrational, or politically inexplicable. They ascribe political rationality to motives if the public managers can see a reasonable relationship between actions and imputed motives. Actions seen to be serving policy-makers' self-interest, organizational goals, or political needs would be considered politically rational. For example, the Department of Defense granted David Eisenhower, son of former President Dwight Eisenhower, early release from military service to marry Julie Nixon, daughter of President-elect Richard Nixon, in 1968; they also granted leave to Vice President-elect Joe Biden's son, who was serving in Iraq, to attend his father's inauguration in 2009. Actions seen as serving personal likes and dislikes are considered politically irrational. They include actions seen to be motivated by personal relationships or policy preferences unrelated to organizational responsibilities. Public managers do say, "That policy-maker likes or does not like me, that other person, my organization, that other organization, a particular idea, or a particular program area." Public managers find many actions by policy-makers politically and otherwise inexplicable, although they may use other language in describing inexplicably motivated actions. The attribution of motives is heavily influenced by available information. Policy-makers appear to believe that they act more politically rationally than subordinate public managers believe they do and that their subordinates do not have or do not correctly interpret available information. Also, various public managers can have different interpretations of the same actions. For example, a university president who chooses to increase expenditures for a sculpture park by hiring a person to oversee it during a period of budget cuts may be seen as having politically rational, politically irrational, or politically inexplicable motives. The chair of the Art Department might see it as a politically rational action because board members express a great deal of interest in the sculpture park; the chair of the Political Science Department might see it as politically irrational because she believes that the university president just really likes sculpture; and the chair of the Physics Department might see it as politically inexplicable because he does not see any motive for the action. Public managers find politically rational and politically irrational motives much easier to understand than politically inexplicable ones as they can accommodate their budgetary choices to those motives. Public managers' interest in organizational grapevines or informal discussion of policy-makers' motives serves their budgetary political concerns.

Public managers have more exposure to their immediate organizational superiors and can ask, if only indirectly, what motivates their actions. Organizational superiors generally share organizational responsibilities and information with their immediate subordinates.

As lower-level public managers look beyond their immediate organizational superiors, they may attribute proportionally more irrational and inexplicable motivations to policy-makers. Within a public organization, higher-level public managers may appear distant to lower-level public managers and more like office-holding policy-makers than like lower-level managers. Executives and administrators who act as executive surrogates have responsibilities to lead public organizations. Executives in governments are elected policy-makers, either elected to executive positions directly or selected from among elected policy-makers. Direct election to a policy-making position responsible for taking leadership actions makes a person an executive. Examples of people holding executive positions include the U.S. president, governors, some mayors, some school superintendents, and other elected officeholders with executive responsibilities (e.g., vice president, lieutenant governor, clerk, treasurer, and sheriff). Some executives, many mayors for example, win election to a policy-making body and then are selected to an executive position by the policy-making body. In contrast, executive surrogates take on the budgetary role of executives without being elected directly to a position having formal leadership responsibilities. Executive surrogates are either employees (hired and fired) or serve in a legislature or on a policy-making board. Examples of people holding executive surrogate positions include city, village, and county managers; some school superintendents; university presidents; executive directors of district governments and nonprofit organizations; and top legislative leaders and chairs of policy boards.

Public managers view executives and executive surrogates as leaders who are responsible for charting courses for future actions and who have a propensity toward making changes when first taking office. Public managers observe and analyze executives' and executive surrogates' proposed courses of actions. They evaluate executives and executive surrogates partially on their relative degree of perceived permanence. In other words, they ask: How long might this executive or head administrator be expected to serve in that position? Fixed term of limited length or a history of turnover in particular positions suggests impermanence, and unlimited terms and a history of continuity suggest permanence. Public managers and others can wait out an executive or executive surrogate who is leading in a direction that is not to their liking when they know that the person in the executive or executive surrogate position will change in the foreseeable future and that they can hope for someone with preferable views. To paraphrase President John F. Kennedy's description of Wilbur Mills, the chair of the House Ways and Means Committee: "He was here when I came, he will be here when I go, he knows it, I know it, and he knows that I know it." Executives and executive surrogates can be compared to the weather, which changes, or gravity, which persists. Otherwise, public managers seek understanding of executives' and executive surrogates' motives. They observe preferred policy areas, overriding themes, and political affiliations. Public managers also evaluate the relative power position of executives and executive surrogates in regard to formal and informal powers; a long-serving, popularly elected executive with strong formal powers is different from one who is unpopular, who has recently been fingerprinted by the FBI in connection with corruption charges, or who possesses little in the way of informal or formal budget powers (e.g., some mayors). Public managers generally assess policy-makers in regard to whether they can and will help or hurt a public manager's budget quest for access to resources.

Public managers view individual legislators and policy board members as representing their constituencies. Legislators elected at-large tend to be viewed as representing all of a government's residents and those elected in a district scheme as specifically representing people in their electoral district. Nonprofit policy board members may be selected by co-optation (by current board members), by election among members, or by default (positions available to whoever is willing to serve). Where elections occur, policy board members may be quite active in urging others to seek election. In the annual public budgeting process, public managers view legislators and policy board members primarily as controlling access to a public organization's resources with secondary interests in supporting specific areas or activities and, less so, in opposing specific areas or activities. Public managers often attribute support or opposition relative to electoral district concerns because representatives are thought to seek advantages for their districts, deflect disadvantages, and express opinions held by people in their district. Public managers see legislators and policy board members as generally more oriented to the status quo and less oriented toward change than executives and executive surrogates. Public managers pay special attention to particular institutional leadership positions in legislatures and policy boards. Those holding these positions include overall leaders, party leaders, and chairs of committees or subcommittees with substantive or budgetary responsibilities for the managers' areas of responsibility, and even specific members with relevant expertise or great interest in those areas. Power differentials within legislatures or in policy boards may determine budgetary results.

Public managers may or may not have perspectives on policy-makers' staff, which refers to individuals, organizational subdivisions, or organizations that serve particular policy-makers. Individual staff members usually report to their organizational superiors directly; subdivisions and organizations usually have at least one person reporting directly to a policy-making superior. An administrative assistant who handles budget matters among other responsibilities is a staff member. An executive's office could contain a budgetary subdivision. The Office of Management and Budget at the federal level and similar arrangements in states and larger local governments are staff agencies. The U.S. Congress relies on the Congressional Budget Office and the Government Accountability Office as staff agencies; congressional committees and subcommittees have staffs; and individual members of Congress, especially leaders, have staff members who deal with budgetary concerns. State legislatures and larger local governments have similar arrangements.

Nonprofit organizations tend not to focus budget responsibilities into the hands of many staff persons; budget concerns tend to be handled by a variety of staff members in a less specialized fashion. To the extent that nonprofit organizations are fee-funded, they tend to have "business" offices that make revenue and expenditure projections for the higher-level administrators and policy-makers. Aside from the specific individuals to whom staff and staff agencies may report and by whom they are directed, staff and staff agencies may develop institutionalized patterns of behavior that extend over multiple occupants of particular positions. For example, in their *Policy and Politics in State Budgeting*, Thurmaier and Willoughby report that state budget offices tend to take an orientation to their work that can be described as tending toward control or toward policy-making (p. 129ff). Such behaviors are probably well noted by public managers who relate to those offices as a basis for forming perspectives. The control-oriented state budget offices scrutinize expenditure requests and closely regulate access to budgetary resources within budget years to minimize spending; the policy-oriented state budget offices focus on long-term policy choices in budget proposals. Newly elected or selected policy-makers, even when they want a different orientation displayed by staff, may choose not to devote their resources to effectuating such changes or even be aware that other choices are possible.

Outside supporters include those who are interested in public organizations' service provision activities, especially those who see themselves directly benefiting. Typical supporters include clientele, employees, suppliers of goods or services, and persons who hold an opinion that the service provision is a good idea. Sometimes, members of the general public exhibit support for public organizations. In many cases, supporters may organize a group that assumes the task of supporting funding for particular public organizations, some subdivision, or specific activities. Public sector employee groups support funding for their units; businesses, individually and collectively, support funding that benefits them. Supporters appear to be motivated by self-interest in respect to specific and concrete material benefits, opinions about the intangible benefits of the public organization, or both. Public managers view their supporters positively for the most part, as means of securing funding goals. Supporters are viewed as being wonderful, enlightened people whose well-being or interests are aligned with the organization's best interests and who can provide political resources in budgetary decision-making. At the same time, however, public managers may be concerned that supporters may have and express preferences that do not coincide with the public managers' preferred courses of action.

Outside opponents of a public organization, organizational subdivisions, or activities are viewed as obstacles, and not necessarily stationary ones, because they strive to block or undercut support for funding. Because of the competitive character of funding decisions, reducing support for something lessens its chances of being funded. Opponents may argue that something is simply undesirable; however, they can win in those cases by making what they oppose appear less desirable. Typically, public managers face relatively few opponents compared to supporters. Although some opponents appear to be motivated by concern for material well-being or personal animosity, most opposition to funding appears to be based on opinions. Public managers tend to view opponents negatively.

Public Managers' Roles

Public managers primarily play the role of spending advocates for their organizations or subunits. Their most inclusive line or expression of that advocacy runs like this: "Please provide funding to my area of responsibility so that we can make important, positive impacts." They advocate with an eye on the general, long-term well-being of their organizations or subunits and fulfillment of their current service responsibilities. They primarily seek funding but with regard to whether gaining funding may cause problems in the future. Public managers do not desire funding for activities that are incompatible with their present responsibilities, ones that are ill advised because they create opponents, or ones that have little chance of being successfully implemented.

They tend to advocate for what they and their organizations prefer or favor, such as definitional or modal personnel types, particular types of equipment, and areas or types of activity. For example, doctors, teachers, and pilots are definitional or modal personnel types in hospitals, schools, and air forces. People in organizations tend to want to increase the number of people like themselves to do the work of organizations.

Public managers express advocacy in a wide variety of manners. The variety of modes of expressing an advocacy role may be thought of as elements, acceptable modes of expression, or subordinate roles. Those elements may overlap in practice. Of the many possible ways of expressing these elements, three that may be found include service provider, policy analyst and proposer, and political entrepreneur. The reform public manager or the reform view of proper public manager behavior on these elements differs from the traditional public manager and those expressing a traditional view of budgetary politics.

The service provision element of advocacy in public budgeting may be overlooked or insufficiently emphasized. Some public organizational work is appreciated and well noted, even if some is taken for granted. The lack of some services or the poor performance of some of those services also is likely to be noticed. Well-done, poorly done, and not-done work obviously will elicit reactions from other participants in a system of budget politics. Well-done work might engender more political support for an organization or an area of activity. Poorly done work and not-done work often cause political support to decline.

Reform public managers express the view and act in service provision as if their concerns are exclusively to perform their work well without any regard to any kind of political consideration. An example of ignoring political influence occurred when a police officer in Omaha, Nebraska, arrested two of the mayor's sons in two separate incidents a few months apart. This view and behavior mirrors the Progressive Movement view of public managers as being technically competent experts. These public managers try to avoid involvement in politics, although other people may become politically involved with such public managers. These public managers might say that their work should speak for itself.

Traditional public managers tend to regard service provision as a part of budgetary political advocacy in that they believe that taking political considerations into account is normal. Some public managers, and especially those in high-level administrator positions, use discretion available to them in operations to make choices that they consider likely to generate support and not likely to generate opposition. They gather political information, particularly in regard to policies that they deal with, and act upon it. The details of exactly what services to perform in what manner and in what places may be subject to political preferences by higher-level public managers, policymakers, interest groups, and members of relevant publics. In implementing this strategic political viewpoint, traditional public managers still are bound by formal policies and ethical requirements that they uphold. Such public managers may be criticized for being excessively flexible or having negotiable ethics. They are likely to argue in turn that their ethics include effectiveness or expediency in carrying out their professional responsibilities and that futility is not properly an ethical standard.

The second element of the budget advocacy role of public managers is proposing and analyzing policy. Reform-oriented public managers take one tack on this element and traditionalists take another. Reform-oriented public managers tend to treat policy analysis and policy proposing as impartially and informationally as they possibly can. They try to analyze policies as neutrally as possible and propose policies that can be justified with evidence and arguments in a rational fashion. If they have or display any bias, it is more likely to be professional rather than political.

Traditionally oriented public managers tend to take political consideration into account in analyzing and proposing policies. They look at the interests and opinions of policy proposers, policy-makers, supporters, and opponents. They have an admitted bias toward their own organization and areas of responsibilities and toward holders of political power, especially supporters and potential supporters. These public managers portray their behavior as a practical necessity. They admit that their analysis and proposals are somewhat negotiable based on political support, which usually is somewhat reciprocal. They believe that their negotiability is in the service of their operations and those they serve and that discretion is inherent in the process of proposing and analyzing policies.

The third element of the advocacy role in the politics of public budgeting is the explicit pursuit of political support. Reform public managers generally avoid politics, including policy politics. They may feel driven to engage in political activity when the survival of their organization, organizational unit, program, or area of work is at stake. Even then, they rely on evidence and rational arguments.

Traditional public managers, in contrast, embrace policy politics. They appear to be just as happy to rely on irrational arguments as rational ones and on arguments based on biases. They appear to believe that pursuing political support requires a willingness to rely on other people's preferences or biases and irrational behavior to serve their own budgetary ends. Their policy campaigns, including budgetary ones, may be designed to resemble private-sector salesmanship and advertising efforts that focus on people's hopes and fears. Traditional public managers are also likely to contend that the truth and rationality are uncertain and therefore negotiable to a degree. If public managers predict a possibly dire consequence or a probably glorious outcome depending on whether their agency or area gets a proper level of funding (i.e., more funding), then only the most extreme claims can be easily debunked, especially by persons without the kind of expert status held by persons in public organizations who can claim expertise. An example of this phenomenon can be seen in spokespersons for higher education, whose general position appears to be as follows: "Fewer people getting college degrees is bad; more people getting college degrees is good. Give us money."

Public Managers' Resources

Public managers possess or have access to a greater variety of resources than they may be able to deploy in the service of securing funding for their organization or area of responsibility in the budgetary process. Public managers vary in respect to how much of these resources they have or have access to. Their resources include formal and informal powers. Formally managers possess discretion in service delivery, as noted above, or, more broadly, discretion in carrying out their official responsibilities, including analyzing and proposing policies. Public managers in some public organizations, mostly governmental ones, can resolve cases brought before them and make rules governing behavior. Informal powers include their ability to influence others through informal actions that may be based on their skills, credibility, prestige, recognized expertise, and information. Like other political actors, public managers participating in budgetary politics prefer to develop a reputation for success in the use of political power and avoid an unsuccessful reputation. Public managers also establish relationships with persons and entities outside their public organizations that may provide them with formidable resources. Public managers may also have personal relationships. However, public managers' political support typically arises from support for the activities that they supervise rather than because of personal relationships. Persons outside their organization and higher in their organization support their area of activity because they desire the provision of particular goods and services. For example, agricultural producers and their organizations support bureaus in the Department of Agriculture because of what they do rather than because of personal relationships with persons in those organizations. Still, personal relationships tend to develop out of these impersonal relationships because of interactions and proximity; people who share the same concerns frequently find it easy to like each other. The outside supporters may be individuals or individual entities (companies or other organizations), unorganized groups of individuals or entities, or organized interest groups.

Public Managers' Decisions

Public managers choose whether to act in particular situations. Like other political actors, they decide whether particular cases justify political action and whether their political power may be more fruitfully applied to other situations. This decision is likely to be influenced by deciding whether an outcome is already determined and whether a public manager's resources would be employed futilely. Regardless of what views public managers hold, they have to make decisions related to budgetary politics. They have to decide what to propose in their budget submissions and what justifications to make on behalf of those proposals. Deciding on their budget proposals also entails deciding how much to ask for. Secondarily, public managers choose how much of their total available expenditure authority to use during each fiscal year. Managers taking a reform view can be expected to spend exactly as much as required by their work and to ask for exactly as much as required by what they are proposing. Managers taking a traditional view can be expected to try to maximize the resources that they obtain. They do so in two ways. First, they use resources made available to them to demonstrate that they required those resources in the first place. They believe that not spending resources would indicate that they did not actually need the resources. Second, they ask for as much as they think appropriate to produce the highest funding possible. In doing so, they take into account their political support and the prevailing situation with policy-makers, including whether revenue is abundant and what level of support they can expect from higher-ups, policy-makers, and outsiders. Wildavsky refers to the political analysis involved here as "calculation."

Traditional managers making proposals try to influence higher-ups to support more spending rather than less because what is proposed is intrinsically appropriate and because the policy-makers will support the higher level of spending. Indirectly they are trying to influence policy-makers to support more spending rather than less because what is proposed is intrinsically appropriate and because outsiders will support the higher level of spending. Traditional managers making proposals are trying to influence outsiders to support their expenditure proposals specifically and their areas of responsibility generally to gain higher levels of spending authority. Both policy-makers and outsiders can act toward higher-level managers, policy-makers, and other outsiders in ways that are barred to public managers. Public managers may be explicitly and formally banned from many activities supporting spending proposals, and they are well advised not to become overly aggressive within their own organizations. However, they may generate sufficient support among policy-makers and outsiders to gain their ends. In contrast, reform managers make proposals based on analysis, propose exactly what they believe they need in funding for those proposals, and expect policy-makers to decide whether to provide the amounts requested on the basis of analysis. They rely on the intrinsic merits of what they propose in the evidence and arguments that they present.

Policy-Makers' Perspectives, Roles, Resources, and Decisions

Policy-makers' perspectives include ones on themselves, other policy-makers, public managers, and outsiders in the process of budget politics. Policy-makers tend to see staff only as extensions of themselves or other policy-makers, although staff can act independently and make a difference in some cases. Policy-makers tend to present themselves as wise guardians of public resources. More specifically, executives and executive surrogates see themselves as taking a comprehensive or overarching view of their public organizations rather than narrower ones taken by legislators (especially those elected by districts) or policy board members, public managers, and outsiders. Legislators and policy board members tend to emphasize narrower concerns and to see themselves as having a firmer grasp of details that they care about, in contrast to executives and executive surrogates, who they believe operate on the basis of relatively superficial knowledge. Both sets of policy-makers tend to see public managers as overly enthusiastic in seeking resources and as insufficiently appreciative of the alternate possibilities for use of resources. Policy-makers regard outsiders as political forces that may support or oppose their specific position or them personally, the organization more generally, and a side on a budget proposal. Reform policy-makers tend to see outsiders as irrational meddlers; traditional policy-makers tend to see outsiders as legitimate participants.

Policy-makers mainly play the role of guardian of the resources of public organizations. Essentially, this role involves telling others that they cannot obtain approval to use as much of a public organization's resources as they would like to have. Policy-makers say no to public managers, outsiders, and other policy-makers. Policy-makers learn to say no because, practically, they are not able to say yes to all the requests they receive. In carrying out this guardian role, policy-makers ask questions about proposals, including why they should be funded. They tend to look for reasons for why policy proposals should not be funded. In some cases, policy-makers advocate for spending proposals. Reform-oriented policy-makers tend to do so because of analysis, and traditionally oriented policy-makers tend to do so because such proposals are part of their public policy agenda, help their constituents or district, are pet causes, or reflect political pressures from outsiders. Traditional policy-makers tend to be more sensitive to the political considerations of dealing with outsiders because they are more likely to be concerned about advancing themselves personally, politically, or organizationally.

The resources available to policy-makers include the formal powers of their positions and the informal powers of influencing others. Executives and executive surrogates generally have opportunities to set budget agendas for legislators or policy boards. Informally, they also might be able to generate widespread support for some proposals or at least the appearance of such support. Legislators and policy board members collectively enjoy more formal power than executives and executive surrogates. However, unless that formal power is expressed collectively, executives and executive surrogates might make a greater impact on budgets by virtue of their informal powers of influencing others. The narrow geographic boundaries of electoral districts or a narrow range of policy interests does not allow policy board members to generate as much informal political power as executives can generate. In the politics of annual budgeting, chief executives individually and legislators or policy board members collectively may be able to prevent spending. When the two kinds of policy-makers collide politically, the side that gathers more outside support tends to win, except when one side decides that political consequences do not matter. In an executive-focused, control-oriented budget political system, executives also may control access to expenditure authority during a fiscal year. That authority can contribute to executives' resources relative to operating units.

Traditionally oriented legislators and policy members may exert power informally by explicitly or implicitly trading support among themselves, their outside supporters, and public managers. Many political scientists have called relationships between elected officials, operating units, and outsiders "iron triangles" or "issue networks." Iron triangles specifically are legislative committees, governmental agencies, and organized interest groups that dominate policy areas by collaborating with one another; executives, executive surrogates, and other policy-makers find it difficult to exercise influence in such areas. Issue networks are more inclusive and less rigid in conception, but their participants also are seen as generally determining policies within their subject matter areas by working out their disagreements and presenting a united front against those outside the issue network. Within budget systems, executives who try to exercise influence over specific triangles or issue networks often have the advantage of being able to choose which sets of policy-makers, outside supporters, and operating units they will work with and which they will oppose. Reform-oriented policy-makers tend to argue the merits of cases rather than proceed politically.

The decisions faced by policy-makers divide between executives and executive surrogates on one hand and legislators and policy board members on the other hand. Executives and executives' surrogates have to decide how much to recommend for funding the various operating units and programs. Elected executives tend to have more latitude on these decisions than executive surrogates because executive surrogates do not have as strong a claim to independent status. Sometimes, however, executive surrogates may claim and be accorded independent status because of their political influence, even if that influence is achieved on the basis of arguments about professional credentials. Unelected school superintendents often exert enormous influence over school boards because of their expert status. Executives with discretion over resources during a fiscal year can use that power to increase cooperation by public managers. By virtue of being able to decide how much of the limited resources specific public managers receive, executives can gain compliance with some of their wishes. Legislators and policy board members, perhaps after committee work, have the ultimate budgetary political power of deciding how much various operating units and programs will be authorized to spend. Executive veto powers enable executives to influence legislators in regard to budgets. Executives negotiate with legislators in regard to what each side will do or forgo doing. Executives offer to forego vetoing specific bills or proposed expenditures in return for legislators supporting executives' preferences and threaten to veto specific bills or proposed expenditures in return for legislators opposing executives' preferences. Contrary to arguments made in favor of line item vetoes, an executive veto power is not unidirectional in the sense of lowering spending. Executive veto power can be used in the service of decreasing or increasing expenditures, depending primarily on each individual executive's preferences. An example of vetoes being used relative to specific legislators occurred in the state of Illinois when a governor vetoed one-half of specific bridge projects in opposing legislators' districts while simultaneously not vetoing the other half of the same specific bridge projects in supporting legislators' districts.

Outsider Perspectives, Roles, Resources, and Decisions

Outsiders are taxpayers, voters, citizens, constituents, or supporters seeking goods and services by participating in the decision-making process for annual budgets. Outsiders also see themselves as the ultimate arbiters of what public organizations decide about public budgets because they are "the public." Outsiders value particular public managers' areas of responsibility that concern them. They see public managers as the people responsible for implementing policies. They see themselves as collaborators in the policy process. Outsiders tend to see policy-makers as those who take pressures from the outsiders and turn them into formal policy, including budget policy. Other outsiders may be viewed as collaborators or opponents. They are likely to see collaborators as rationally pursuing the same ends; they are likely to see opponents as being rational, irrational, or inexplicable in much the same way that public managers view administrators, depending on whether they see a reasonable or unreasonable connection between opponents' views and behaviors and whether they see any logic in opponents' behavior at all.

Outsiders see their own role as creating and directing pressure onto policy-makers to support the outsiders' own policy positions. This activity can be fairly described as partisan, even when no organized groups are involved. Political parties and interest groups gather those motivated to exert pressure and channel the pressure into policy processes. They do so by lobbying, influencing others to lobby, engaging in electoral activities, and providing resources to others. In lobbying, they provide policy-makers with information and arguments. Outsiders may have expertise, favorable public standing, or skills that make their information and arguments particularly persuasive. Scientists, academics, and military officers are experts. Military veterans and mothers generate sympathy. Lawyers and people in show business present cases skillfully. Outsiders influence others to lobby by making public pronouncements and mounting campaigns to encourage others to lobby. Such campaigns generally take place through the media, but they also may take place within the confines of outside groups or organizations without directly engaging broad-based media. Outsiders might engage in electoral activities by voting and by supporting particular candidates or positions with their reputation, money, or campaign work. Large groups (e.g., the American Association of Retired Persons, with more than 40 million members), labor unions (e.g., the American Federation of State, County, and Municipal Employees and the Service Employees International Union), and groups that are especially focused on single issues (e.g., Mothers Against Drunk Driving and the Sierra Club) can deliver large numbers of votes in particular elections. Endorsements by individuals or groups may be helpful, money can be deployed to advantage in many campaigns, and campaign work is done to make a difference in electoral outcomes. Outsiders might voluntarily provide resources to organizations, policy-makers, and potential policy-makers. Although campaign contributions come to mind here, nonprofit organizations and even governmental agencies may be influenced by direct contributions of resources. Outsiders are willing to make suggestions about how public managers can exercise their discretion in order to better serve outsiders and to hear from public managers how additional funding might be used to provide goods and services. Outsiders can influence policy-makers in ways that public managers cannot even attempt.

Reformers prefer not to pay a lot of attention to outsiders unless they are technical experts or so politically powerful that they cannot be ignored. Reformers tend not to think that a person wearing a shoe is the best person to tell whether shoes are comfortable, serving their purpose, or well made. Traditionalists tend to accept and encourage outsiders who support their preferred policies or area of responsibility.

The decisions for outsiders are what to support, what alliances to make, and how hard to push on funding particular programs. They select the funding choices they want to support from those available within their range of interests, and they make alliances because of the fragmentation of political power and the need to acquire majorities in various places in order to achieve policy goals.

In a traditional annual budgeting political system, a common phenomenon understood by participants is that budget proposals are initially inflated or padded beyond the level that budget proposers can expect to gain. The purpose of the padding is to provide inflated amounts of budget requests that higher-level managers, executives, and legislators or policy board members can cut from spending proposals. In either case, a person operating on a different set of expectations than those common in the annual budget political system will appear out of step with others by asking for either far more than would be expected or too little.

Conclusion

Politics understood as deciding what public organizations will do creates situations in which public managers are directed to act. Most politics associated with public organizations have little room for an extremely active role by public managers acting as public managers. With some specific exceptions, public managers avoid overtly taking part in basic, partisan, and personal politics. They do engage in policy and organizational politics that relate to their areas of responsibility. Budget politics is essentially a subdivision of policy politics as it relates to the allocation of resources needed to carry out organizationally decided policies.

In budget politics, public managers ask for funding for their areas of responsibility by preparing budget proposals as well as decide how much currently available budget authority to spend during a fiscal year. Executives and executive surrogates decide how much to recommend that public managers be authorized to spend, and legislators or policy board members decide how much public managers should be authorized to spend. Outsiders often attempt to influence public managers and policy-makers concerning budgetary decisions. In turn, public managers and policy-makers may attempt to influence outsiders in regard to what public budgeting decisions to support.

The reform and the traditional views are two general views on the participation of public managers in annual budget political systems. The reform view emphasizes that public managers are and should be technically competent experts who are politically neutral. Reformers argue that the preparation of budget proposals should be based on rational analysis, with proposals limited to the exact amounts necessary to operate. Reformers oppose the use of discretion in operations for the sake of gaining political support, what they see as the use of appealing but misleading arguments, and the attempt to influence outsiders and policy-makers through political means. Traditionalists suggest that politics is the overriding process of making decisions for public organizations and that some politically oriented behavior is required for public managers to succeed in their work. Traditionalists argue for taking political circumstances into account in proposing budgets and implementing them; for making politically appealing arguments for funding their areas of responsibility; and for trying to influence others to support funding for their areas of responsibility. Room for variation is likely to exist within any annual budget political system; however, it may be nearly impossible for a public manager to operate successfully while being opposed completely to the ethos of an annual budget political system, whether that ethos is highly traditional or highly reform oriented.

Additional Reading and Resources

Print

Aaron Wildavsky provided the basic perspective for this chapter. He reacted to the almost universal pro-reform bent of scholarship on public budgeting with an evaluation of how public budgeting occurs in the political sphere. His perspective, usually referred to as budgetary incrementalism, is linked with the doctrine of pluralism, which generally means that gradual adjustments are made in public policies. His often-cited classic expression of budgetary incrementalism was initially published in 1964:

Wildavsky, Aaron. *The Politics of the Budgetary Process.* 4th ed. Boston: Little, Brown, 1984.

A continuation of the budgetary incrementalism perspective before and after Aaron Wildavsky's death in 1993:

Wildavsky, Aaron. *The New Politics of the Budgetary Process.* Glenview, IL: Scott Foresman, 1988; 2nd ed. New York: HarperCollins, 1992.

Wildavsky, Aaron, and Naomi Caiden. *The New Politics of the Budgetary Process.* 5th ed. New York: Longman, 2003.

The earliest and most concise expression of budgetary incrementalism by Wildavsky:

Wildavsky, Aaron. "Political Implications of Budgetary Reform." *Public Administration Review* 21 (Autumn 1961): 183–190.

Authors expressing critical views of Wildavsky:

Meyer, Roy T. *Strategic Budgeting.* Ann Arbor: University of Michigan Press, 1996.

Rubin, Irene S. *The Politics of Public Budgeting: Getting and Spending, Borrowing and Balancing.* 5th ed. Washington, DC: CQ Press, 2005.

Schick, Allen. "Systems Budgeting and Systems Politics." *Public Administration Review* 29 (March/April 1969): 137–150.

A comprehensive review of criticisms of incrementalism in a collection of perspectives on explaining budgetary decisions:

Swain, John W., and C. Jeff Hartley Jr. "Incrementalism: Old But Good?" In *Evolving Theories of Public Budgeting*, ed. John R. Bartle, 11–27. Amsterdam: JAI Press, 2001.

A book discussing political perspectives and behaviors expressed by state budget offices:

Thurmaier, Kurt M., and Katherine G. Willoughby. *Policy and Politics in State Budgeting.* Armonk, NY: M.E. Sharpe, 2001.

6

Organizing Concepts
for Expenditure Budgets

Formats and Approaches

The terms "format" and "approach" relate to how information is organized in public budgeting and the concepts and terms used to communicate about expenditures. "Format" refers to information in a document, including what information is included, what terms are used, and how the information is displayed. "Approach" refers to the general manner in which expenditure information is gathered and processed. Approaches are tools used to facilitate making decisions; they reflect different ideas about how budget decisions should be made. Specific formats reflect the budgeting approaches used to prepare expenditure information. Policy-makers often require specific formats and approaches.

Although this chapter speaks generally about formats and approaches, each government and nonprofit organization decides what formats and approaches to use for its own purposes. Exceptions occur when local governments have to follow requirements from their state government for particular documents and when governments granting nonprofit status require nonprofit organizations to submit documents. Public organizations display great disparities in their formats and how they use approaches. Contrasting budgeting formats and approaches with card games may clarify how various public organizations use budget formats and approaches. Unlike card games, budget formats and approaches do not operate according to generally recognized rules. Card games have many local variations, but players may clarify matters by consulting standard rules, "according to Hoyle." Any budget format or approach in an actual organization may be a unique local variation and quite different from any other organizations' formats and approaches, even though they may be labeled similarly.

Formats and approaches figure most prominently in expenditure proposals as they are prepared and approved, but also they affect the implementation and the reviews and reports stages of the budget process. Formats and approaches set the conceptual terms in budget documents and processes. Here, we emphasize preparing expenditure proposals.

The purposes and uses of formats and approaches vary widely. Among other things, policy-makers and administrators use formats and approaches to control overall levels of expenditure, specific expenditure categories, and an organization's ability to act in particular ways; to promote efficiency, effectiveness, and planning; to portray an organizational image; and to make choices. Formats and approaches present information aligned with the purposes selected. Sometimes, a required format may symbolically endorse a particular purpose or pretend that a particular purpose is being served. Different formats and approaches require gathering and processing specific kinds of information.

This chapter discusses budget formats, revenue formats, five different approaches (lump-sum, line-item, performance, program, and what-if budgeting), mixing approaches, and ends with a commentary on the approaches. The discussion of each approach describes and explains a format example, key ideas associated with that approach, how the approach is used in preparing an expenditure proposal, activities related to that particular approach that may occur after preparation, some possible advantages and disadvantages of using that particular approach, and situations in which the use of that particular approach may be beneficial. The commentary frames the approaches in regard to arguments about them and their actual impacts and assesses them generally.

General Discussion of Formats

People decide what information to include in budget documents and how to organize that information. People preparing budget documents use conventions so that locations and relationships on a page convey meaning to those reading the document. For example, this book page reflects conventions associated with the English language—reading from left to right and top to bottom and using words and punctuation organized according to standard English rules.

Information in a budget format can be divided into headings and main bodies, as indicated in Figure 6.1. Heading information is located mostly at the topmost portion of documents or pages. Headings provide specific information in regard to the organization, time, and document. First, the organization information identifies the government or nonprofit organization and possibly a subdivision. Subdivisions often are organizational units, but also may be other categories. Second, time information indicates a time period or a specific point in time. Third, document information indicates the character of the information in the main body, such as a proposed, approved, or implemented budget. Although the organization, time, and document information may

```
Figure 6.1   Elements of Budget Formats

Headings
• Organization
• Time
• Document

Main body
• Revenue
• Expenditure
```

appear to be self-evident from within an organization, they certainly are not self-evident from outside an organization, and they can be easily confused within an organization (especially time and document information). Budget formats employ other common organizing conventions: page designations, tables of contents, and subject matter headings.

The main body of a budget document contains expenditure and possibly revenue information in words and numbers. Words indicate the categories of the information that are used to divide a budget document conceptually into parts and provide narratives. To classify is to group information, and a classification refers to a system of categories. Public organizations classify information in a variety of ways, using different specific categories and different combinations of specific categories. Common expenditure categories for subdivisions include organizational unit(s), purpose(s), fund(s), and operating or capital. Numbers indicate dollar amounts and other indicated quantities. Any budget format readily should supply answers to these questions: What organization? When? What kind of document? What categories? How much?

Narratives are words strung together to form sentences, complete thoughts. They range from one sentence within a specific area of a format or notes to possibly several pages found in introductory material: for example, executive policy statements. Narratives provide explanations that are often part of broader persuasive efforts.

Deciphering particular budget documents can be difficult. Some documents are intimidating because of their sheer mass of details spread over hundreds of pages. The most important difficulty is interpreting the words, especially unique ones or ones not used uniformly. Some common terms, such as "fund" and "year-to-date," are used consistently. "Fund" is an accounting term that refers to a conceptual category for recording and reporting on financial transactions. "Year-to-date" refers to amounts of revenues and expenditures from the beginning date to some specific date during a fiscal year, although the beginning and the specific dates vary. Some terms, however, are used inconsistently. Words such as "program," "function," and other general terms might represent an organizational subdivision or another budget category. Specific examples of misleading terms are "ad valorem taxes" and "obligations." In some states, the term "ad valorem taxes" is used to mean property taxes, even though the Latin term "ad valorem" means "according to value" or "measured in monetary terms." Ad valorem taxes could be all taxes measured in monetary terms, such as property, income, sales, inheritance, and estate taxes. For the federal government, the term "obligation" is used to mean that a federal entity has made some kind of a commitment to spend money; however, federal commitments frequently can be reversed. The federal use of the term "obligation" is misleading for people familiar with the term in the private sector and the rest of the public sector, where "obligation" generally means a legally binding commitment that cannot be reversed. Inconsistency in the use of budget terms arises from the lack of generally accepted or enforced conventions, a desire to craft a positive appearance at the expense of accuracy, and customs and language that have developed over time.

Although budget formats tend to be mostly words and numbers in tabular form, they are frequently accompanied by narratives that string words together into sentences and sometimes paragraphs. Narratives especially can be helpful in understanding budget documents. Narratives include transmittal letters or memorandums, descriptions, explanations, glossaries of terms, and even notes. For example, the real meanings of the words and numbers in an audit are frequently spelled out in the notes.

Revenue Formats

Revenues occupy a small portion of most budget documents within which they appear. For revenue formats, heading information contains the words "revenue," "forecast revenues," "estimated revenues," or functionally equivalent terms such as "receipts" or "income." "Estimated" generally means "forecast" in the context of budgeting. The main body of the document lists revenues and their dollar amounts classified by main categories and possibly subcategories and sub-subcategories. The main categories and their subdivisions represent a revenue measure or a group of related revenue measures. The terms used may clarify whether an entry is a main category or a single revenue measure, but in some cases a category in a document remains ambiguous in the absence of further information.

Table 6.1 displays a state budget proposal format example for revenues. The heading provides the crucial information of organization, fiscal year, and document (forecast revenues in a proposed budget). The main body shows main categories, subcategories, and individual revenue measures. The far left column of the table lists the main revenue categories: sales taxes, income taxes, and fees. Subcategories appear for the first two main revenue categories, and

Table 6.1

Revenue Format Example

Delaware

Proposed budget Estimated revenues (in millions of dollars)			Fiscal year 2009
Sales taxes			$100
General retail		70	
Selective		30	
Alcohol	5		
Gasoline	15		
Tobacco	10		
Income taxes			200
Personal		160	
Corporate		40	
Fees			50
		Total	$350

sub-subcategories for selective sales taxes. Each column inset, where one or more entries appears one column to the left of the immediately preceding entry, means that the inset entries are subdivisions or parts of the preceding entry. General retail sales and selective sales taxes are the two parts of the sales tax category; the three entries under selective sales taxes are the three parts of that entry. A quick review of the numbers involved indicates that the sum of the entries for the inset items is equal to the preceding item in each case. In some cases, formats show only larger subdivisions of particular revenue categories.

Lump-Sum Budgeting Approach

Table 6.2 displays an example of a lump-sum budget format. This example and the ones that follow in this chapter illustrate some of the basic concepts of the budget formats and approaches. The heading information indicates that the document is a proposed budget for a city for the 1891 fiscal year. In the main body, the Police Department is an organizational unit, and "Elected officials' salaries" is a purpose. A lump-sum budget answers the question of how much the organization will spend for each category of expenditures and in total. In a lump-sum budget, information is classified into lumps.

The key ideas are lump sums and general accountability. Lump sum means a round dollar amount for a general expenditure category. General accountability means that those spending the money are accountable in a general way to those who approve the expenditure amount.

Table 6.2

Lump-Sum Budget Format Example

Springfield, Massachusetts	Fiscal year 1891
Police Department	$10,000
Elected officials' salaries	1,000
Total	$11,000

Those preparing a lump-sum budget, whether that is a public manager, policy-maker, or group of policy makers, start first by choosing one or more general concepts of what is being budgeting for (e.g., new revenues after the Magna Carta in England, a war, an organization or organizational subdivision, or some general purpose). Second, someone forecasts how much money is required for each general category. Third, someone seeks approval. Lump-sum budgets can be open-ended in respect to time, but typically they are limited to one fiscal year. Lump-sum budget proposals contain relatively little information and, therefore, are easily understood.

After preparation, which is obviously not technically sophisticated, budget-related activities for a lump-sum budget are minimal. Those approving can accept, reject, or adjust the lump sums. Those implementing a lump-sum budget have a wealth of discretion. That level of discretion implies a high level of trust, direct observation of budget implementation, or both. At best, lump-sum budgets place a general upper limit on spending by managers. In some cases, specifically in many local governments, legislators collectively approve each specific payment for expenditures. Lump-sum budget reports are useful for determining that implementing officials have stayed within their assigned spending limits and establishing a record of expenditure levels.

The limited amount of information found in lump-sum budgeting provides advantages and disadvantages. The advantages are that managers and policy-makers devote little time and effort to formal budget preparation and approval, that those implementing a lump-sum budget make the detailed budget decisions, and that policy-makers control expenditure totals. When and where detailed control is desired, another budgeting approach or additional control devices are necessary. Examples of other control devices are approving each payment, prohibiting specific expenditures, or limiting the number of personnel or positions. The disadvantages are insufficient control and planning by policy-makers and too much discretion by managers.

The lump-sum budgeting approach may be employed usefully by organizations in which the dollar amounts are so small that trust makes the most sense, direct observation of expenditures is common, and other control devices exist.

These conditions exist for small public organizations, of which there are many. Additionally, the federal and state governments do use lump-sum formats for appropriations and when transferring money and granting discretion to operating agencies. Generally, though, the lump-sum budgeting approach lacks attention to details that many find appropriate in public budgeting.

Line-Item Budgeting Approach

Table 6.3 displays a line-item budget format example that resembles and contrasts with the preceding lump-sum example. In the authors' experience, most people expect budgets to be in a line-item format. The heading information differs in four respects from the previous example. First, the fiscal year differs. Second, "Police Department" now appears in the heading information rather than as an information category in the main body. Where organizations are subdivided into units, their budgets tend to be organized by the same subdivisions. Managers typically oversee budgets for their organizational areas. Third, the words "General Fund" indicate that this city uses that category to account for police department expenditures. Fourth, the word "operating" appears, which indicates in this case that capital expenditures are not dealt with here. Capital expenditures might include vehicles, a communications system, and buildings.

The information in the main body concerns only the Police Department's operating expenditures. The example shows three expenditure categories and a department total. The three expenditure categories and their dollar amounts are spoken of as line items or "lines" (how much did you propose for that line?). Only the two personnel categories are, strictly speaking, items, and the patrol officers' line is for four positions (at $4,000 each). Even though the line for supplies is obviously for multiple items within a general category, such entries usually are spoken of as line items. Line-item entries range from very specific items to general categories such as supplies or personnel. Implied, if not stated, is the idea that the items themselves are specific ones that can be examined. A line-item format is characterized by a list of what will be purchased (in varying levels of detail). Sometimes, lines are referred to as objects of expenditure. Line-item budgets resemble shopping lists. Line-item budgeting provides at least minimally detailed information that is easily understood. Even simple line-item budgets are more detailed than lump-sum budgets. Line-item budgets answer the same questions as lump-sum budgets (how much for the whole organization and for specific lumps—usually organizational units in line-item budgeting) and the additional question of what will be purchased. In line-item budgeting, information is classified by organizational units and then line items. Budgets usually use organizational units as an organizing category.

Table 6.3

Line-Item Budget Format

Springfield, Oregon	Fiscal year 1911
General fund	

Police Department
Proposed operating budget
Line items

Chief	$8,000
Patrol officers (4)	16,000
Supplies	1,000
Total	$25,000

The degree of specificity of lines in line-item budgeting ranges very widely. Specific items are the theoretical basis for each line. Some lines distinguish themselves from lump sums only by identifying a general expenditure category, such as personnel. Also, in some cases, specific lines are identified as parts of broader categories or subcategories. For example, a budget document may identify dental insurance as included in the more general category of fringe benefits, which may be identified as included in the category of personnel.

The key ideas are line items, control, detailed accountability, and honesty. Line-item budgets enable those approving budgets to control those implementing budgets by specifying what can and cannot be purchased, necessarily restricting what can be done. Detailed accountability means that those implementing a budget have to adhere to specific limits for particular line items. This detailed accountability of items purchased allows policy-makers and administrators to exercise oversight and the public to scrutinize. Honesty refers to people not taking unfair advantage of public organizations. Reports and financial audits contribute to honesty.

Those preparing a line-item budget have to first determine the different line items needed. Ordinarily, previous budgets or experience provides that information. Second, preparers forecast an amount for each line that appears in their budgets either directly (this much) or indirectly by forecasting the quantity and the price of those items (e.g., four patrol officers at $16,000). Third, they calculate the monetary values involved by multiplying and adding. Forecasting is the primary technical area for the preparation of a line-item budget.

After preparation, those approving, implementing, and auditing and reviewing a budget often deal with line-item details. Those approving have details to consider, question, and adjust. Those implementing a line-item budget have to pay attention to line items as approved, as purchased, and as used.

Managers adjust operations when the prices of line items increase or when a larger than expected quantity of a line item is being used. An approved line item places an expenditure limit that may be exceeded only by using appropriations from another line item (with prior approval) or by getting approval from administrators or policy-makers to gain more expenditure authority. Managers monitor particular line items and deal with situations to keep within the approved amounts or seek more spending authority. During the reviews and reports stage, line-item information appears in annual reports and audits and may be the specific focus of review efforts.

The advantages and disadvantages of line-item budgeting tend to revolve around the ideas of control and accountability, although line-item budgeting can be useful also as a planning exercise. Line-item budgets allow policy-makers to control managers and to make them accountable for purchases. Additionally, policy-makers can infer operating methods from proposed line items. Many policy-makers see greater control, accountability, and information as advantageous. Managers find themselves constrained from exercising discretion by line-item limits. They also spend time forecasting and dealing with line items in implementing their budgets. Some argue that line-item budgeting is disadvantageous because it misdirects policy-makers' and administrators' efforts to constraining managers in cases where discretion would be preferable and by directing attention to the less important details of purchases instead of more important concerns. Those concerns can be characterized as involving what public organizations do (outputs), the results of those activities (outcomes), and the policy choices available to public organizations. Early twentieth-century proponents of executive budgeting expressed a preference for lump-sum budgeting because it afforded managers and executives more discretion. Proponents of later budgeting approaches argue for paying attention to outputs, outcomes, or choices rather than line items in using budgeting and budget documents in policy-making.

Line-item budgeting is generally suitable. Line-item budgeting is by far the most commonly used budgeting approach and is likely to remain so. The approach is simple and familiar.

Performance Budgeting Approach

The performance budget format example displayed in Table 6.4 resembles the immediately preceding example; the differences are primarily additional information. This performance budget format example covers only a portion of the Police Department expenditures, in contrast to the two previous examples, which included the whole Police Department. The only differences in the heading information are the fiscal year and the word "Patrol." Patrol in this

Table 6.4

Performance Budget Format Example

Springfield, Ohio	Fiscal year 1951

Police Department
Proposed operating budget: Patrol

Activity unit: One person–one vehicle–one hour
Annual units: 4,500

Line items	
Patrol officers (3)	$45,000
Vehicle	10,000
Vehicle supplies and services	8,000
Total	$63,000
Unit cost: $14.00	

example refers to an activity, which is a "performance." In other cases, patrol might represent an organizational subdivision. The words and numbers in the line following "Activity unit" indicate that patrol performance is measured by one person in a vehicle for an hour, and the line following "Annual units" proposes 4,500 hours of one person patrolling in a vehicle. Other terms for performances include "classes of work," "functions," and "projects." The line items are similar to those in the previous example. The inclusion of line items in Table 6.4 reflects the fact that most performance budgets include line items and that line items have to be forecast as to quantity and price in order to propose a budgeted amount for a performance. Including line items also enables those looking at performance budgets to review "production functions," which are the amounts of different resources required to produce the outputs. The unit cost at the bottom of the table ($14) expresses the inputs (total proposed expenditure of $63,000) divided by the outputs (annual units of 4,500). A measurement of unit cost is one way of expressing the efficiency of providing the proposed activity. In addition to the questions answered by the two previous budget formats, performance budgets answer the questions of what is being done and what are the associated costs. In performance budgets, information is classified into organizational units, then performances, and then line items.

The key ideas for performance budgeting are output, means, and efficiency. Output or outputs refer to what will be done: the performances. The preceding budgeting approaches focus attention on inputs in gross monetary terms (lump sums) or in a detailed fashion (line items). Although those two approaches rely on the usually unstated assumption that inputs will produce positive outputs, performance budgeting explicitly indicates the outputs. By focusing attention on outputs, performance budgeting raises the question of how outputs will be produced, the means, and whether other means might be better. Performance budgeting tends to be associated with concern for operating efficiently. As in Table 6.4, efficiency is generally thought of in terms of the relationship between the input costs and the outputs.

Preparing a performance budgeting proposal involves several steps:

1. Figuring out how to categorize the work involved, which sounds much easier than it is.
2. Forecasting performance levels by predicting a level of demand or proposing an appropriate service level.
3. Dealing with line items (which ones, how many, and what prices).

The third step is very similar to the process of line-item budgeting; however, in performance budgeting, the proposed line items are constrained by the output levels. Obviously, records of previous expenditures and performances would be very helpful in preparing a performance budget. Those preparing a performance budget use some form of work analysis as well as forecasting techniques associated with line-item budgeting. The relationship between line items themselves and the performance can be called production functions; that is, how much or how many of particular line items are required to produce a performance.

After preparation, those approving, implementing, and auditing and reviewing a performance budget have more information to deal with than those dealing with a line-item budget. Those approving can direct their attention to the performances, the means of producing those performances, and the efficiency. Those approving a budget can accept, reject, or revise the performances and the associated lines. However, the explicitness of performance budgets in respect to outputs and inputs constrains those approving budgets from falsely arguing that one can simultaneously reduce line items and increase outputs. Those implementing a performance budget need to keep track of performances and associated expenditures. Tracking performances and associated expenditures complicates the work for managers because it multiples the categories of information that must be recorded. However, unless performance and expenditure information is tracked, managers cannot relate an implemented budget to a proposed or an approved performance budget and hold operating units accountable for their budget implementation. When a performance budget has been implemented or in other cases where performance information is available, managers and policy-makers also can report, audit, and review performances. Operating units and their managers might be held accountable for achieving the proposed levels of performance and efficiency.

The advantages of performance budgeting include explicit treatment of policy choices and great attention to operational efficiency. The disadvantages are its difficulty and costs. Performance budgeting requires that managers explicitly state what work their operating units will perform. Policy-makers, then, can consider the appropriateness of the work, its quantity, and related operating methods. Performance budgeting puts managers in the position of defending or justifying their operations through their budget proposals. Attention to operations by managers and policy-makers is expected to lead to greater efficiency. On the other side, performance budgeting is difficult in regard to the variety of ways that performances can be expressed and understood and in regard to the forecasting process. Performance budgets are difficult to prepare and implement because of the difficulties in crafting and selecting performance measures. Performances expressed as functions (patrol) tend to be imprecise, and those expressed as activities (one person patrolling in a car for so many hours) tend to be highly precise. Still, much of what patrol officers do could fit into other performance categories (crime investigation, public relations, crime prevention, traffic enforcement, parking enforcement, and responding to incidents). The difficulties with forecasting work involve either imprecisely formulated performances (functions) that may become little more than line-item forecasts with a performance heading or precise forecasts that rely on accurate forecasting of events (e.g., number of crimes) and knowledge of production functions (e.g., the average amount of time that an investigator spends on a crime). Precise and accurate forecasting is difficult. The costs of performance budgeting include the much greater costs of gathering and processing information, especially in the preparation stage but also in the approval and implementation stages. The real costs of preparing performance budgets are the other tasks that go unperformed because of its requirements. If the number of lines in a budget is seen as a way of roughly forecasting cost relationships, the budget format examples in Tables 6.2 to 6.4 show that the much greater length of a performance budget makes it much more costly than either lump-sum or line-item budgeting.

Performance budgeting is particularly suitable in two kinds of circumstances. First, it is suitable when the performances can be meaningfully measured. Second, it is suitable when attention to performances is desirable for the sake of concern for outputs or operational efficiency.

Program Budgeting Approach

The program budget format example in Table 6.5 resembles earlier examples. The heading information duplicates what already has appeared in the earlier examples, except for the later fiscal year and the line indicating that the

Table 6.5

Program Budget Format Example

Springfield, Arkansas	Fiscal year 1967

Police Department
Proposed budget

Solving Crimes Against Persons Program

Line items

Twenty percent of chief's time	$10,000
Detective	25,000
Vehicle (and supplies and services)	10,000
Facility (and supplies and services)	5,000
Total	$50,000

Projected Outcomes of Solving Crimes Against Persons Program

Category	Number	Number solved	Percentage solved
Murder	1	1	100
Robbery	5	2	40

document is for a program called "Solving Crimes Against Persons." A program is a systematic set of activities designed or intended to accomplish one or more outcomes. In this example, a crime investigation program is expected to result in solving crimes against persons. Sometimes, programs are subdivided into subprograms. The line items differ in two ways from earlier line items. First, the line item for 20 percent of the expenditure for the police chief's time recognizes that the chief uses that much time for the purpose of crime solution. Dividing line items is more common in program budgeting than in other approaches. Second, the two line items involving vehicles and facilities appear to include capital expenditures on those items. Including capital and operating information together is common in program budgeting. The material under the "Projected Outcomes" heading indicates forecast levels of crimes against persons, the number solved, and the percentage solved. The service provided, crime solution, depends on the level of demand for service. The police department can only solve the crimes committed and reported. Program budgets are especially likely to contain supporting documents concerning the analysis of projections or levels of services, choices of operational methods, and levels of outcomes. The supporting documents are likely to include or reference multiyear plans. In addition to the questions answered by lump-sum and line-item budgets, program budgets answer the questions of what the purposes or goals are, how much is being spent on those purposes or goals, and what forecasted outcomes are. In program budgeting, information is generally classified into organizational units, then programs, perhaps subprograms, and then line items. In some cases, programs cross organizational unit lines so that the classification is program, organizational unit, and line items.

The key ideas of program budgeting are outcome, goals or purposes, effectiveness, planning, rationality, and analysis. Outcome refers to what is accomplished in the sense of an ultimate desired result. In the illustrative example, the outcomes are solved crimes; other examples of outcomes are reducing poverty or pollution and increasing levels of educational attainment or voluntary public service activities. Program budgeting renders explicitly what citizens expect of public organizations: positive results. Expected outcomes may be also thought of in terms of goals or purposes. Outcomes can be seen as measuring the effectiveness of pursuing particular goals or purposes. Program budgeting embodies the logic of rational decision-making as displayed in planning efforts, as will be seen shortly in the discussion of preparing program budget proposals. Finally, program budgeting promotes the idea of analysis because that justifies choices made in program budgeting.

Preparing a program budget presents many challenges:

1. Adopting a rational decision-making model.
2. Selecting the goals or purposes to pursue. Often people disagree about specific definitions of goals or purposes, and even slight apparent differences in their definitions might result in significant practical differences. Also, in many cases, a stated goal or purpose is only an intermediate one rather than the final or ultimate goal. For example, crime solution may be a goal, but the ultimate goal may be to make the public safe from crime.
3. Prioritizing the goals or purposes.
4. Selecting desirable outcomes that serve as measures of achieving goals or purposes.
5. Analyzing and choosing the means to achieve the desirable outcomes.
6. Deciding on the desired level of outcomes given resource constraints.
7. Forecasting line items using the production functions associated with the means in the fifth step and the level of outcomes selected in the sixth step.

Line-item information is necessary for forecasting costs accurately. As in any rational decision-making or planning process, information acquired or developed later in the process may require rethinking earlier steps. For example, resource constraints examined in the sixth step may result in the realization that a specific goal is not achievable with the resources available to the organization. Preparing a program budget involves analytical techniques, such as cost analysis, systems analysis, and hypothesis testing; a variety of planning techniques; and forecasting techniques for work programs, outcomes, and line items.

Preparation of a program budget tends to reveal that people have diverse opinions about goals, purposes, outcomes, and the means of achieving outcomes; that knowledge on these matters is limited; and that budget decisions are political. Diverse opinions on goals, purposes, outcomes, and the means of achieving outcomes tend to become more apparent as people move from abstract to more concrete situations. Diverse opinions give rise to concrete policy proposals, including budgets, about which policy-makers decide. Limited knowledge about producing outcomes means that managers and policy-makers have to make decisions based on opinions and assessments of probabilities rather than settled knowledge.

After a program budget is prepared, policy-makers review it and decide what to approve. Most policy-makers lack a background that would make them comfortable with analysis. Also, from the perspective of policy-makers, analysis has the unfortunate tendency to provide evidence for positions at odds with either their own personal opinions or those of their constituents or supporters. Because time is limited, policy-makers probably first examine analysis that interests them. During implementation of a program budget, the available resources are segregated by and accounted for relative to the various approved programs. Outcomes are tracked. During the reviews and reports stage, auditors can use the outcome records to assess program effectiveness. Managers can review their programs for effectiveness.

The advantages and disadvantages of program budgeting stem from its rational character, association with analysis, and emphasis on effectiveness. The advantages include the opportunities that program budgeting affords to public organizations to examine what they are doing in terms of goals, purposes, outcomes, and means. Those opportunities may lead to useful analysis, to greater attention to effectiveness, and better decisions. The disadvantages are the difficulties and costs. Program budgeting is difficult because it requires a tremendous amount of information and calculations to create and analyze programs, because many managers lack the skills to create or usefully consume expert analysis, and because no one has yet figured out how to adequately analyze many public policies. The costs of program budgeting include the extra expenses of analysis (including analytically skilled personnel), an increased amount of time devoted to budgeting activities, and the conflict that arises when goals, purposes, outcomes, means, and analysis are the objects of budgetary attention. In many cases, program budgeting is not a practical possibility.

Program budgeting is suitable in situations that play to its strengths, when effectiveness or planning is a major concern or when planning or analysis can be expected to improve budget decisions.

What-If Budgeting Approach

What-if budgeting occurs when an executive, other policy-makers, or administrators decide to prepare and approve budget proposals on the basis of "what if we did things this way." Situations that give rise to what-if budgeting tend to be negative: within-year budget shortfalls and long-term financial declines. Some situations in which what-if budgeting arises represent an attempt to facilitate change through reallocation. In those situations, the what-ifs for managers are simultaneously: (1) What would you give up if your budget were reduced by some percentage—say, 5 percent? and (2) What would you like to do that you are not presently doing if you could increase your budget by some percentage—say, 2 percent? Reallocation processes use reductions to fund increases. Finally, when revenue shortfalls occur, what-if budgeting helps in deciding how to decrease expenditures. We see what-if budgeting as including what others have called zero-base budgeting, decremental budgeting, cutback budgeting, and sometimes incremental budgeting.

Table 6.6 provides an example of a zero-base budget format, the most well-known version of what-if budgeting. The heading information is mostly the same as in previous examples, except for the fiscal year and the term "Decision units," which identifies the subject of the budgeting information. Decision units can be organizational units, performance areas, programs, or any other manner of subdividing an organization's finances for the purpose of budgeting. The decision unit in this example is the investigation of crimes against property. Other new format features include decision packages, ranking numbers, results, costs, cumulative results, and cumulative costs. Two or more decision packages are created for each decision unit. Each decision package contains some kind of a result or consequence statement, a ranking indication, a cost, and associated line items. All these elements are included together as a decision package. The key aspect of any decision package is the result or consequence statement because it states what difference funding a decision package will make. Results or consequences can be expressed negatively or positively; as outputs, outcomes, or something else; and generally or specifically. Everything else in a decision package depends on the results or consequences statement, which justifies funding a decision package. The line items are those items required to produce the results or consequences, and the cost is the total of the line items for the decision package. The ranking numbers, "1 of 2" and "2 of 2," indicate the relative importance of the decision packages within a given group ranking, such as a decision unit, and the number of packages in a group. The first number indicates a rank position, and the second number indicates the number of packages in the group. By convention, the highest rank is 1 and the second highest is 2. The ranking numbers along with a decision unit name give each decision package a unique name. In some cases, packages are ranked for more than one decision unit, for example, an organization-wide ranking of decision packages. The cumulative results and the cumulative costs appear in the second decision package in the example and would appear in a third and any lower-priority decision package. The cumulative categories result from adding the costs and the results for the first two packages together to indicate running totals. For a third or even lower-priority decision package, the costs and the results from that package and every higher-priority package are added together to give that running total. The line items in the two decision packages are similar to what appeared previously. In addition to questions answered by line-item budgeting, what-if budgeting answers the questions of what choices are offered and preferred by managers and which ones are preferred by managers and executives. In zero-base budgeting, each decision package can stand alone, somewhat like items on an à la carte menu. Levels of authorized spending are determined ultimately by the sum of expenditures of the decision packages selected by policy-makers.

In other versions of what-if budgeting, indications of the budgeting approach might be most visible in the headings, budget instructions, accompanying narrative material, or a comparison with the previously approved budget. Most such budget documents are likely to display a line-item format.

What-if budgeting answers the question of how an expenditure budget differs from a previous budget in addition to the questions answered by line-item budgets. Those answers may also include program, performance, or other consequence information; increases or decreases; and alternatives choices. In what-if budgeting, the classification of information is generally organizational units and line items. In zero-base budgeting specifically, the classification is organizational units, decision units, decision packages, and line items.

The key ideas of what-if budgeting are choice, consequences, and preferences. Choice defines what-if budgeting. Consequences may be expressed explicitly or be inferred from lump-sum or line-item information in conjunction with an existing budget. Preferences are seen in the recommended and approved choices (from all possible choices).

The instructions in specific situations direct how a what-if budget is prepared. The instructions indicate required choices, that is, whether and how much cutting, increasing, or reallocating a budget is required:

Table 6.6

Zero-Base Budget Format Example

Springfield, Tennessee	Fiscal year 1979

Police Department
Decision unit: Investigation of crimes against property
Decision package 1 of 2
Results: Investigation of burglaries, thefts, and motor vehicle
   thefts for 40 hours a week
Costs: $78,000

Line items	
Detective	$40,000
Vehicle	30,000
Supplies	8,000
Total	$78,000

Decision package 2 of 2
Results: Investigation of burglaries, thefts, and motor vehicle
   thefts for 40 hours a week
Cumulative results: Investigation of burglaries, thefts, and motor
   vehicle thefts for 80 hours a week
Costs: $78,000
Cumulative costs: $156,000

Line items	
Detective	$40,000
Vehicle	30,000
Supplies	8,000
Total	$78,000

1. Reviewing the instructions
2. Reviewing the situation
3. Formulating choices
4. Picking choices to recommend
5. Forecasting line items

Cutting budgets is more common and not at all pleasant. Cuts within a budget year present special problems as it is impossible to cut expenditures after they have been made; an overall cut of 4 percent within a year might require that some areas of a budget be cut by 10 to 20 percent simply because they are still available to be cut. The difficulty of handling cuts increases as the size of the cuts increases. Dealing with budget increases is more pleasant. Reallocation processes are mixed, largely depending on whether a manager expects to have an overall budget increase or decrease.

Also, budget preparation instructions may exempt certain categories of expenditures from being decreased or increased. The choices of what to recommend cutting or augmenting are based on existing responsibilities, programming or alternatives possibilities, and guidance from policy-makers or administrative superiors.

In formulating choices for budgetary decreases or increases, the starting point is generating possible changes and choosing which of them to recommend. A manager can start at zero as in zero-base budgeting and add choices or start with all possible choices available and subtract from them. Second, adding up or subtracting down, a manager has to forecast the expenditures for the recommended choices and have some idea of the consequences caused by the change in expenditures. Managers responsible for operating units frequently argue that cuts will cause more consequences than administrators are willing to believe. Implementing cuts is the only way to find out which side in such a dispute is correct. Zero-base budgeting makes the consequences of choices more explicit but does not stop such disputes from occurring. Preparing what-if budgets involves forecasting techniques and perhaps analytical techniques concerning outputs or outcomes.

After the choices have been proposed, then they have to be approved, rejected, or revised. In many cases of in-year budget cuts, policy-makers with formal approval power essentially delegate the power to approve budget cuts down the organizational hierarchy and intervene only when the cuts are objectionable from their perspective. Many policy-makers avoid taking formal responsibility for the specifics of budget cuts by allowing their subordinates to take that responsibility. Cuts frequently are allocated down a hierarchy; organizational units are told how much they have to cut their budget, and in some cases, the cuts are handed further down the hierarchy until they come to the smallest units with budget authority. Proposals to increase budgets more frequently are solicited by policy-makers or administrators and decided on at the higher levels of an organization. Budgetary politics plays a role in what-if budgeting decision-making as it does in any budgeting situation, but the focus here is on the budgeting approach.

Ranking is the zero-base budgeting mechanism for making choices. Managers preparing decision units rank their choices; administrators take decision packages from more than one decision unit and rank them; and policy-makers rank decision packages for all the decision units. In approving decision packages, the ranking process sorts out decision packages into groups depending on how important the decision packages are to the organization. In some cases, administrators or executives aggregate decision packages into labeled groups. The most important decision packages will be funded, the least important decision packages will not be funded, and the decision packages in the middle will be scrutinized closely. Most approval attention is likely to be given to those decision packages right around the point at which the organization's desire to fund decision packages is exhausted. Approving a budget using what-if budgeting takes more time than approving a budget without choices or major changes.

After approval takes place, managers implement the changes. Budget cuts tend to create a lot of work. Operating units have to figure out how to operate without certain resources. Managers get to help people learn different ways of operating. Also, managers and administrators may impose additional requirements for documenting resource usage (such as photocopying, telephone, or vehicle usage) or for gaining approval for expenditures (such as purchases, hiring, travel, and raises). Budget increases produce more work as well, although someone usually champions increases and willingly takes on some of the work burdens. During implementation, managers typically pay close attention to changes, supervising those work areas closely and gathering and reviewing budget-related information, because those areas are most likely to have problems. If the consequences of the changes are at issue, managers may gather and review consequence-related information. Zero-base budgeting may reduce difficulties in implementation by relating changes in expenditures and consequences. When a form of what-if budgeting other than zero-base budgeting is used, the subdivisions of a budget are likely to be organizational units, choices, and lines.

In the reviews and reports stage of a budget process, more concern is likely to be displayed for changes instituted using a what-if approach than otherwise. Managers, especially, review changes for the differences the changes make for their operations.

The advantages of the what-if budgeting approach are that it involves managers in making changes, informs choices, and facilitates change. Managers offering choices for change are likely to produce choices that are grounded in reality as opposed to changes simply imposed from the top down. The choice information is likely to produce better choices. The production of choices makes it easier to change a budget. The disadvantages are the difficulties and costs, which include developing, learning and teaching, and putting the approach into practice. Many people find it hard to learn a new budgeting approach because it requires new concepts, information, and information processing. If trust is not very high and people think that decisions are being made on another basis than information put into budget proposals, then they are not terribly enthusiastic about learning a new budgeting approach. The costs involve the time required to gather and process information in order to make decisions and the time required to approve and to implement changes. Budget cuts and reallocations, more than budget increases, require that managers rethink their current operations and policies. Budget implementation is more time-consuming for changing situations.

What-if budgeting is suitable for making choices. Certain kinds of situations lend themselves to choices, such as those involving grants, research and development, or budget changes, whether cuts, reallocations, or increases. Otherwise, what-if budgeting is not suitable because generating choices without picking among them wastes resources. Zero-base budgeting appears particularly suitable when major changes are contemplated because it exposes information about production functions and policy choices.

Mixing Approaches

Despite the compartmentalized presentation of the five budgeting approaches here, public organizations frequently mix them together. The mixing takes different forms.

In some cases, different units, levels, or branches in a public organization use different approaches to develop, present, or review a budget. Nonexecutive policy-makers tend to be partial to line-item budgets, and reformers using performance, program, or what-if budgeting approaches tend to be executives and administrators. Where different approaches are used, some budget information has to be converted from one set of information categories to another.

In other cases, an organization may supplement a primary approach with one or more elements from another approach. Performance measures, which are more often outcomes than outputs, have been particularly popular as a supplement to line-item budgets in recent years.

In some cases, elements from one approach informally supplement another approach, as in narratives or oral presentations. For example, narratives or oral presentations can use wording such as: "If our unit is given this much more money, we will provide this much in additional services"; "This initiative will result in these performances or efficiency measured in these terms"; "This program is directed at this goal or will produce these outcomes"; or "Analysis shows that this choice is the best." These statements illustrate ideas associated with performance, program, and what-if budgeting approaches.

Finally, in some cases, words such as "analysis," "program," "performance," and "zero-base" are added to line-item budgets to give the appearance or impression of budget reforms that are not practically existent. Without intensive scrutiny of such situations, it is impossible to determine whether the persons responsible for the appearance but not the reality of reform think they are fooling others or are really only fooling themselves.

A Commentary on Approaches

Controversies in many fields mystify until people know the terms and the stakes involved. Budgeting approaches have been at the center of many intense budgeting controversies. The stakes generating the intensity of those controversies include deeply held values, political power, economic advantage, and personal exposure to change.

The first two budgeting approaches, lump-sum and line-item budgeting, are associated with two sets of revolutionary events, the development of a constitutional monarchy in England and successful popular government in the United States. Both reforms contributed to political power being more broadly shared, and they express the view that constraining governing authorities in the gathering and use of resources is wise. The overwhelming majority of public organizations have found these two budgeting approaches sufficient for their purposes. Lump-sum budgeting easily facilitates political accountability, but provides limited information for decision-making. Line-item budgeting facilitates control and can provide extensive information for decision-making. Most public organizations have used these approaches for long periods of time.

These two approaches can be considered successful by the standard of widespread use. In contrast, the three later budgeting approaches developed in the twentieth century—performance, program, or what-if budgeting—have been used primarily in public organizations that are large, complex, and reform-oriented, with the federal government providing the most prominent examples. Generally, the logic presented on behalf of these three budgeting approaches is that using more information and analysis leads to better budget decisions. However, those approach reforms also have involved the stakes mentioned above.

Proponents of these three later budgeting approaches share the Progressive Movement values of rationality, reliance on experts, executive leadership, and active government. Interestingly, those proponents appear to assume that the goals of the first two approaches, to make government accountable to the public and to control the operations of government, are no longer a matter of concern or that those ends can be obtained using the later budgeting approaches. Rationality and expertise are reflected in agencies gathering and analyzing data, and executive leadership is reflected by executive guidance of the agencies. Also, the emphasis on executive leadership is a reaction to the tendency of legislative bodies to make marginal or incremental adjustments in budgets over extended periods of time and to diffuse responsibility. Executives concentrate responsibility when they propose and implement approach reforms using experts under their supervision. Often, approach reforms are coincidental with efforts to shift expenditure patterns. Analysis can be used to justify change.

The stakes at issue in budgeting approach controversies typically divide disputants in ways that are reinforcing rather than crosscutting. The value cleavages tend to be between more and less rationality, government activity, and executive leadership. The power divides involve executives and legislators, agencies, political parties, and holders of the different values. Economic advantages and disadvantages arising from government actions or inactions provide another set of motives for contention: for example, initiating or concluding particular programs. Agencies and their managers feel crosscutting pressures more than other participants as they tend to share the progressive values with the executives and therefore hope that reforms will pay off, but also they see that increased executive power may come somewhat at their expense, that executive-driven policies tend to be more ephemeral than legislative ones, that legislatures appropriate, and that past reform efforts often have been disappointing. Finally, public managers and legislators are exposed to the greatest possible changes in budgeting. Legislators can collectively ignore budget reforms wrought by executives. Public managers do not have that luxury and must attempt to comply when they are told that a new budgeting approach is required.

Assessing the three later budgeting approaches is much harder than assessing the two earlier ones. The later budgeting approaches suffer from being harder to grasp, from being at the center of controversies that have not been permanently resolved, and from the uncertainty of their inherent utility. Proponents appear to oversell the later budgeting approaches, and opponents appear to discount them excessively. A fair assessment probably lies somewhere between those extreme assessments.

The three later budgeting approaches are more ambitious in character than the first two. They all aim at improving decisions by increasing information rather than facilitating political arrangements. The later budgeting approaches pose more technical challenges in implementation than the earlier approaches and more naïveté in suggesting that people can adequately identify and agree on better decisions. Diversity of political views and disparity of preferences makes agreeing on better decisions difficult, if not impossible, to achieve in all but trivial cases. The technical challenges of the later budgeting approaches are developing and implementing new information categories to arrange line-item information, analyzing, and making analytically based decisions. In some cases, adoptions of budgeting approaches have been reforms primarily in name because the analysis is missing.

In most cases, the decision to adopt a particular budget approach is made by individual organizations or by specific public officials within those organizations. Individual organizations may adopt a performance, program, or what-if budgeting approach, but those adoptions tend to occur in bunches or small waves, contributing to the impression that they are fads. Although "fad" is probably too harsh a word, only a fraction of governments or nonprofit organizations have ever adopted any of the later three budgeting approaches. Furthermore, to our knowledge, no public organization has ever used one of the later budgeting approaches for ten years or more. The later budgeting approaches have not become widely entrenched in public organizations the way that the first two are even though some elements of a budgeting approach have endured in particular governments: for example, functional accounting categories in the federal government.

The three later budgeting approaches continue to receive attention from public administration academics and enthusiastic support from some reformers who want more from budgeting than they believe they can get from the first two approaches. Also, they have had enduring residual impacts, including awareness of a wide range of budgeting concepts and supporting informational and analytical techniques applicable within the context of budgeting. Whether a budgeting approach is widely adopted or becomes entrenched is probably less important than whether a public organization seriously considers its outputs, outcomes, and policy choices and gathers and analyzes information in the service of making its budget decisions. The three later budgeting approaches contribute to the general movement of public policy and public administration toward greater rationality.

Conclusion

Managers prepare budgets using particular budgeting approaches and present them in particular formats. Those budgeting approaches and formats determine the choice of information to communicate that guides managers in their preparation and influences the decisions made when budgets are being approved and implemented.

Additional Reading and Resources

Print

A symposium on performance budgeting:
"Performance Budgeting: Has the Theory Worked?" *Public Administration Review* 20 (Spring 1960): 63–85.

The latter portion of this article discusses program budgeting:

Schick, Allen. "The Road to PPB." *Public Administration Review* 26 (December 1966): 243–258.

The instructions to agencies on producing proposed budgets are a good introduction to a budgeting approach. The U.S. Bureau of the Budget, the precursor of the U.S. Office of Management and Budget, published instructions for program budgeting that can be found in the following sources:

U.S. Bureau of the Budget. "Bulletin No. 66–3," "Supplement to Bulletin No. 66–3," and "Bulletin No. 68–2." In *Planning Programming Budgeting: A Systems Approach to Management*, ed. Fremont J. Lyden and Ernest G. Miller, 405–443. Chicago: Markham Publishing, 1967.

U.S. Bureau of the Budget. "Bulletin No. 68–9" (April 12, 1968). In *Government Budgeting: Theory, Process, Politics*, ed. Albert C. Hyde and Jay M. Shafritz, 129–141. Oak Park, IL: Moore Publishing, 1978.

An assessment of program budgeting at the federal level:

Schick, Allen. "A Death in the Bureaucracy: The Demise of Federal PPB." *Public Administration Review* 33 (March/April 1973): 146–156.

The inventor of zero-base budgeting discusses its application to government:

Phyrr, Peter A. "The Zero-Base Approach to Government Budgeting." *Public Administration Review* 37 (January/February 1977): 1–8.

An investigation into the application of zero-base budgeting in Georgia:

Lauth, Thomas P. "Zero-base Budgeting in Georgia State Government: Myth and Reality." *Public Administration Review* 38 (September/October 1978): 420–430.

An account of zero-base budgeting in a city:

Singleton, David W., Bruce A. Smith, and James R. Cleaveland. "Zero-Based Budgeting in Wilmington, Delaware." *Government Finance* 15 (August 1976): 20–29.

The U.S. Office of Management and Budget instructions for zero-base budgeting:

U.S. Office of Management and Budget. "Bulletin No. 77–9" (April 19, 1977). In *Government Budgeting: Theory, Process, Politics*, ed. Albert C. Hyde and Jay M. Shafritz, 306–321. Oak Park, IL: Moore Publishing, 1978.

The contemporary approach to using a variety of concepts of performance in budgeting can be found in the following:

Kelly, Janet M., and William C. Rivenbark. *Performance Budgeting for State and Local Government*. Armonk, NY: M.E. Sharpe, 2003.

Redburn, F. Stevens, Robert J. Shea, and Terry F. Buss, eds. *Performance Management and Budgeting: How Governments Can Learn from Experience*. Armonk, NY: M.E. Sharpe, 2007.

Two articles assessing the prospects for performance-based budgeting:

Joyce, Philip G. "Using Performance Measures for Federal Budgeting: Proposals and Prospects." *Public Budgeting & Finance* 13 (Winter 1993): 3–17.

Willoughby, Katherine G., and Julia E. Melkers. "Implementing PBB: Conflicting Views of Success." *Public Budgeting & Finance* 20 (Spring 2000): 85–120.

Internet

National Governors Association—Center for Best Practices

Many states engage currently in activities that the National Governors Association refers to as results-based management and results-based budgeting, which we refer to here as performance-based budgeting. A variety of reports, including state-by-state accounts, and links can be found at these two pages, respectively, on management and budgeting at www.nga.org/portal/site/nga/menuitem.9123e83a1f6786440ddcbeeb501010a0/?vgnextoid=22bdb00978e b4010VgnVCM1000001a01010aRCRD&vgnextchannel=4b18f074f0d9ff00 VgnVCM1000001a01010aRCRD and www.nga.org/portal/site/nga/menuite m.9123e83a1f6786440ddcbeeb501010a0/?vgnextoid=cae0303cb0b32010V gnVCM1000001a01010aRCRD.

Also, the website's Center for Best Practices can be searched for publications using the terms "Managing for Results" and "budget" or using budgeting-related terms.

Minnesota Office of the Legislative Auditor

Minnesota engaged in program budgeting starting in 1969 and performance-based budgeting in 1992. The Program Evaluation Division of the Office of the Legislative Auditor of the State of Minnesota issued a 108-page report and four-page summary in 1994 on those efforts, which can be found at www.auditor.leg.state.mn.us/PED/1994/perform.htm.

A Performance-Based Federal Budgeting Approach
Documentation for the latest federal budgeting approach (performance-based) using the Program Assessment Rating Tool can be found at the Program Performance Page and in Part 6 of the current OBM Circular A-11 (federal budgeting instructions to agencies), respectively at www.whitehouse.gov/omb/performance_default and www.whitehouse.gov/omb/circulars_a11_current_year_a11_toc.

Planning-Programming-Budgeting System
A brief article from a staff member of the U.S. Bureau of the Budget on using program budgeting for the Special Library Association starts on page 21 of the following PDF file:

Willard Fazar. "Program Planning and Budgeting Theory: Improved Library Effectiveness by Use of the Planning-Programming-Budgeting System." *Special Libraries* 60 (September 1969): 423–433, www.sla.org/speciallibraries/ISSN00386723V60N7.PDF.

7

Analysis in Public Budgeting

Analysis refers to efforts to understand particular phenomena, which usually means asking and answering questions. Public managers conduct analysis for themselves and consume analysis undertaken by others. People concerned with public organizations conduct or consume analysis for the sake of informing themselves in making choices among alternatives or in persuading someone else which alternative(s) to prefer. The basic question for any kind of analysis for public budgeting fits into the formula: "Is alternative A or alternative B preferable?" Although one can analyze almost anything, analytical efforts related to public budgeting involve matters of significant value. Public policy-makers and public managers analyze because they have to make choices involving large amounts of resources and serious consequences. Analysis contributes to the achievement of better results.

The basic analytical question of the preferability of alternative A or alternative B can be extended to any number of alternatives. Alternatives typically concern what to do (policy broadly understood) or how to do it (operations). Analysis of policies tends to focus on whether to start, continue, stop, or adjust a policy. Analysis of operations tends to focus on different ways of accomplishing a policy. Although policy-makers decide on major policies, public managers frequently contribute to those decisions and make decisions on related or subordinate issues and operational matters.

The scope of analysis for public budgeting differs from the scope of other kinds of analysis. First and most important, relevant publics are within the scope of public sector analysis. For a government, the relevant publics include its citizens, residents, and revenue payers. For a nonprofit organization, the relevant publics include its clients, members, and financial supporters. While private sector entities analyze only how alternatives affect them, public organizations need to pay attention to how alternatives affect their publics. Second, analysis for public budgeting only involves matters directly affecting budget decisions.

Public managers can conduct analysis informally or formally. The basic analytical ideas are the same. Formality in analysis tends to arise when the purpose of the analysis is to communicate the results to someone else or when the analysis is particularly complicated. Formal analysis usually is reserved for important issues because of the costs of gathering, creating, manipulating, recording, and communicating information. The choice of formal analysis usually results or arises from situations involving requests, requirements, or persuasion. Formal analysis tends to be presented in written form, uses a lot of evidence, and affords opportunities to correct errors. Many more decisions result from relatively informal analysis performed by policy-makers, administrators, public managers, and line personnel in public organizations. Informal analysis is more common than formal analysis because it is within an organization's control and less costly. Although one might expect analysis to coincide with budget preparation, analysis occurs outside of that context because issues can arise at any time and more time for analysis may be available then.

The Analytical Process

Analysis is a multistep process. The steps, though varying, follow a typical pattern. First, analysis starts with a person noticing, opining, or imagining something. Some phenomenon or idea is identified. The phenomenon or idea may be new, newly important, or long known. In many cases, the phenomena chosen for analysis carry emotional connotations.

Second and third, someone conceptualizes a question, and someone posits alternatives. Alternatives are essential for analysis related to public budgeting because alternatives are required in order to make a choice. After a question and alternatives are considered, they may be revised or abandoned. For example, some alternatives are obviously politically or practically infeasible. The development of alternatives is particularly important as the range of alternatives defines the possible choices. Analyzing a large number of alternatives, however, is often not practical. When many alternatives are available, analysts may do multiple rounds of analysis after starting with representative alternatives to exclude some portion of the less desirable alternatives. When alternatives are posited, only real choices should be considered. Observe the following two sets of personal conditions: (1) rich and anonymous, or (2) rich and famous. The only real choice between the two sets is between being anonymous and being famous, since being rich is included in both. Similarly, two statewide park development plans might differ only on a few specific projects; a comparison of those two plans would focus only on the differences in specific projects.

Fourth and fifth, analysts gather and process information. Gathering information may involve measuring or counting, and processing information may involve calculating.

Sixth and seventh, analysts compare alternatives and reach conclusions.

Sometimes, comparison leads to the elimination of alternatives as poor choices. Sometimes, comparison leads to the conclusion that choices are moderately different. Sometimes, comparison leads to the conclusion that analysts cannot detect significant differences among the alternatives.

Eighth, analysts may communicate their analysis in more or less detail. Ninth, one or more decisions may be made on the basis of the analysis. Analysis informs rather than leads mechanically to decisions.

Many factors can influence how any particular analytical process unfolds. Perceptual or conceptual screens and value structures, which all people have, are two obvious examples. The selection of alternatives and analytical tools is less obvious but may be equally influential.

The division of the analytical process into steps helps analysts focus on the tasks at hand and not become diverted by some specific interesting phenomenon, such as their own initial opinion on the better alternative. People doing analysis find it surprisingly easy to come to the end of an analytical process by concluding that their first opinion was correct without adequately carrying out each analytical step. Also, analysts may retrace their analytical steps, so to speak, or iterate the analytical process as new information becomes available.

Analytical Techniques in Public Budgeting

Only some ways of conducting analysis clearly apply to public budgeting. Four kinds of analysis useful for the purposes of public budgeting are covered here: political, empirical, cost, and system analysis. Although public budget decision-making may benefit from moral and legal analysis as well, those kinds of analysis extend beyond the scope of this work. Still, the analysis of moral and legal questions is quite appropriate.

The four kinds of analysis discussed here can be associated with particular disciplines or areas of human knowledge: (1) Political analysis is based on knowledge of political events found in historical, journalistic, or political science accounts of public affairs. Analysts consider options relative to politically relevant actions and reactions. The analytical question of preferability also includes the question: "Is an alternative politically acceptable?"; (2) Empirical analysis is based on sense observations that analysts deploy to describe, explain, and predict phenomena. Empirical analysis starts with defining a phenomenon in terms of sense observations. Analysts frequently examine the magnitude of a particular phenomenon, whether phenomena are related to one another, and the strength of those relationships; (3) Cost analysis concerns choices involving the relative costs of alternatives, mostly expressed in monetary terms; (4) System analysis, representing an engineering perspective, focuses on change relationships between and among different phenomena. Roughly speaking, when one phenomenon in a system changes, one or more other phenomena change. The change in relationships is key.

Many specific versions of these four kinds of analysis are found under a wide variety of other names. Each of the four kinds of analysis provides one or more frameworks within which analysis takes place. Frameworks include concepts and procedures to assist analysts in focusing attention on evidence concerning factors of particular importance within a particular framework and in coming to characteristic results. Frameworks are theoretical constructs that analysts use to represent real situations with all their attendant details in an abstract fashion so that the situations can be analyzed. Frameworks also can be called perceptual screens because each kind of analysis asks only certain questions, considers only certain kinds of evidence, and arrives at particular kinds of answers.

The general analytical question is whether one or another particular policy or operational choice is preferable. Interestingly, people generally assume or opine that positive consequences will result from particular choices. Generally, people have to make assumptions and rely on opinions because they are unable to analyze everything that they do. However, analysis may confirm or refute assumptions and opinions or leave particular questions unresolved.

An example of an initially unexamined assumption occurred in the early days of civilian emergency medical services. The assumption was that anyone who suffered from a medical emergency was best treated by being rushed to a hospital, a practice that was sometimes referred to as "snatch and run." That assumption was proven incorrect after the results of that practice were analyzed. Today, people suffering from medical emergencies usually are given treatment where they are before being transported to a hospital. Over time, analytical efforts find that some policies and operational choices that appeared to be good ones are inferior to other options.

In the following sections, the techniques associated with the four kinds of analysis can only be discussed generally because of space limitations.

Political Analysis

Political analysis means considering the alternatives in respect to their political acceptability and preferability. Some potential alternatives can be eliminated from consideration because they are unacceptable. Others may be singled out for greater consideration because of political preferences. Political acceptability and preferability can be assessed based on opinions, values, goals, or purposes. In other words, political preferences mean that people will tend to support, oppose, or stay neutral on particular alternatives.

In assessing political acceptability and preferability, analysts think about the most likely reactions of relevant actors within a political community or an organization. Political communities, including those involving nonprofit organizations, display institutional features; that is, regular patterns of behavior (institutions) that have a meaningful impact (features) on the life of a political community or an organization as evidenced in the decisions that are made. Examples of institutional features include groups, organizational hierarchies and subdivisions, offices, positions, voting, elections, selections, and other decision-making processes.

Public managers and their agencies generally have the goal of maintaining and increasing their budgetary resources. The choices available to any public manager and any public agency can be examined in light of which choices will generate more support for funding.

Of course, in political communities and organizations, different actors are interested in particular subject matters, and some actors are more powerful than others because of their institutional location or possession of resources. Political analysis involves identifying particularly interested and potent political actors. Groups and persons often state their views and interests. Persons in policy-making positions, such as chief executives, chief administrators, legislatures, and policy-making board members, are obviously potent political actors, as are people in the higher levels of organizations. Single-issue interest groups in the United States provide examples of small groups that have greater influence on public policy than members of the general public. Such groups are organized and active participants in policy matters affecting their issue. Similarly, policy-makers exert great influence by virtue of their positions. Although public managers may have the greatest expertise in particular areas, they should recognize that political power can and does overrule expertise.

As a matter of course, public administrators and public managers responsible for budgeting notice the actions and pronouncements of particularly interested and potent political actors as those pronouncements occur, especially those that are directly relevant to a particular agency or organizational subdivision. They also generally assess the stances of particularly interested and potent political actors in order to interpret how they might stand on issues on which they have not yet acted nor pronounced.

The process of conducting political analysis can start with asking and answering a few simple questions about alternatives. These questions are similar to ones attributed to Paul Appleby regarding what administrators should ask before making important decisions (expressed by Grover Starling in his textbook, *Managing the Public Sector* [p. 43]):

- Who will be glad?
- Who will be mad?
- How glad?
- How mad?

These questions may sound too simple to be useful. However, their purpose is to provide a framework for sorting out the possible supporters and opponents of a particular alternative and the intensity of their support or opposition. After these four questions are answered, two more questions may be relevant:

- What can those who are glad do?
- What can those who are mad do?

The range of possible activities obviously includes budgetary support, neutrality, or opposition. Those with considerable resources, useful skills, or strong policy-making positions are likely to have much more impact than others without those advantages. For example, federal programs for young Americans tend to be treated much less favorably than those for older Americans. Young Americans either lack the right to vote or exercise that right at a much lower rate than older Americans do, and the number and size of organized interest groups speaking on the behalf of younger Americans are dwarfed by those representing older Americans. Older Americans who are mad or glad therefore have more clout and can vote accordingly, influence others to do the same, and engage in lobbying efforts in the policy-making process. An extreme possibility, more common within organizations than political communities, is the elimination of a policy or an organizational subdivision, but only certain actors have the power to produce that result.

General public opinion plays a part in political processes. However, general public opinion tends to set general boundaries for policy-making rather than determine the specific choices of alternatives.

The consequences of political analysis are to discard alternatives that generate more opposition than support and to focus attention on more politically viable alternatives. Political situations are not completely static, and an alternative that is not acceptable or preferable in one time period may become acceptable or preferable later.

Public managers who do not conduct political analysis may believe that they are acting appropriately. However, they do so at the peril of generating unnecessary political opposition and failing to garner sufficient amounts of political support. Norton Long expresses this point extremely well in his 1949 article "Power and Administration" published in *Public Administration Review*:

There is no more forlorn spectacle in the administrative world than an agency and a program possessed of statutory life, armed with executive orders, sustained in the courts, yet stricken with paralysis and deprived of power.

The lifeblood of administration is power. Its attainment, maintenance, increase, dissipation, and loss are subjects that the practitioner and the student can ill afford to neglect. . . .

Analysis of the sources from which power is derived and the limitations they impose is as much a dictate of prudent administration as sound budgetary procedure.

Political analysis differs from the other three kinds of analysis discussed here in relying much more on interpretation of events rather than direct observation. In analyzing political situations, what people think about a situation may be more important than what really happened. Those interpretations often take the form of narratives or stories that express thoughts, values, preferences, and beliefs. Political analysts observe what people think or express about situations as that provides insight into how they might react to different alternatives.

Much political analysis reflects a wary appreciation of past events. For example, the attitude of city officials in Chicago about snow removal is based on a lesson learned well from a mayoral election in 1979. In the winter of 1978–1979, frequent large snowfalls and bitter weather led to many impassable streets, public transportation delays, and the inability of city crews to make timely garbage collections. The public expressed its dissatisfaction with the city government by voting out the incumbent mayor. Subsequent administrations have paid a great deal of attention to snowfalls.

Political analysis can be proactive as well as reactive. During a budget standoff between President Clinton and the Republican Congress in 1996, the two sides refused to compromise over budget legislation. The Republicans' political analysis of the situation appears to have been that the public would not mind and might approve the federal government not having funding to act. President Clinton prevailed in that situation by offering the narrative that vital public services would be neglected if the standoff continued.

Empirical Analysis

Empirical analysis uses information from sense observations, including instrument-based ones. Sense observation provides indisputable evidence. All competent observers following competently created procedures for observation and reporting will report the same. Empirical analysis cannot address issues that rest on anything other than sense observations. Analysts can report the existence of disputed beliefs, opinions, and accounts of particular events using sense observations and analyze those sense observations relative to other sense observations, but cannot speak authoritatively to the truth of the beliefs, opinions, or the disputed events using empirical analysis. One can observe a person communicating a sighting of or a belief in the existence of an unidentified flying object. One cannot sense a belief or an opinion, however, and not all competent observers see unidentified flying objects.

Analysts obtain sense observations from existing records or procedures set up solely for the sake of a particular analysis. For other recording purposes or for the sake of analysis, particular qualities are observed and recorded. Those qualities may be said to be present or absent, to be more or less, or to be measurable on a particular scale. Also, the number of phenomena may be counted.

Analysts address four kinds of empirical questions:

- What is this phenomenon?
- What is the magnitude of this phenomenon?
- Are phenomena related?
- How strongly are phenomena related?

Sequentially, these questions seek to identify, describe, explain, and predict observable phenomena.

What Is This Phenomenon?

This question seeks to identify or define a phenomenon so that it can be distinguished from all other phenomena and placed in any appropriate classification scheme related to other phenomena. Answering this question enables analysts to get beyond unstated or unspoken assumptions about a phenomenon and, if necessary, to develop a precise definition for further analysis. Describing a phenomenon enables analysts first of all to gain an understanding of what is involved. Does a phenomenon have a public dimension? Is a phenomenon a problem or an opportunity that a public organization should consider engaging? Is it within the scope of a public organization's mission and capabilities? Focusing on identifying a phenomenon means discerning its essential features or qualities. Identification precedes further empirical analytical efforts.

What Is the Magnitude of the Phenomenon?

This question concerns its size, quantity, or scope. Gauging the magnitude of a phenomenon means finding and reporting the phenomenon in numerical fashion. Frequently, the numbers represent either the number of phenomena within some context (e.g., per year within a jurisdiction) or a measurement of the phenomenon. Measuring the size, quantity, or scope of a phenomenon enables analysts and others to assess whether a phenomenon is sufficiently common or large in some sense to be a concern to a public organization. Such measurements of magnitude enable analysts to evaluate claims of importance objectively.

Identifying and gauging the magnitude of a phenomenon helps analysts and others in a public organization avoid the common tendency of making decisions based on anecdotes, personal stories, or media accounts of phenomena. Stories that people read or hear tend to have a strong impact. However, anecdotes may not be perfectly accurate, and personal stories and media accounts of phenomena may not provide an accurate or adequate account of situations. A personal story of something heard, seen, or reported may involve an unusual situation. Generally, carefully collected information is more accurate than impressions formed from stories. Media accounts are especially prone to bias because the news media emphasize the unusual or extreme situation. A general rule for journalists is that a dog biting a man is not news, but that a man biting a dog is news. A famous newspaper headline captures the media's orientation to the sensational: "Headless Body Found in Topless Bar." Of course, public organizations can use that tendency to the advantage of their programs. The U.S. Consumer Product Safety Commission issues press releases with provocative labels: "Top Five Hidden Home Hazards." However, the commission identifies hazards and measures their magnitudes. For example, furniture and appliances tipping over claimed thirty-one lives in 2006 in addition to an estimated 3,000 injuries.

Are Phenomena Related?

This question concerns whether one phenomenon is associated with or connected to one or more other phenomena. For example, water in the solid form is associated with cold temperatures. Analysts use information to test this question; they may refer to this procedure formally as hypothesis testing. A look at data or information may show that two or more phenomena are invariably or nearly invariably related, apparently have no relationship, or may have a relationship. For example, a coin that when flipped always comes up heads suggests a relationship between the act of flipping and heads. Likewise, a coin that when flipped averages about 50 percent heads and about 50 percent tails suggests a lack of a relationship between flipping and heads (almost even between heads and tails, as would be expected). However, a flipped coin that comes up 70 percent heads suggests a possible relationship between flipping and heads. Analysts can address the question of a possible relationship using statistical analysis; they hypothesize that two or more phenomena are not related and then calculate the probability of the data on hand occurring by chance if that and other assumptions, such as a random collection of data, are correct. The most common cutoff point for relationships is .05, meaning that something occurs by chance in one of twenty cases or less often. A relationship between two phenomena may exist without that relationship being at all useful in any meaningful way to a public organization.

It should be noted that statistical analysis can produce false reports of relationships or the lack of relationships. If one conducts many tests of significance, one in twenty occurs by chance alone. If the data do not have a random distribution or are not collected by a random sampling method, the results may be inaccurate. If there is a gap between what people say they do (e.g., they say they always wear a seat belt) and what they actually do (e.g., they do not always wear a seat belt), then the results may not be accurate. Also, as the number of cases increases, the possibility of statistical significance increases.

U.S. military analysts during World War II found a good example of a useful statistical relationship. Analysts examined many factors relative to success in pilot training and other phenomena because success in pilot training was considered a key aspect of military effectiveness on account of the amount of resources required to train pilots. Statistical tests revealed that trainees from urban locales succeeded at a higher rate than those from rural backgrounds.

How Strongly Are Phenomena Related?

This question speaks to how much change in one phenomenon is associated with how much change in one or more other phenomena. In other words, how much does one phenomenon change relative to change in another phenomenon? The idea underlying this kind of analysis is that phenomena can be manipulated to produce better results. Analysts can calculate answers to this question using various statistical routines. Relationship statistical routines include processes for "controlling" for particular phenomena, which means to eliminate the effect of the variation of the control phenomena so that other specific relationships can be examined. In election polling, for example, when pollsters report "likely voters," they are controlling for the probabilities that some people who gave them answers will not vote, based on historical evidence and on answers to various questions. One point to emphasize about statistical analysis is its accuracy if done properly. In contrast, people inaccurately perceive probabilities of events occurring in widely varying manners, depending on their own viewpoint more than the actual probabilities of events occurring.

Cost Analysis

Cost analysis addresses the relative merits of alternatives by estimating costs for current situations or forecasting them for future situations. Costs are negative impacts. Most costs, but not all, are measured in monetary terms. Positive impacts are included in some forms of cost analysis. Positive impacts take the form of effects in cost-effectiveness analysis or benefits in cost-benefit analysis. Analysts produce estimates or forecasts so that alternatives can be evaluated using a comparable basis. Cost analysis has three common forms, each of which uses a different comparison basis. Simple cost analysis compares costs alone, cost-effectiveness analysis compares the costs per common unit of positive impact (output or outcomes), and cost-benefit analysis compares the net difference between benefits and costs (benefits minus costs). From the first to the last listed, they tend to become increasingly inclusive, difficult, and inaccurate. Cost-effectiveness and cost-benefit analysis build on simple cost analysis.

Simple cost analysis can be broken down into six steps:

1. Developing alternatives
2. Listing costs
3. Quantifying costs
4. Valuing costs
5. Calculating costs
6. Comparing and deciding

Using various categories in listing costs divides a broad topic into smaller ones with cues on what might be included. Categories may overlap. One set of categories divides costs into those for the organization and those for its relevant publics. A second set includes direct expenditures, lost income or revenue, and nonmonetary costs. A third set includes overhead, capital, and operating costs. Generally, being more inclusive is preferable in this step as costs of little consequence can be discarded later in the process.

Nonmonetary costs are most easily overlooked. A classic example of a frequently overlooked cost is the cost of land that a public organization already owns. Sometimes a single cost may be mistakenly represented in two or three different ways. For example, the cost of a farm flooded by a dam could be listed as the cost of the land, the cost of the crops, or the cost of the farmer's income from the land. Costs may be listed for one year or for multiple years when costs are distributed unequally across years for different alternatives, usually capital expenditures in the first year. When listing costs for multiple years, analysts posit a life span for a capital item and then list costs for the various years for each alternative. Sometimes negative costs are recognized. Negative costs are increases in value that lessen the costs of an alternative.

Quantities can be determined in four ways. First, quantities may be already known and recorded in some fashion. Determining those quantities is a matter of accessing records and making appropriate calculations. Second, existing phenomena can be observed and counted or measured. Third, for existing phenomena that are too numerous to count or measure, analysts can sample (observe and count or measure some subset of all the phenomena) and extrapolate an estimated quantity for the rest based on reasonable assumptions. Finally, analysts can forecast future values. Forecasting is briefly discussed in Chapter 8. The last two ways of determining quantities are inherently and increasingly less certain than the first two. When quantifying costs, those with small quantities and without obviously great values can be discarded from an analysis. For example, one cost in an analysis of two garbage collection modalities might be dog bites on collection personnel; however, the number of bites is likely to be small; without obviously great values, the cost of dog bites on collection personnel can be discarded.

The value of costs can be dealt with in one of three ways depending on two sets of distinctions. First, costs ordinarily handled in terms of money are monetary costs, and analysts ordinarily get those values from actual events, usually markets. Monetary costs usually can be found and estimated or forecast just as are revenues and expenditures. Second and third, costs not ordinarily handled in terms of money are nonmonetary costs that for the sake of analysis are valued in money terms (monetized) or not (nonmonetized). Analysts assign money values to monetized nonmonetary costs based on similar or analogous cost phenomena. The process usually involves finding something similar to the nonmonetary cost that is priced, obtaining a value for the priced phenomena, and relating that price to the nonmonetary phenomena. Market-based values are preferred because those values have been revealed through human behavior. Often this process involves examinations, identifications, assumptions, and analogies. Analysts examine costs to identify relevant aspects or features. They think about and look for similar costs for which prices are or can be established. They assume or assert some relationship between the listed cost and the analogous cost. One can probably best understand the process through considering an example: the loss of an attractive view could be a cost of an alternative. Questions asked and answered likely would include: What kind of a view? Is the view seen from inside buildings, outside, or both? The kind of view would guide the selection of analogous costs. People value views of mountains, oceans, canyons, woods, meadows, and junkyards differently. The cost of a view from inside buildings could be based on some relationship with different building prices or different hotel or motel room rates or property values. The cost of a view outside of buildings could be based on some relationship with vacation costs for people who travel to similar scenic locations. Another way of approaching the cost of a view is what people "pay" or are paid to live in a scenic or a nonscenic area based on differential average wage scales by geographic area. After an analogous cost is found or determined, then analysts assume or assert how the alternative's cost and the analogous cost are related. For example, the total cost of a vacation trip cannot be entirely attributed to a scenic view; however, some portion could be attributed to a scenic view. A classic example of an alternative cost and an analogous cost not being the same is the value of people's time when an alternative affects relatively small portions of many people's time: for example, twenty minutes a week. A portion of a market-based wage rate could be applied, 50 percent for example, to value people's time. Key concerns for choosing money values are consistency, reasonableness, and fairness in regard to the alternatives under examination. The ultimate standard for the value of costs is what people willingly would pay to avoid a cost or require in pay to suffer a cost. Nonmonetized nonmonetary costs are simply listed; examples include the loss of a species, a historic landmark, or human life. Nonmonetized nonmonetary costs are considered significant, but valuing them in money terms is considered inappropriate or impractical. Trivial costs can be discarded at this stage.

When alternatives differ in the distribution of costs over a multiyear period, analysts select a discount rate to treat all the costs as equivalent in terms of time. The process is known as discounting because people value things in the future less highly than the same things in the current period. All monetary and monetized costs at different points in time are rendered into their "net present value," which is the current value of future values based on the market value of money at various points in the future. A future payment of money at a specific point in time is equivalent to a lesser value at the present time because of interest payments that can be gained from the ownership of the money at the present time or that will be paid for the use of the money for the period of time. The sources of discount rates are usually interest rates in debt markets in which public organizations borrow. Because interest rates typically vary according to the time period for which money is borrowed, an appropriate time period should be selected. When they are used, discount rates can affect the results more than any other factor in cost analysis. A low rate increases costs; a high rate reduces costs. For a three-year period, an analyst using a discount rate of 10 percent would get a discount factor of 100 percent for the current year, 90 percent for the second year (100 percent − [100 percent × 10 percent]), and 81 percent for the third year (90 percent − [90 percent × 10 percent]).

Analysts calculate the total costs for each alternative by multiplying all of the cost numbers and values and adding the results (by year, if appropriate) to get a total cost. If the alternatives involve multiple years, calculations are made for each year and discounted before the results for all years are added. In situations where the distribution of values is not uneven over years (including capital costs in the first year) for the alternatives, analysts can compare them without discounting. Discounting is recommended in that situation so that the net present values of alternatives can be compared with the often unstated alternative of not proceeding with a policy or operations because the cost is excessive. Discounting is required to compare alternatives appropriately where the distribution of costs over years is uneven; those differences might include different numbers of years, capital costs, and operating costs.

Comparisons of alternatives may or may not allow clear-cut conclusions. In some cases, analysts and policy-makers may believe that the positive consequences of alternatives differ greatly. If the positive benefits and monetary, monetized nonmonetary, and nonmonetized nonmonetary costs all favor one alternative to a significant degree in the opinion of an analyst, then the analyst could reach a clear-cut conclusion. Minor differences or differences that favor different alternatives muddy the conclusiveness of cost analysis. In some cases, one or more alternatives will be clearly superior or inferior. In any event, cost analysis can provide a useful understanding of the alternatives and allow analysts to point out clear conclusions.

Cost-Effectiveness Analysis

Cost-effectiveness analysis goes beyond simple cost analysis in including a single effect that analysts use to create comparable measures of efficiency, which are unit costs. "Cost-effectiveness" is an economic term that has the same meaning as "efficiency" for most people. The additional analytical work includes choosing and quantifying one effect and then using that information to calculate the unit cost. That additional work is in bold type in the following list based on the six steps in simple cost analysis. Otherwise, the steps are essentially the same:

1. Developing alternatives
2. Listing costs **and choosing one effect for all alternatives**
3. Quantifying costs **and the effect**
4. Valuing costs
5. Calculating **unit costs**
6. Comparing and deciding

Choosing one effect in step 2 might require eliminating some alternatives from consideration or reworking them to conform to the analytical requirement of one effect. Sometimes two or more effects can be quantified as if they were one effect (using a single scoring scale). Calculating the unit cost in step 5 usually involves dividing the quantity of effects from step 3 into the value of the costs in step 4. Discounting is required when the costs or the effects are unevenly distributed over years. The order of calculations is multiplying quantity times values for each year to produce annual costs, discounting by year, totaling of years, and then dividing the total costs by the number of effects.

Cost-Benefit Analysis

Cost-benefit analysis uses the same basic steps as simple cost and cost-effectiveness analysis, but goes beyond cost-effectiveness analysis by including multiple effects and their values. Benefits are positive effects. The following list shows cost-benefit steps with the differences from simple cost analysis and cost-effectiveness analysis in bold type:

1. Developing alternatives
2. Listing costs **and benefits**
3. Quantifying costs **and benefits**
4. Valuing costs **and benefits**
5. Calculating **net difference between benefits and costs**
6. Comparing and deciding

In steps 2 to 4, analysts deal with benefits as they do costs in the other two forms of cost analysis discussed here. Costs, though, tend to be borne by public organizations (at least initially), and benefits tend to be enjoyed by those served by a public organization. In the case of capital expenditures, costs tend to be more near-term, and benefits tend to be more evenly distributed over time. Benefit estimates and forecasts, therefore, tend to be less precise and less certain than cost estimates and forecasts. Valuing benefits can be a very creative undertaking. In step 5, discounting is usually necessary. The proper calculations are benefits minus costs. In step 6, as always, policy-makers can consider any other information they consider relevant.

System Analysis

System analysis focuses on relationships. A system can be defined as two or more elements that interact: when one element changes, one or more other elements change. Categorizing ways of using time offers a simple example of a system: students might spend their time studying, sleeping, socializing, and doing other activities. Increasing one's use of time decreases the amount of time available for other uses.

System analysis is particularly concerned with the relationship of elements. Analysts define the boundaries of each system; boundaries sometimes appear arbitrary. The elements within a system are expected to be related, and analysts look at the environments of systems only in respect to interactions with system elements. Systems may occur naturally or as a result of human artifice. Natural systems may display tendencies, and artificial systems can be understood in terms of their intended purposes. We call many things systems: for example, ecological, nervous, plumbing, and criminal justice systems. Analysts can develop abstract models of systems and manipulate the relationships within models.

Analysts apply system analysis to address a variety of questions, frequently focusing on capacity or limits, thresholds, balance, and optimization. System analysis is particularly useful in complex situations and where results are counterintuitive, that is, different from those expected. For counterintuitive results, system analysis focuses on the reactive or adaptive qualities of systems.

Systems have capacities or limits. When some elements in a system increase, they may exceed a system's expansive capacity or substantially change the system. A bottleneck is a limiting element on pouring from some bottles that is applied to some systems. The same concept expressed in another fashion is that the strength of a chain is the strength of its weakest link. Although the capacity or limit concept appears simple, it applies to many phenomena. For example, mandatory sentences are a common suggestion to solve the problems of crime. Mandatory sentences appear likely to run into the limited capacity of prisons to hold more prisoners, the willingness of taxpayers to fund more prisons, the willingness of courts to allow prisons to stack prisoners like cordwood, and the reactions of the rest of the criminal justice system. When prisons are crowded to capacity, police, prosecutors, and judges may choose to act in ways that avoid putting individuals into prison with mandatory sentences. The capacity of criminal justice systems now depends on the willingness of criminal defendants to enter into plea bargains to avoid trials. Without plea bargains, criminal justice systems can only process a fraction of the criminal defendants who now choose to bargain pleas rather than be tried.

Elements in systems may be balanced, and changes in one element may need to exceed particular thresholds before another element changes. Natural ecologies provide various examples of balances and thresholds. For example, waterways in nature teem with life that maintain various balances. They display balances between predators and prey and between life forms that take in or give off oxygen and carbon dioxide. Those balances can be upset in various ways. Although the exact balances fluctuate, predators and prey tend to increase and decline together. The predator-prey balance can be upset by a significant growth or decline in numbers on either side of the balance. A small number of prey may render a species extinct by predators, and a large number of prey may result in a species' extinction through exhaustion of its food supply. Waterways' balance of life between organisms taking in or giving off oxygen and carbon dioxide can be upset by phosphates. Although waterways can tolerate certain levels of phosphates, beyond certain levels phosphates strip waterways of living things. The phosphates fertilize plant life that grows very rapidly, depleting the water of carbon dioxide for plants, which has the effect of depleting the water of oxygen for animal life.

Efforts can be made to optimize systems. Optimization may involve maximizing, minimizing, or balancing one or more particular aspects of a situation. Human-constructed systems may be optimized relative to their purposes. For example, a main purpose of a heating or a cooling system is to make people feel comfortable. That purpose is achieved when those systems maintain set temperatures levels. Similarly, traffic systems are designed to move traffic. The flows of traffic systems can be optimized by synchronizing traffic lights and continuous traffic light adjustments.

System analysis helps in thinking through complex situations, especially ones in which the results of prior actions are counterintuitive. For example, for many years public officials pursued the strategy of building more roads to satisfy the public's demand for driving. Unfortunately, more roads generated more driving rather than satisfying a static level of demand. Similarly, big-city officials supported interstate highways to connect the cities with other large cities and to funnel traffic away from their downtowns. The results include urban sprawl and reliance on automobile transportation. Efforts to change those results now have to take into account currently existing land use and transportation systems. Similarly, the public's awareness and thinking on environmental matters generally evolved from concern with the most conspicuous consequences of pollution, such as dirty air and the spontaneous combustion of the Cuyahoga River in Cleveland, Ohio, to a more holistic, systems-oriented approach. For example, the country now has several choices of what to do about waste products: avoid or minimize producing waste products, allow natural processes to remediate waste products so they become harmless, artificially remediate waste products, or put waste products into the air, water, land, or outer space.

Consumers of Analysis

Various people present their or others' analytical efforts to public managers and policy-makers with the expectation or hope that the analysis will affect choices, particularly in regard to the use of resources. Those people provide analysis, and public managers and their superiors consume it. When public managers deal with budgetary decisions based on analysis supplied by others, they are likely to test the plausibility and correctness of that analysis by considering the same sorts of things that they might use for any kind of information brought to their attention: the motives of the sources, the kinds of evidence, and whether the information makes sense on its surface. Motives for analysis range from producing accurate analysis to creating persuasive, politically useful narratives to be used as political ammunition. However, even those who seek accuracy in analysis may be led astray by their preferred alternatives. Neutral analysts are much more likely to be passionate about accuracy and dispassionate toward the various alternatives. The greater the amount of evidence and the greater the care that can be shown in its collection, the more likely it is that analysis is accurate. Information that makes sense on its surface is generally more acceptable than information that contradicts what people already believe. Still, consumers of analysis can look further to avoid being misled.

Public managers and others can ask questions that address whether any particular analysis provides or serves as the appropriate basis for a budgetary decision. One question is whether the question addressed in the analysis is appropriate for the decision being made. A common version of the wrong question being addressed occurs when a preferred alternative is examined in comparison with one or more obviously inferior alternatives (straw man alternative).

A second question is whether the analysis is complete in the sense of including all necessary relevant information. Analysis based on incomplete information may reach incorrect conclusions. Some analysis may only go through the motions. This kind of analytical effort may produce "results" that are as useful as cargo cult science, described by Richard Feynman, a Nobel laureate in physics, as going through the motions. The phrase was based on the behavior of natives of the South Pacific islands who emulated the U.S. military's building of landing strips and control towers in order to produce cargoes from airplanes. They went through the motions, but no planes landed to deliver cargoes.

A third question is the appropriateness of the assumptions made, which should be evident in the analysis. Those assumptions include any numerical values not based on observations and the assumption that nothing of obvious significance is missing. Artificially high or low discount rates can swing the final results in cost analysis toward one alternative or another, as can choices of values.

Finally, if the analysis appears reasonably correct, the last question is whether all the procedures have been handled correctly, including the mathematical ones. Although checking these procedures may be tedious, addressing this question protects against inadvertent procedural errors.

Conclusion

When all is said and done, and perhaps analyzed, people make decisions. The analytical concepts and frameworks presented here can be helpful in providing better understandings of situations worth analyzing. Political analysis particularly assists in the formulation of decision alternatives based on political feasibility. Empirical analysis particularly assists in determining the size or scope of a phenomenon and whether and how strongly it is related to other phenomena. Cost analysis, which resembles expenditure forecasting, provides a basis for expressing the costs of various consequences, whether a singular result broadly stated, unit costs of specific numbers of an effect, or the net benefits after costs and benefits have been taken into account. Systems analysis is particularly helpful in tracing how various aspects of a situation may be related to one another, especially when results are contrary to expectations. Although the literature on these analytical techniques tends to stress using them in a formal fashion, they can be used fruitfully in an informal fashion as public managers cope with day-to-day decisions or as they formulate policies or budget proposals.

Additional Reading and Resources

Print

An introductory public administration textbook, which is currently still in print, with especially good coverage of the relationship between politics and administration:

Starling, Grover. *Managing the Public Sector.* Homewood, IL: Dorsey Press, 1977.

A classic exposition of the need for agencies to analyze their political power:

Long, Norton E. "Power and Administration." *Public Administration Review* 9 (Autumn 1949): 257–264.

A more general classic account of the power position of agencies:

Rourke, Francis E. *Bureaucracy, Politics, and Public Policy.* 3rd ed. Boston: Little, Brown, 1984.

A general account of doing policy analysis:

Irwin, Lewis G. *The Policy Analyst's Handbook: Rational Problem Solving in a Political World.* Armonk, NY: M.E. Sharpe, 2003.

Two practically oriented empirical analysis books:

Macfie, Brian P., and Phillip M. Nufrio. *Applied Statistics for Public Policy.* Armonk, NY: M.E. Sharpe, 2005.

McNabb, David E. *Research Methods in Public Administration and Nonprofit Management: Quantitative and Qualitative Approaches.* 2nd ed. Armonk, NY: M.E. Sharpe, 2008.

A good introduction to systems analysis:

Gibson, John E., William T. Scherer, and William F. Gibson. *How to Do Systems Analysis.* Hoboken, NJ: John Wiley, 2007.

A chapter-length treatment of cost analysis for nonspecialists:

Reed, B.J., and John W. Swain. "Cost Analysis." In *Public Finance Administration*, 135–168. 2nd ed. Thousand Oaks, CA: Sage, 1997.

A critical view on the limits of the utility of analysis in budgeting:

Wildavsky, Aaron. "The Political Economy of Efficiency: Cost-Benefit Analysis, Systems Analysis, and Program Budgeting." *Public Administration Review* 26 (December 1966): 292–310.

Internet

North Carolina General Assembly's Cost Analysis Page
The General Assembly of North Carolina maintains a fiscal note (cost analysis) web page for pending legislation at www.ncleg.net/gascripts/fiscalInfo/fiscalInfo.pl.

U.S. Congressional Budget Office—Cost Estimates
The U.S. Congressional Budget Office provides cost estimates for many pieces of federal legislation. The page noted here provides background; clicking the Cost Estimate tab allows users to browse or search through cost estimates at www.cbo.gov/CEBackground.shtml.

U.S. Government Accountability Office
The U.S. Government Accountability Office (GAO) has a particularly robust search system on its website and does much analytical work; here, the home-page address is given along with some of the features that can be used to locate useful material at www.gao.gov.

Search results. The search box is in the upper right-hand corner of the home-page. A search on a term will usually produce results. The results that appear may show up to five boxes containing information, in addition to parts of the home page template. One box contains the results, and the other four are oriented toward providing tools to improve search results. Toward the center top is the returned search box including the search term and alternative ways of dealing with a search: for example, Help, Start Over, and Advanced Search. Both Help and Advanced Search provide information on options available for searching. The search results show up in the middle box, underneath the search box. They include clickable links to organize the results by date or relevance and to provide access to GAO documents. If a clickable link is not visible, it is under a Quick View pull-down tab.

Narrowing results. On the left side, a box headed Narrow Results provides options for limiting the results to subsets within the categories of date, topic, and type. The date periods, topics, and types of GAO documents are listed. If a user narrows a search, the search parameters stay narrowed until the narrowing criteria are removed from the returned search box.

The search results box below the search box provides the option of narrowing the search among Publications, Entire Site, Bid Protest Docket, and Federal Rules. On the right side, a box may appear headed Suggested Searches that shows alternative, related, or narrowed search terms.

Searching for analytical techniques. In searching the GAO website for analytical techniques, various formulations of search terms are frequently useful. Good search terms at the onset for the content of this chapter include: analysis, hypothesis, program evaluation, performance measures, cost analysis, cost benefit analysis, cost-effectiveness analysis, systems analysis, and operations research. One example of a search result document is "Combating Nuclear Smuggling: DHS's Decision to Procure and Deploy the Next Generation of Radiation Detection Equipment Is Not Supported by Its Cost-Benefit Analysis," GAO-07–581T, March 14, 2007.

8

Routine Operating Techniques in Public Budgeting

Many operating technique activities are integral to public budgeting. Techniques literally refer to ways of doing things. Operating techniques in public budgeting relate to money and resources. Often operating techniques initially are set up as systems, frequently by or at the direction of technical experts and reflecting written policy decisions, and then public managers carry out or direct the day-to-day activities. These operating techniques serve typical purposes, go through a typical set of stages in a process, and reflect specialized concepts. Chapter 8 examines major purposes, typical processes, central concepts, and actions of the operating techniques commonly used in public budgeting. Operating techniques reflect the idea that resources will be handled economically, efficiently, effectively, and appropriately by public organizations, whether a nonprofit organization without any employees or a major government. Operating techniques are discussed here under the headings of accounting, forecasting, handling resources, purchasing, dealing with personnel, auditing, dealing with risks, and capital budgeting.

Accounting

The accounting discipline connects accounting, reporting, and auditing with one another. We concentrate on accounting and related aspects of reporting here and discuss auditing later in the chapter.

Accounting is monetarily related score-keeping. Accounting for public organizations is called fund accounting. Accounting comes first in this chapter because it relates to the other operating techniques; one finds most of the information used in other technique areas in accounting systems. One major purpose of accounting is to make useful financial information available. Fund accounting is particularly oriented to tracking the flow of resources (especially money) into and out of public organizations.

Accounting can be described simply as gathering, manipulating, storing, and reporting relevant financial information. Gathering information takes place when relevant events occur as defined relative to the accounting system. Those events are called transactions. When transactions occur, then an electronic system captures or a person writes down relevant information. Manipulation refers to the handling of information as it is moved into and out of an accounting system, moved from one place to another in an accounting system, or used in calculations. Storing information means keeping it in a way that makes it retrievable. Reporting means that information is made available to people, often in a summarized fashion.

Fund accounting uses standard concepts that may be customized for specific organizations. Different kinds of public organizations use accounting standards promulgated by various national organizations: for example, the Governmental Accounting Standards Board. Customization occurs when accounting systems are set up or something changes. Customization typically reflects specific details rather than fundamental concepts; for example, what things are accounted for and what their names are. The standard concepts involve funds, accounts, reports, the annual accounting cycle, bases, and the mechanics of operating an accounting system.

Public sector accounting systems are divided into funds. Information is segregated into funds for the sake of tracking information within particular areas, such as capital projects, business-like activities, and revenues that are restricted to being used in particular ways. One fund is used to account for whatever is not accounted for in any other fund; that fund may be called the general fund or operating fund. Small organizations may have only one fund.

Each fund is divided into accounts. Accounts can be organized into seven basic kinds of accounts in three groups. Accountants label the three groups real, budgetary, and nominal accounts. The real accounts are asset, liability, and fund balance accounts. Assets are things that are owned, such as cash. Liabilities and fund balances are things that are owed. Liabilities are owed to others, such as notes payable. Fund balances are owed to the organization itself. The budgetary accounts are estimated revenues and appropriations (authorized expenditures), such as estimated property tax revenues and appropriations for supplies. The nominal accounts are revenue and expenditure accounts that show the financial actions of collecting and spending money, such as property tax revenues and supplies expenditures. Budgetary and nominal accounts often are divided further according to organizational subdivisions and objects of expenditure, such as the admissions office, personnel expenditures, and detailed areas of personnel expenditures. The actual number of accounts ranges from a few to hundreds. Formalized accounting systems organize accounts by group and kind, assign each account a name and a number based on the kind of account, and list them by name and number in a "chart of accounts." Table 8.1 shows the groups and related kinds of accounts. Charts of accounts are organized by the kind of accounts.

Table 8.1

Basic Accounts in Fund Accounting

Groups	Kinds
Real	Asset, Liability, and Fund Balance
Budgetary	Estimated Revenue and Appropriation
Nominal	Revenue and Expenditure (or Expense)

For instance, all of the asset accounts are in one sequence of numbers, often beginning with the number 1.

Fund accounting also uses subsidiary accounts that combine information from two or more of the seven basic kinds of accounts. Subsidiary accounts are either revenue-related or expenditure-related. Subsidiary revenue accounts show amounts of estimated and actual revenues, as well as the difference between the two. Subsidiary expenditure accounts show appropriations and expenditures and the difference between the two. Subsidiary expenditure accounts may also display other restrictions on expenditure authority. Subsidiary accounts track budgets' implementation. Information placed in a subsidiary account is also placed in the appropriate basic kind of account at the same time: for example, revenue, estimated revenue, expenditure, and appropriation accounts. In those cases, the basic kind of account is called a control account.

Public organizations use an annual accounting cycle of opening, operating, and closing "the books" (the accounting system). Opening the books at the beginning of a fiscal year starts with nothing in any of the accounts and involves placing information in specific accounts for real (assets, liabilities, and fund balances) and budgetary accounts. Real account information comes from annual financial reports for the previous year. Budgetary account information comes from an approved budget.

Operating the books over the course of a fiscal year mostly involves recording transactions having to do with real and nominal (revenues and expenditures) accounts. When the books are in operation, information is placed in the budgetary accounts only if a budget is changed.

Closing the books for a fiscal year involves sequentially closing or removing accounts from the accounting system, with the nominal and budgetary accounts being closed before the real accounts. Annual financial reporting relies on the completing of the annual accounting cycle.

Any information observed or taken from an accounting system is a report, however informally that information may have been obtained. Many public organizations produce standard formal reports. Reports vary by scope, level of detail, and type. The scope of a report may be a single transaction,

Table 8.2

Example of Accounting Report

Organizational Unit K—General Fund
Monthly Expenditures Report for March, fiscal year ending October 31

| | | Expenditures | | |
| | | During | Year-to- | |
Account number	Amounts Appropriated	month	date	Available
1	$500	$70	$240	$260
2	$300	$10	$230	$ 70

a particular fund, a particular organizational unit, or an entire organization. Narrower scope reports tend to be more detailed and broader scope reports less detailed. The two types of reports represent a particular point in time or a specified time period. For example, annual reports typically show real accounts at the point of time at the end of the fiscal year and nominal accounts for the period of the fiscal year. The period reports are created by comparing two points in time: for example, the beginning and end of the fiscal year for revenues and expenditures. Public managers mostly deal with reports for particular organizational units with the most details in period reports that also contain information on the latest point in time available. Table 8.2 provides a simple report example of two subsidiary expenditure accounts.

Fund accounting systems use various sets of rules about what information to record that also indicate by implication when to record an event. Those sets of rules affect what accounts are used and what they mean in reports. Public organizations may use one or more of four common sets of rules. Each set of rules is called a "basis." The cash basis is best to discuss first because it is simple and probably familiar to readers. The cash basis relies on the concept of money transactions. Transactions are recorded when money is collected or payments are made. People keep track of their checking accounts on this basis. Some small public organizations use this basis because of its intuitive simplicity. Still, accounting standards do not approve the cash basis.

Accountants prefer and accounting standards approve the accrual basis for certain funds. The idea of obligation distinguishes the accrual basis from the cash basis. Accruals are recorded obligations. Transactions are recognized when obligations occur, and then specific accounts show what those obligations are. The most easily recognized obligations are bills being sent or being received. Accounts showing obligations include accrued revenue, expense (accrued expenditures, which are bills received), receivable, and payable accounts. Accrual basis accounting also records cash transactions, but many

Table 8.3

Accrual and Cash Basis Accounts

Accrual basis accounts				Cash basis accounts
Revenues receivable (billed)	−	Accrued revenues (billed but not collected)	=	Revenues (collected)
Expenses (billed)	−	Accounts payable (billed but not paid)	=	Expenditures (paid)

of those cash transactions liquidate or eliminate obligations, which means showing reductions in accrued assets (owed to) and liability (owed by) account amounts. The accrual basis provides a forward view into bills that probably will be paid and collected, which undoubtedly contributes to a more complete view of an organization's financial situation. Table 8.3 illustrates how accrual and cash basis accounting accounts differ and relate. They differ in that accrual accounting has two accounts to show what is displayed in one account in the cash basis, and they relate in that the difference between each pair of the two accrual accounts equals the cash basis accounts. The transaction events in the time sequence for the accounts in Table 8.3 are billing, collection or payment, and the calculation that follows payment. In other words, what is billed minus what is collected or paid results in a calculation of what is still owed. Generally, when dealing with fund accounting, the key focus is on the meaning of categories of information more than the internal mechanics of producing the information that are discussed below.

Accounting standards also approve the modified accrual basis for certain funds. The modified accrual basis differs from the accrual basis because many public organizations collect revenues that cannot be practically accrued in advance of payment or billing. Income and sales tax returns are essentially bills, and many other revenue payments are essentially cash events in the sense that payments and amounts to be paid are decided at the time of payment. The most notable of accruable public revenues are property taxes, utility and other billed services, and pledges to nonprofit organizations. The modified accrual basis means that some to virtually all revenues are accounted for on the cash rather than the accrual basis. For those making decisions for or about a public organization, modified accrual accounting means diminished reported revenues relative to accrual accounting.

The encumbrance basis, which is not approved by accounting standards, only can be used in conjunction with one of the first three bases discussed, which are literally alternatives to each other in the sense that only one of those three bases can be used for accounts in a fund at any one time. The encumbrance basis concerns only expenditures or expenses, not revenues. The key concept is a commitment or decision to spend. An encumbrance is recorded when a commitment or decision to spend is made and removed when either the commitment or decision is reversed, the expenditure has been made, or the expense has been recognized. One can tell the encumbrance basis is being employed when encumbrance accounts appear in the fund balance category or subsidiary expenditure accounts. Encumbrances in reports mean commitments or decisions to spend have been made, but have not yet been finalized (reversed, billed, or paid). Encumbrances frequently are recorded based on purchase orders that some public organizations require.

The mechanics of fund accounting refers to how information is handled in a fund accounting system. The basic rules specify what information goes where. The mechanics are relatively easy to deal with on a general level. They involve equations, balances, the mathematical operations of adding and subtracting, and double entry.

The seven basic kinds of accounts are organized on the two sides of an accounting equation, with one equation for each fund. The two sides of an accounting equation are equal in recorded monetary value, and accounting rules are designed to keep them equal. An inequality between the two sides indicates an error has been made. The basic fund accounting equation is Assets (includes Accrued Assets) + Expenditures (or Expenses) + Estimated Revenues = Liabilities (includes Accrued Liabilities) + Revenues + Appropriations + Fund Balance.

Each account in a fund accounting equation with a numerical value can be said to have a "balance." Accounts without any value are called zero balance accounts, but that status is usually temporary as the whole purpose of accounts is to hold information. Accounts on the left side of the fund accounting equation have debit balances, and accounts on the right side have credit balances. A zero balance usually indicates no entries have been made into an account. Other balances may result from one entry (most budget accounts), a series of similar entries that are additive (most nominal accounts), or additive and subtractive entries (cash, accrual, and subsidiary accounts).

The mathematical operations of adding and subtracting arise from what entries are made into which specific accounts for each transaction. When entries are made to accounts, deciding what entries to make to which accounts is called "analysis." Analysis encompasses both selecting the accounts and deciding whether to add or to subtract. In some cases, analysis decisions are easy. Money going into an accounting system is an addition to a cash account, and money going out is a subtraction from a cash account. In all cases, set rules indicate what is added to or subtracted from which accounts. General rules on adding to and subtracting from accounts are that an additive

Table 8.4

Entries for Sample Transactions

Transaction	Debit-balance accounts	Credit-balance accounts
Cash collected	Cash + debit $5	Revenue + credit $5
Bill sent	Revenues receivable + debit $5	Revenue + credit $5
Bill paid	Cash + debit $5 and revenues receivable – credit $5	

entry to a debit-balance account is a debit and that an additive entry to a credit-balance account is a credit, and conversely, that a subtractive entry from a debit-balance account is a credit and that a subtractive entry from a credit-balance account is a debit. In other words, entries and account balances that are alike are added, and entries that differ from account balances are subtracted from the balances. As noted in the previous paragraph, the location of an account in the accounting equation determines the kind of balance that an account has.

Double entry means that two aspects of each transaction are recorded in two or more accounts as debits and credits. A single value based on a bill, a check, or other monetarily valued item is entered into two accounts in an account equation. A standard way of demonstrating double entry is to display a physical item such as $5 and show how a single transaction with that item produces two entries into an accounting system. For example, a money transaction has a cash account entry and an entry in some other account, for example, revenue. A more complicated example involving recording a revenue payment on the accrual basis means using both a revenue receivable account and a revenue account when a bill is sent and using both a cash account and the same revenue receivable account when a bill is paid. Each set of double entries includes equal values for debits and credits so that the accounting equation maintains its equality.

How double entry works is illustrated in Table 8.4, which displays the debits and credits for the two examples in the preceding paragraph using a value of $5 for the transactions in the table. First, the Cash account is a debit-balance account that is added to with debits and subtracted from with credits. The choice of a debit or credit entry for the cash account means that the other account or accounts involved would have countervailing entries so that the debits equal the credits. The Revenue account is a credit-balance account that receives an addition in the form of a credit, which means more revenue has been collected. This first example represents what would appear using the cash accounting basis accounting. The second example involving the revenue bill requires a debit entry for the Revenue Receivable account and a credit entry for the Revenue account when billed and a debit entry for the Cash account and a credit entry for the Revenue Receivable account when the bill is paid. This second example represents what would appear using an accrual accounting basis.

Debits and credits are part of the mechanics of accounting related to the accounting equation, adding and subtracting, and double entry that are details rather than the meaning of accounting. Aside from the mechanical aspects that are useful for people operating accounting systems, knowledge of debits and credits is not very useful for people who consume accounting reports. The initial concern in consuming accounting reports is the reported categories and the meaning of the values in those categories. Accounting report users need to know what the values in categories mean so they know what is happening with a public organization's operations and finances.

Forecasting

Forecasting refers to predicting the future. People forecast in terms of monetary values in public budgeting, most notably annual revenues and expenditures. Much of the information used in forecasting comes from an organization's accounting system. How forecasting applies in other operating technique areas can be seen later in this chapter.

The purpose of forecasting, also called estimating or projecting, is to provide reasonably accurate information in advance of actual events for the sake of financial decision-making. That decision-making also can be called planning. Annual budgets require estimates of required expenditures forecasts that depend in some measure on annual revenues.

To forecast is to err. Errors vary only in direction and degree. This perspective reminds us that forecasting accuracy is limited and that we can acknowledge and deal with errors. Three ways of dealing with forecasting errors are intentionally building a bias toward safety in the forecasting techniques, monitoring actual values relative to forecast ones, and preparing for unfavorable forecasting errors by making arrangements for or actually taking corrective actions.

Building a bias toward safety in forecasting techniques means slightly biasing or slanting forecasts toward whichever direction would leave an organization with more money or resources on hand. For example, slightly higher expenditure forecasts and slightly lower revenue forecasts increase the likelihood that a public organization will have resources remaining at the end of a fiscal year. In this context, a slight bias means one that is within the range of what a forecaster can reasonably expect a forecast value to be. Biases in forecasting may exist for other reasons as well. Policy-makers who favor particular programs might bias expenditure forecasts low to make the programs more acceptable, and people with opposing views might do the opposite. Likewise, some policy-makers who want to spend more money bias revenue forecasts up and expenditure forecasts down; other policy-makers take the opposite stance.

Monitoring means observing actual values to see how closely they con-form to forecast values and being open to deciding that forecasts erred. If forecasts diverge in a direction that causes difficulty, monitoring helps in deciding whether to monitor the forecast values more closely and to see whether changes need to be made in financial decisions. Early observations of possible problems and early reactions might make the required corrective actions less severe.

Unexpected events might make corrective financial actions necessary. In addition to monitoring and forecasting biases, some corrective actions can be implemented before problems actually arise: they include central offices or administrators retaining some expenditure authority or other financial reserves, making contingency plans for reducing expenditures or increasing revenues, and making arrangements for credit. Corrective actions to imple-ment after problems arise include implementing prepared plans, as well as rescinding expenditure authority, freezing expenditures, and reformulating expenditure plans.

The forecasting process involves recognizing a need for a forecast, choosing forecasting techniques, gathering information, producing predicted values, and monitoring actual events relative to the predictions. Many forecasts, such as those for annual budgets, are either obviously necessary or regularly scheduled. People in some public organizations are not aware of the value of forecasts that might be helpful in particular areas or become aware only when they are introduced to a financial management concern, sometimes painfully—for example, cash flow, pensions, or dealing with risks.

The choice of forecasting techniques determines what information is re-quired to produce predictions and how people arrive at particular predictions. All forecasting techniques rely on some kind of initial opinions or assump-tions; some also use mathematical calculations. Forecasting techniques can be grouped into three types: opinion, trend, and causal.

Opinion forecasting uses one or more opinions. Whoever provides the opin-ions decides what information is relevant and how that information relates to the prediction. Forecasts based on multiple opinions may go through sequential or mathematical processes, such as a review of initial opinions, averaging, or selection of a predicted range or median value. Opinion forecasting is quick, easy, and cheap, especially when it involves one opinion. This technique probably works best for public organizations in situations involving a high degree of uncertainty or small monetary values, such as specific grants and minor revenues and expenditures.

Trend forecasting techniques rely on the assumption that the future will resemble the past for the items predicted. Accordingly, one or more actual values for an item serve as the basis for a forecast. The simplest trend forecast is that a future value will be the same as a past value. French monarchical finance officials forecast revenues by the rule of the penultimate year: next year will be the same as the prior year (i.e., prior to the current year). More complex trend forecasts use averages, weighted averages, or mathematically more complex calculations that practically approximate averages. Trend forecasting consistently implemented is politically neutral.

Causal forecasting techniques rely on the opinion that one item can be predicted on the basis of one or more other items. Causal forecasting requires two quantitative specifications: first, a mathematical relationship between what is being predicted and the predictor variable(s); and second, a value or values for the predictor(s). The simplest causal forecasts rely on one value that is relatively stable over time and serves as a predictor variable. For example, changes in Social Security payments to retirees can be predicted based on the changing numbers of retirees; changes in the amount of money that a school system will spend on kindergarten teachers can be predicted on the basis of the changing numbers of children in the relevant age group. Causal forecasting techniques involve the solution of mathematical problems involving a range from two variables in one equation, as in the examples given here, to many variables in many equations. The most complex causal techniques use econometric equations to predict sales and income taxes based on economic variables.

Handling Resources

People in public organizations pay attention to handling resources, especially money. In doing so, they might self-consciously engage in a variety of processes that may be governed by sets of regulations. Collecting revenues and spending money are two very basic processes that are distinct, even though they both connect to a treasury that holds money. Both processes may be subject to a set of rules that are called internal controls, designed to safeguard resources and to enhance the accuracy of accounting information. Internal controls are frequently designed by accountants. Large, formal organizations may engage in additional processes associated with their treasuries: dealing with cash flows, investing, and borrowing. All these processes may have special sets of rules or regulations associated with them.

Public organizations collect revenues for the sake of funding their operations. Revenue collection follows a typical sequence of steps, even though some revenues do not require all steps and some steps occur in different orders depending on the particular revenues. Policy-makers establish a policy to collect revenues, such as taxes, payments, or contributions. In many cases, those revenue policies persist unless and until they are changed. Public organizations notify people about revenue policies. They locate revenue bases (especially taxes) and relate to people who communicate with them about revenue bases. Someone measures revenue bases (including exemptions and deductions), decides which revenue rates apply, recognizes applicable revenue credits, and calculates payment amounts. Someone takes payments on behalf of public organizations and makes deposits into a treasury. Public organizations resolve disputes about revenue payments, particularly the size of the payments, and make efforts to ensure that revenue policies are being followed.

Public managers probably deal with expenditures more than any other resource-handling process. They communicate expenditure authority, use expenditures to accomplish the work of the organization, and follow substantive and procedural rules to make sure expenditures are made properly. Dealing with expenditures relates closely with purchasing and personnel-related expenditures, which are discussed later in the chapter. Policy-makers decide on authorized expenditures in budgets or expenditures related to goods or services that public organizations sell. When expenditures are budgeted, the authority to spend is communicated from central offices and down hierarchies (allotment) until it arrives in the hands of managers. In many public organizations, executives and administrators retain some of the budgeted expenditure authority granted to them beyond the amounts required to support their operations. That retained expenditure authority constitutes reserves that can be used to deal with contingencies as they arise. Such reserves make it much easier to cope with specific events that cannot be predicted. In cases where expenditures are not authorized by objects of expenditure, someone may determine how to divide up expenditure authority among different groups of objects (allocation). Some public organizations, including the federal government, have a formal process for organizational subdivisions requesting that they be allowed to make expenditures (apportionment). In the apportionment process, organizational subdivisions request and are granted expenditure authority by general expenditure categories for specific time periods (frequently quarterly). Usually, some portion of budgeted expenditure authority is retained centrally in a public organization until central authorities are comfortable with releasing that expenditure authority to operating units late in fiscal years. Apportioned expenditure authority not used earlier in fiscal years can be used later. Apportionment impedes executives, administrators, and public managers from spending furiously to create a coercive deficit, a situation in which a public organization has to spend more than originally budgeted to continue a vital service.

Someone (generally starting very high or very centrally in a public organization) communicates budgeted expenditure authority until some of it ends up in the control of the persons who actually do the spending (generally public managers). The people who directly do the spending may purchase goods and services or make other kinds of payments that are mostly transfers of money. Those doing the spending are formally responsible for how the money is spent. They spend by authorizing payments, frequently by signing documents that contain information about the purchase of goods or services, the payees, and account names and numbers. They follow substantive and procedural rules. Substantive rules concern what can be purchased, and procedural rules concern how one goes about spending money: for example, when, who signs, what forms are used, and what information must be provided for spending. Some public organizations require special approval for certain expenditure categories, such as large amounts and travel.

Most public managers enthusiastically support spending in their operational areas because they believe their work is important. Spending by public organizations generally goes through one or more other persons who exercise oversight over spending. These overseers review spending efforts, enforce restrictions on spending found in budgets, communicate expenditure authority and various rules, and actually make payments. The overseers, particularly those in central finance offices, work in specialized roles, such as accounting, purchasing, and payroll. Sometimes tension arises between those advocating spending and those enforcing the rules. Both sides do useful work.

Internal controls is a term especially associated with accounting that generally applies to handling resources, particularly money. Internal controls are sets of procedures designed to protect organizational resources, mostly through information-related routines, that also protect the accuracy of information in the accounting system. Very small public organizations may not use internal controls. Internal controls feature formal written rules concerning many details of handling resources, including procedures to follow, responsibility for the custody or control of resources, assignment of different people to deal with different aspects of resource-related processes, and reviews of those assignments and the information they generate. Required signatures for approvals, required documents and information, the requirement that different people take in money and make out deposit slips for financial institutions, and managers reviewing their subordinates' handling of resources all exemplify internal controls. Rigorous implementation of internal controls prevents errors and facilitates the correction of well-intentioned and ill-intentioned errors.

Occasionally, internal controls exceed common sense; for example, requiring receipts for the reimbursement of small highway toll amounts.

Public organizations with substantial amounts of resources may regulate their cash flow within a fiscal year. The purposes of regulating cash flow include gaining investment income, paying bills in a timely fashion, and avoiding debt costs. Initially, a cash flow system may be designed to collect revenues as early as reasonably possible and to make expenditures as late as reasonably possible. Revenue billing, collecting, and depositing may be moved up in time; purchasing and bill paying may be moved back. Then, revenue and expenditure flows are forecast so that short-term investments and debt can be planned. Generally, a central finance official or office deals with cash flow issues. One important cash flow caveat is that moving revenues too early or expenditures too late may cause the other parties in those transactions to react because of the size of the financial costs that they may have to bear. For example, members of the public may react politically to having revenue payment due dates advanced too far, and vendors may choose not to do business with a public organization, provide inferior service, or increase their prices to recoup the financial value of late payments.

Investments are temporary placements of resources in a form that is expected to provide a gain in value. For investments, as well as debts discussed, public organizations generally consider the purposes and the expected time periods involved in making decisions. Public organizations invest to increase their resources. Short-term investments, within a fiscal year and related to cash flow, also have to be available to make expenditures. Public organizations almost always use short-term investment devices that are essentially a payment of money at one point in time by the investing party for which a larger payment is promised for a later point in time. Regardless of the name of the device—bond, money market account, interest-bearing checking account, certificate of deposit, or repurchase agreement—these investments are essentially loans from public organizations to others for promised future payments. Because promises to pay are dependent on who exactly is making the promise, public organizations tend to take care that the parties to whom they loan can pay them back.

Public organizations sometimes use mid-term investments, longer than a year and up to five years in length, and long-term investments, more than five years in length, in connection with capital budgeting or dealing with risks (both of which are discussed later in this chapter). Long-term investments are a financing technique relative to making future payments. Payments can come out of current revenues, debt, or investments. Investment financing makes the most sense when a public organization has uneven revenue flows (large gifts or tax revenues) or large future payments that are related to current operations (pensions and risks). When investing for long time periods, more than five years in length, public organizations often buy assets rather than loan money. Assets vary in value more than loans and generally involve more risks, but over long periods of time they generally provide greater investment returns. Asset investments by public organizations are mostly shares of stocks, which means that the organizations have an ownership interest in companies. Asset investments provide returns by distributing profits or increasing values. Public organizations use long-term investments to facilitate making payments in future years, primarily for pensions or operations.

Public organizations use short-term debt, less than a year, to deal with short-term financial shortages, that is, to pay bills. They use mid-term debt, longer than a year and up to five years in length, and long-term debt, more than five years in length, to finance larger amounts over extended periods for capital budgeting, dealing with risk, or pensions. Only the federal government routinely finances current operations from long-term debt; other public organizations cannot do so. Debt is borrowed money that is owed with some kind of a fee for the use of that money. Debt means that public organizations are promising others to make future payments for loaned money. Public organizations' debt is someone else's investment.

Besides the time periods, short-term debt on the one hand and mid-term and long-term debt on the other hand differ in a variety of ways. Short-term debt is much more likely to represent a relatively simple contractual relationship between a borrower and a lender (financial institution) to finance cash flows. Mid-term debt and long-term debt tend to be much larger in value and more complicated, involve many more parties, and change hands more than once. The complications stem from the size of the debts, the time periods, and the variety of aspects affected by the size and the time periods. For example, large debt amounts mean greater care in assessing repayment ability, and long time periods mean that one of the parties might desire to have the loan repaid early. Typically, when public organizations borrow for a long period, the party initially loaning the money plans to sell the future promises to pay to others, who in turn may sell the debt to others. Long-term promises to pay are contracts that usually are called bonds.

The process of borrowing money involves forecasting the amount required and the time period for which it is required, locating a willing lender, reaching an agreement on borrowing terms and debt contracts, getting money, following any restrictions on the loan, and repaying the money. Key concerns of the parties providing money are the obligation of the borrowing party, its ability to repay loans, and the tax status of the future payments. Lenders prefer unlimited obligations for future payments; they charge more for limited liability loans. They also charge more for borrowers who have less ability to repay loans. Most payments on state and local government debt are exempt from federal income taxes, which make those debt contracts valuable to investors. For that reason, state and local governments pay significantly less in interest costs than private individuals or companies for their borrowing.

Purchasing

Purchasing relates to buying things, specifically what is bought, from whom, for how much, and how that is done. Dealing with expenditures focuses on the payment process. Those purchasing strive to buy the most appropriate goods and services in an appropriate manner at the best prices. Budgets restrict what goods and services can be purchased, but they seldom say exactly what will be purchased, from whom, or how those decisions are actually made.

The act of deciding what to buy starts with determining the characteristics of the goods and services to be purchased. The characteristics are called "specifications." Many different kinds of specifications describe goods and services. Varieties of specifications include physical properties (eight feet long), process qualities (baked in an oven), product equivalencies (like a brand-name product), performance capabilities (400 miles per hour), service provider qualities (certification), and vendor qualities (prequalified vendor or small business).

Public organizations locate vendors in a variety of ways depending on situational factors, such as what is being purchased, how much money is involved, and legal and policy restrictions. Relatively informal processes work well in many situations, and many small public organizations generally purchase informally, simply finding and buying a good or service. Highly formal processes may be required as legal restrictions and larger dollar amounts come into play. The four formal purchasing processes include competitive bids, competitive proposals, negotiated bids, and noncompetitive negotiations.

For competitive bids, public organizations prepare and distribute solicitations for vendors to bid on products. Those request-for-bid documents include specifications and procedural details; that is, bids are held sealed and opened publicly at an appointed time and place. Competitive bidding tends to be used for goods and services that are essentially commodities, which means that the products are much more alike than not, and that involve relatively large amounts of money. Bid evaluations tend to focus mostly on prices.

Competitive proposals differ from bids in that the specifications in requests for proposals are not as specific or detailed as in requests for competitive bids. Proposals tend to be used for services and unique goods, which cannot be specified as precisely as items involving bids. Proposal evaluations tend to focus initially on what is proposed. The public organization indicates what it wants accomplished, but does not specify exact methods. In other words, vendors indicate in proposals what they will do or how the desired results will occur. The competitive proposal process is like the competitive bid process in that the public organization plans on making a purchase choice from the submitted alternatives.

Negotiated bids start out like competitive proposals. They differ in that the purchase choice is not made simply on the basis of the proposals submitted. The public organization uses the proposals to make an initial or preliminary vendor choice. The public organization negotiates with a vendor about the price and details of the proposal. If the two sides cannot reach a mutually acceptable agreement, the public organization negotiates with the vendor that submitted the next best proposal. The process ends when the public organization and a vendor agree or when the public organization gives up on making the purchase based on the submitted proposals.

Noncompetitive negotiations are used when only one vendor can supply or is interested in supplying a purchase. Factors that may make noncompetitive negotiations necessary are location, the size of a purchase, or unique qualities.

The purchasing process involves the steps of specifying, locating vendors, deciding on vendors, ordering, receiving, testing, and using purchases. Purchasing in the right or appropriate manner includes following applicable laws and ethical guidelines, especially in regard to conflicts of interest. In situations involving substantial amounts of purchases, the centralization of purchasing activities into one person's or one office's hands is appropriate. Centralized purchasing tends to be carried out economically and appropriately because specialized personnel are familiar and facile with those activities, and they can operate easily in a standardized manner.

The best price for a purchase may appear to be relatively simple to determine. However, in many cases, related costs loom much larger than the price difference between two purchase options. Related purchasing costs may include the costs associated with ordering, transporting, financing, storing, replacing, operating, servicing, removing, and disposing of purchases. Other cost factors include the relative usefulness of a purchase option compared to the other options and money that a purchase option might bring during disposal. Multiple costs may be associated with each of these activities. For example, the costs of storing a good may include those for the physical space, the money value of the product (borrowing cost or loss of investment cost), and losses from products becoming less useful, obsolete, or missing. Operating purchases may vary in respect to the cost of supplies, personnel, training, and associated equipment. Decisions on large purchases can benefit from examining the life cycle costs of products, from when an organization specifies or orders a product to when the organization is done with it.

Dealing With Personnel

Personnel costs constitute a majority of expenditures for many public organizations. Observing and analyzing those expenditures can be very beneficial. Personnel costs, such as those forecast for annual budgets, can be viewed or examined in various ways. Payments associated with personnel go to employees for their labor (salary) and benefits (health insurance), to governments on account of workers' employment (taxes), and to vendors for the things purchased that are necessary for personnel to be effective (equipment). Missing any of these costs in a forecast can lead to an inadequate assessment of personnel costs. One way of looking at personnel costs is cost per hour of labor, which includes the costs of pay earned by employees even if the direct payment will be paid in the future. Benefits to be paid in future years (paid leave, some pensions, and postretirement benefits) have been an increasing concern for governments in recent years because those benefits might accumulate to levels higher than imagined. Also, such benefits increase future costs without necessarily being visible in the years before payments are required. In many cases, the future costs have created difficulties for governments that were unaware of all the financial consequences of their actions when employees started taking paid leave prior to retirement, retirement payments, and postretirement benefits. Accounting standards increasingly require accounting and reporting of employee benefits to be paid in the future.

Pensions are payments made to employees or their heirs as a result of ending their labor service to an employer under certain qualifying conditions. Pensions are both a matter of fairness for employees engaged in risky occupations and a form of compensation to attract employees. Pension systems vary in regard to what defines them, which is especially important. Pension systems vary depending on whether an employer provides defined benefits or defined contributions.

A defined-benefit pension plan is a commitment by an employer to pay employees or their dependents or heirs certain amounts of money under specific conditions. The benefits are defined by employees' salaries or wages, years of service, age, and manner of leaving an organization, including retirement, death, or disability. Payments are usually calculated based on a formula. Employees may be required to contribute to pension plans. Another condition for payments is a required minimum time period of employment after which employees are said to be "vested" in the pension plan, which means that they have a legal ownership right to payments. Before vesting, employees have an ownership right only in what they may have contributed to a pension plan. After vesting, they have a legal right to the employer's contributions as well. Vesting periods and levels of payments usually differ depending on the various ways employees leave an organization. The level of payments for retirees typically rises according to the years of employment; promised payments per year of employment for the first five or ten years of employment are less per year than those for the later years of employment. Defined-benefit plans place the financial responsibility for making payments on the employer. The proper way to run a defined-benefit plan is to forecast numerical levels of employment, salaries, vesting, and how and when employees will leave an organization to ascertain the likely levels of future payments. Then, money is set aside annually and invested in appropriate forms for long-term payment of the promised benefits. Failure to do so creates underfunded pension plans in which employers owe their employees more in future payments than they have made provisions for paying. Future obligations, then, can be met only by increasing payments into defined-benefit pension plans. Unfortunately, many policy-makers want to start making extra payments to underfunded plans in the future rather than in the current fiscal year.

Defined-contribution pension plans are an alternative. Defined-contribution plans deal with retirement, death, and disability issues separately. To provide for employee retirement pensions, employers make periodic payments to third-party organizations on behalf of specific employees. The third-party organization collects the money, accounts for the payments, invests the money on behalf of the employee, and makes retirement payments. Employer obligations cease after the payments are made. The size of retirement payments is a result of the initial payments, investment choices made by the employee and the third party, and payout choices made by the employee. Death and disability payments may or may not be covered by an employer with a defined-contribution plan. When they are covered, the employer or the employer and the employee together buy insurance policies to cover those possible manners of leaving the employment of an organization.

Auditing

Despite a public image to the contrary, auditing is not generally oriented toward investigating wrongdoing. When investigations of the possibility of criminal wrongdoing take place in regard to financial records or accounting systems, the term is *forensic auditing*. Auditing more generally is the review of matters related to financial resources by persons who are not handling the resources. Audits provide assurances that financial resources are being handled properly. Audits can be divided into pre- and postevent audits and internal and external audits. Pre-event audits tend to be associated with reviewing whether expenditure authority is available; a pre-event audit of expenditure authority precedes a purchase order. Postevent audits primarily rely on documentary evidence. Persons employed by an organization, under the direction of the administrative hierarchy, conduct internal audits, which are generally narrow in scope and within or across fiscal years. Parties outside of an organization or agency conduct external postevent audits, usually for a fiscal year period. Most states require their local governments to have financial audits annually. The federal government and many states have external auditing agencies. Some local governments and nonprofit organizations hire private accounting firms to conduct external audits. Auditing standards for external audits require the auditors to be independent of those they are auditing. External audits result in formal reports that go to the top policy-makers and perhaps the public.

Although many public managers appear to have an aversion to auditors, audits can be seen as opportunities to gain insight into public organizations and to find ways to improve public managers' decisions. A more positive attitude toward audits might make public managers' work results better and their relations with auditors smoother.

The audit process starts with the decision to audit, which may be established in law or initiated as the result of an inquiry. Internal auditors may independently determine what to audit, follow directives from policy-makers, or both. Policy-makers may select external auditors to undertake required or optional audits. Deciding on the scope of an audit is a key step. The scope refers to what questions are examined for what range of information (more on scope later). Internal audits tend to involve relatively narrower scopes than external audits. Internal audits may look at specific organizational units, procedures, or questions. External audits tend to be oriented to whole organizations and broader questions. After the scope is determined, auditors learn about the organization and the information that they will audit, and they plan what they will examine. Auditors document their plans in writing. Then, specific information is examined or gathered, usually on a sample basis. After auditors have examined the information, they prepare and issue a report to top-level policy-making officials, often in the form of a letter, which is sometimes made available to the general public.

The scopes of external audits are one or more specific questions for a specifically defined range of information. The specific questions and the range of information determine what evidence is examined and what kind of answer is given in a formal report. The range of information identifies the organization, the parts of its financial resources (funds or programs), and the time periods subject to review. Auditors typically focus on one or more of four specific questions relating to financial, internal control, compliance, and performance audits. Financial audits are the most common, followed by internal control and compliance audits. Performance-related audits are much less common.

Financial audits focus on the accuracy of an entity's annual financial reports. The auditor examines whether the entity follows "generally acceptable accounting principles," which primarily means required accounting standards. The formal report for a financial audit indicates whether the annual financial reports "present fairly in all material respects," which means that a few minor deviations might have been ignored. If the annual financial reports do not meet accounting standards, the auditor may report the deviations in terms of specific exceptions (except for whatever is specified) or indicate that the auditor can offer no opinion. Financial audits for public organizations are similar to audits of private businesses. Recent reforms require auditors to assess internal controls and compliance sufficiently to provide assurances that the risk from problems in those areas is low relative to the fair presentation of the financial reports.

When focusing on internal controls, auditors determine whether they are sufficient to protect resources and the accuracy of accounting information. Here, *protect* means to create a low risk of resources being used incorrectly or information being inaccurately reported from the accounting system. When audit reports discuss problems discovered in internal controls, they generally also identify possible corrective measures. These kinds of audits sometimes are referred to as management letters, as in the private sector.

Compliance audits review evidence to ascertain whether relevant laws, regulations, and guidelines have been followed in handling resources. Compliance audits may be conducted in connection with grant funding.

Performance-related audits concern whether an organization or a program is operating economically, efficiently, or effectively; they may involve prospective analysis of whether the entity will operate economically, efficiently, or effectively. Performance-related audits are essentially analysis, which was covered in Chapter 7. Federal and state auditing organizations have moved in the direction of conducting analysis from their initial focus on accounting and financial transactions. More often than not, performance-related audits focus on effectiveness.

Dealing With Risks

Some public organizations deal very proactively with risks. Risks refer to situations that have the potential for significant losses and liabilities. Potential losses and liabilities may become actual losses and liabilities. Organizations deal with risks to prevent harm and to deal with the financial consequences that may arise from losses and liabilities. Losses refer to the loss of resources (money, buildings, and equipment) that can be measured in financial terms. Liabilities in this context refer to financial resources owed to others as a result of harming others. For example, any public organization that operates vehicles is exposed to potential liabilities that arise from vehicular operations. Public organizations can protect against some potential losses through some operating technique activities (accounting, internal controls, and purchasing). Still, public organizations' exposure to risks increases with the scope of their activities. Obvious risks include accidents and natural disasters.

Public organizations may deal with risks in either an ad hoc or a formal fashion. A formal process of dealing with risks starts with identifying risks and then assessing them according to their frequency and severity. Many risks, once identified, can be eliminated or reduced by changing policies and practices or shifting them to other parties. Then, a public organization can figure out how to pay for the remaining risks. Finally, organizations monitor their exposure to risks as events occur. Because risks affect a whole organization, it makes good sense to have one office or one person supervising an overall process for dealing with risk.

How public organizations choose to pay for potential risks that become actual losses and liabilities can impact their financial situation mightily. Public organizations can finance risks in three ways: self-financing, pooling, and insuring. Self-financing means that public organizations pay for losses and liabilities as they occur from current resources, investments, or debt. Self-financing works best for public organizations with large resource bases or little risk exposure and for frequent but relatively lower-consequence risks.

Pooling means that similar public organizations join together to pay collectively for losses and liabilities. The organizations pay appropriate amounts into a pool from which payments are made. The pooling of resources allows each member organization to spread out its payments for losses and liabilities over an extended period of time and handle the financial consequences of severe losses and liabilities more easily than otherwise.

Insuring involves transferring some of the financial consequences to an insuring entity, usually a commercial insurance company, in return for payments and compliance with company rules concerning those risks. The phrase "some of the financial consequences" means that insurers limit how much they will pay for precisely defined risks by amounts and by circumstances. Insurance companies do not assume the financial responsibility for some risks (e.g., acts of war). The insured has to pay for some portion of losses and liabilities beyond an insurance payment (e.g., deductibles, co-payments, and payment ceilings). Insurance contracts may specify which circumstances eliminate or limit a company's responsibility to make payments (e.g., coverage per year, per event, or per occurrence; the behavior of the insured party). Insurance companies place these limits because of two concerns. The concern for profit is obvious. The second concern, which also affects risk pools and self-insured organizations, is called "moral hazard," which refers to the tendency of people not to be concerned about the consequences of things that are "insured." Losses and liabilities increase costs to an organization regardless of how they are financed, even though some people may not understand this fact.

Purchasing insurance can occur without sufficient attention to the technical details of insurance policies. Insurance policies make the most sense for risks that occur infrequently and have high severity because they are not easily financed. High-frequency risks with low severity are probably best self-financed. Investing effort into purchasing insurance wisely is beneficial. Public organizations should define carefully what is being insured and what is not being insured. Public organizations also can lower the cost of insurance in various ways. Generally, higher deductibles or higher co-payment levels mean lower insurance premiums. Minimizing the number of policies for the same extent of coverage lowers costs; for example, buying one insurance policy for a fleet of vehicles rather than a policy for each vehicle.

Capital Budgeting

Some public organizations pay special attention to budgeting for capital items because they are relatively costly and have long-term effects on an organization and its clientele. Although the definition of capital items varies by organization, they typically include buildings, other large physical structures, and expensive pieces of equipment that have useful lives of multiple years. Capital items may have large effects on operations and are major investments of resources. Capital items may pose financing issues and may require multiyear financing from investments, debt, or both. The purpose of capital budgeting is to consider the selection of capital items carefully. Some public organizations run a capital budgeting process separate from their general or operating budget process. Some simply devote increased attention to capital items during their general budgeting process.

The process of capital budgeting involves developing, choosing, financing, and implementing alternatives. Anyone may make suggestions about capital items. Public managers are most likely to suggest and exercise some discretion on capital items that relate to their areas of responsibility. Some organizations require detailed cost estimations and justifications for capital item alternatives. Policy-makers and administrators rather than public managers generally make large capital items decisions. Some organizations choose capital items and put them in a multiple-year capital improvement program. Financing capital items frequently involves debt. Debt financing allows a public organization to purchase a capital item that it could not otherwise obtain and spreads the payment of costs over time. Implementation ranges from simple purchases to supervising multiple-year construction projects.

Conclusion

Although operating techniques may become very complex in regard to specific details, their purposes reflect the ideas expressed in Chapter 1 in regard to themes. The techniques were applied or developed to enable public organizations to be controlled, managed, and planned to further such goals as efficiency and effectiveness. For the most part, the operating techniques were introduced to public organizations in the twentieth century as technical reforms because reformers, public officials, and members of the general public came to desire and expect a high level of accountability for public organizations because of the high levels of activity by governments and nonprofit organizations. The expectations included the requirement that public organizations create, use, and provide information to others about their operations and operational choices and that public organizations would be constrained in how they operated to increase the likelihood that resources would be used wisely.

Reformers particularly advocated gathering and providing information for the sake of improved decision-making in concert with the three advanced budget approaches discussed in Chapter 6 and the modes of analysis discussed in Chapter 7. Traditionalists and policy-makers in public organizations appear to favor reforms for the sake of greater oversight and control over operations. The publics in most places in the United States appear to expect greater openness and reasonable restraints on operations.

These operating techniques place many responsibilities on public managers and constraints on their behaviors, and they require more managerial positions in public organizations. Public managers devote much of their work time to operating techniques, producing and consuming information, and following appropriate operational restrictions. Public managers are well advised to become very familiar with their organization's information system and other technique areas.

The daunting appearance of rules, regulations, and explanations for operating techniques can be off-putting. Coping with them proceeds best from understanding their purposes, their major concepts, and the processes through which they march. The reward for understanding operating techniques is being able to do the technical work of a public manager as well as possible.

Additional Reading and Resources

Print

A comprehensive treatment of all the topics covered in this chapter and some other topics:

Reed, B.J., and John W. Swain. *Public Finance Administration.* 2nd ed. Thousand Oaks, CA: Sage, 1997.

Treatments of most of the topics in this chapter by economists:

Aronson, J. Richard, and Eli Schwartz. *Management Policies in Local Government Finance.* 5th ed. Washington, DC: ICMA Press, 2004.

Internet

Government Finance Officers Association
The website of the Government Finance Officers Association—a local government-oriented group with links to state chapters, a host of publications on operational techniques, and best practices—is at www.gfoa.org.

The Ohio State Auditor
The Ohio State Auditor, at www.auditor.state.oh.us, audits state and local government and maintains a searchable website that provides links to performance audit information, local government resources, and a variety of publications:

- Taylor, Mary. Village Officers' Handbook at www.auditor.state.oh.us/lgs/Publications/LocalGovernmentManualsHandbooks/village_officers_handbook.pdf
- "Performance Audits" at www.auditor.state.oh.us/services/performance/default.htm
- "Local Government Resources" at www.auditor.state.oh.us/lgs/default.htm
- "Publications" at www.auditor.state.oh.us/Publications/Default.htm

U.S. Office of Federal Financial Management
The U.S. Office of Management and Budget provides web pages for information for federal agencies. This includes information on purchasing, internal controls, and accounting and auditing requirements for federal agencies and federal grantees. Information can also be found at the website of the

Office of Federal Financial Management at www.whitehouse.gov/omb/
financial_default. Circulars from that office are at www.whitehouse.gov/omb/
financial_offm_circulars.

U.S. Government Accountability Office
The U.S. Government Accountability Office provides a variety of key ref-
erences on the bottom of the right-hand side of its homepage, including
Government Auditing Standards, Principles of Federal Appropriations Law,
Internal Controls Standards, and Financial Audit Manual at www.gao.gov/
index.html.

Audits can be found on the U.S. Government Accountability Office website
under the Document Collection heading at www.gao.gov or the U.S. Government Printing Office website under GAO Reports at www.gpoaccess.gov/
gaoreports; both pages have category lists and search facilities.

Conducting Searches
Please refer to page 165 in Chapter 7 for further information.

9

Economic Explanations
in Public Budgeting

Economics refers to human beings producing, distributing, and consuming resources and to an academic discipline devoted to studying those phenomena. An economy refers to how a community uses resources. Economists divide their discipline into microeconomics and macroeconomics. Microeconomics involves studying individual entities (people, firms, and other entities) as they interact with one another in regard to resources. Macroeconomics involves studying whole economies, especially national economies. Economics provides many useful insights into public budgets and public budgeting.

Although often underappreciated, the economic discipline's core ideas are especially useful. Three important core ideas in economics are opportunity cost, incentives, and scarcity. Opportunity cost refers to the fact that all alternatives have costs and that the choice of doing one thing means not being able to do other things. Economists use the concept of opportunity cost to focus attention on real choices. People respond to changes in incentives, often predictably. Relative scarcity is the basis for the economic value of many goods and services; the prices of products vary relative to their scarcity.

Economic Rationales for Public Organizations

Although economic activities are surely coeval with human existence and governing arrangements in all of recorded history, applying economic reasoning as it is presently understood is a more recent phenomenon. Adam Smith fathered modern economics with his publication of *An Inquiry into the Nature and Cause of the Wealth of Nations* in 1776. The title highlights the concern for economic wealth, and the text itself presents a very sensible analysis of economics and government. Since then, economics has developed into a formal academic discipline. As Smith aptly pointed out, governments provide goods and services that private individuals cannot provide. Economists as a general rule strongly favor the use of markets for making resource decisions; they see certain situations as exceptions in which government actions may be preferable.

Economic arguments provide rationales for creating public organizations and for those organizations acting in particular ways. Economists offer two groups of rationales, both of which are based on values. The concern of the first group of rationales is market failures, by which the economists' primarily valued outcome, serving individual preferences, is thwarted. Secondly, under various terms, economists discuss collectively valued goods of various kinds. Proponents of particular policies may invoke two or more rationales in many cases.

Market failure rationales are based on a positive view of the value of serving individual preferences. Based on a number of assumptions, economists can prove that free markets provide the greatest possible satisfaction of individual preferences compared to any other arrangement for allocating resources. A perfectly working free market would produce maximized "allocative efficiency"; that is, individuals would get as much of what they wanted as possible based on the original distribution of resources. Such situations are also referred to as "Pareto optimal" or "Pareto efficiency," for Vilfredo Pareto, the economist who introduced the idea.

When free markets do not exist for some reason or where free markets do not maximize individual satisfaction, economists say that a situation is a "market failure." Market failures at least potentially justify action by public organizations. Discussions of market failures can be found in the areas of welfare economics and public finance economics. Here, we will discuss market failures based on a list given by a distinguished economist, Joseph E. Stiglitz, in his textbook *Economics of the Public Sector* (p. 85):

- Public goods
- Externalities
- Imperfect competition
- Imperfect information
- Incomplete markets
- Macroeconomic disturbances

Although most economists generally agree with Stiglitz, they show more consensus and tend to focus much more on public goods, externalities, imperfect competition, and macroeconomic disturbances than on imperfect information and incomplete markets.

The public goods rationale applies to many public policies. Public goods have properties or characteristics that make them peculiarly appropriate for governmental provision, which can be stated positively and negatively. Positively, governments are especially suitable for providing communal goods and services, ones that economists label public goods. Negatively, individual entities (persons or companies) may lack incentives or capacity to benefit from the provision of public goods or even to reveal their preferences for those goods accurately. Public goods typically have one or two characteristics that set them apart from other goods that are usually called private goods. Public goods are most easily understood in contrast to private goods. Personal consumption items, such as food or clothing, provide clear examples of characteristics of private goods, which are subtractability and exclusivity. Subtractability literally means that a good is no longer available after it has been consumed. Exclusivity refers to whether someone can be practically excluded from benefiting from a good. Food products are both subtractable and exclusive. In contrast, public goods are nonsubtractable, nonexclusive, or both. Nonsubtractable goods are ones that many people can consume without subtracting from the ability of others to consume that good. Nonexclusive goods are ones for which excluding people from consuming is not practical. Lighthouses that warn ships about hazards are both nonsubtractable and nonexclusive.

Public and private goods also differ on demand revelation. The demand for private goods is obvious: it is revealed when they are consumed. Producers exclude people from consumption unless payments are arranged, and consumed goods are subtracted. For example, someone who wants to consume a candy bar pays for and eats it. In contrast, either or both of the qualities of nonsubtractability or nonexclusivity mean that the demand for public goods is not revealed through consumption choices. For example, a lighthouse sends out light signals and does not exclude anyone in the vicinity from consuming those signals. Decisions about providing a lighthouse or other public goods are usually decided by collective or group decision-making. When groups decide about public goods, they simultaneously decide on one level for both supply and demand. A group decides about providing one or more lighthouses. Collective decision-making differs from free market decision-making, which involves different parties independently deciding whether to buy or sell products. Also, the process of indicating preferences differs for public goods. Preferences for private goods are indicated by prices for which people will supply or purchase goods. Collective decision-making also means collective funding for public goods. In this kind of a situation, economists note that individuals, if they are supposed to pay in proportion to their preferences, have an incentive to understate their true preferences with the hope that others will pay for the good. Economists refer to this situation as the free-rider problem. The free-rider problem helps explain the existence of taxes; people would not voluntarily pay enough for public goods for them to be provided at the level that people truly desired. In many cases, goods can be partially public goods and partially not. A generally underappreciated public good is governmental provision of a framework within which free markets can operate (political stability and public order).

Externalities refer to market situations in which the consequences of buying and selling affect others beside buyers and sellers. Economists call such impacts external effects or externalities. Negative ones are external costs, and positive ones are external benefits. Economists commonly cite pollution as a negative externality and the pollination of crops by bees as a positive externality. Because buyers and sellers do not bear the burdens of negative externalities or benefit from positive externalities, they do not take them into account when deciding whether to buy or sell. Consequently, negative externalities will be excessive and positive externalities will be undersupplied relative to the sum total of individual preferences. Public organizations may be able to step in and make situations better by increasing positive externalities and decreasing negative externalities.

Imperfect competition refers to situations in which sellers or buyers of a product do not compete with one another because only one or a few sellers or buyers exist or because the buyers or sellers work together to avoid competing. One seller constitutes a monopoly. (Where two or more sellers act together as a monopolist would, they constitute a duopoly or an oligopoly.) One buyer is a monopsony, which can have similar impacts as monopolies. Monopolists can be expected to maximize their own welfare at the expense of buyers by supplying less of a good than buyers would like and would be willing to pay for in a free market. Some situations appear to be "natural" monopolies: one producer of a good will lower total production costs, especially when production requires a large investment in infrastructure, as is the case for public utilities. Governments can prevent the formation of monopolies, regulate monopolies to seek to maximize consumer satisfaction, or take over the provision of a good.

Imperfect information refers to situations in which parties to economic transactions have vastly different information or incentives to gather and use information. These situations violate the free market assumption of free and equal access to information. The consumer in such situations is thought to lack information, sufficient ability to gather information, or sufficient incentive to gather information. Public organizations can provide information or require the provision of information by private parties to remedy such situations.

Incomplete markets refer to situations in which free markets do not work to provide goods for which the willingness of consumers to pay exceeds the cost of providing the goods. The federal government has been active in providing various kinds of insurance and loans based on this rationale.

Macroeconomic disturbances occur when unemployment is high, when economies decline rather than grow, or when prices increase or decrease at high rates. Economists see those phenomena as indicating that a whole economy is not working properly. Macroeconomic policies relating to those situations are discussed later in this chapter.

Economists advance a second group of rationales based on communally held values rather than individual preferences. Economists refer to these rationales in terms of merit goods, equity, and redistribution. It should be noted that economists are less committed to advancing these rationales since they are not as central to the discipline as the value of satisfying individual preferences.

Merit goods generally are considered of such obvious benefit that collectivities decide that those goods will be provided for consumption regardless of individual preferences as expressed in a marketplace. Seatbelts, public education, the avoidance of addictive substances, charitable actions, and childhoods free of formal work responsibilities are examples of merit goods. Cultural heritage goods, which also may reflect individual preferences, are portrayed as merit goods; for example, libraries, museums, and cultural events such as those with ethnic, geographic, or historical themes.

When economists use the term *equity*, they may mean fairness generally or more specifically the distribution of resources in society, which is a special case of fairness. When they use the term generally, they are referring to situations in which persons would be unfairly disadvantaged by circumstances; that is, Shakespeare's "slings and arrows of outrageous fortune." The remedies for unfair disadvantages are corrective measures by public organizations, most notably welfare, poor relief, or financial relief of some kind for especially harmful events. Federal income tax deductions for catastrophic losses and extremely large health-care expenses are two examples of financial relief. However, economists are generally reluctant to take the unfair disadvantages rationale very far beyond exceedingly obvious cases of harm befalling individuals.

When economists refer to equity as a distributional issue, they speak of the unequal distribution of resources in a free market economy. Those economic inequalities may be divided into those that occur due to human life cycles and those due to diversity among human beings. Inequality due to human life cycles refers to the inability of the very young and the very old to sell their labor. Both groups must therefore rely on others or on savings of some kind to live. Inequalities also might arise due to diversity among human beings, such as illness and disability, which produce the same kind of inequality as that of the very young or very old, and the varying capacity of a people or their ancestors to acquire wealth in a free market economy. Economic inequality due to age, illness, or disabilities also can be seen as a special case of harm befalling individuals because they are unable to succeed in a free market economy. Such inequalities are generally seen as justifying public provision of a minimum level of economic support where necessary. This rationale tends to emphasize preventing human suffering. Thanks to economic inequality arising from the diversity among human beings, some people become extremely well endowed with economic resources while others are much more modestly endowed. The contrast is the relative difference between the rich and the poor. This rationale tends to emphasize relative inequality rather than absolute human want.

The rationale of preventing human suffering and that of preventing excessive inequality sometimes get wrapped together, but they are clearly two different arguments. Economists support the first rationale more than the second, although many support the second rationale. The first of the two rationales indicates correctly that free market economies produce distributions of resources that can have extremely harsh consequences for some individuals. Public actions to avoid harmful consequences can be harmonious with a free market economy. The second rationale generally creates a conflict for economists in that it conflicts with their disciplinarily induced preference for individual satisfaction. Anything that reduces individuals' capacity or inclination to advance their own interest without directly harming others is seen as advancing human well-being. Anything involving redistribution of economic resources is sometimes equated to Robin Hood's robbing the rich to give to the poor; for example, progressive income tax rates result in more taxes being taken from the rich than from the poor. If such redistribution involves taking from one or more identifiable economic groups and giving to one or more other individuals or groups, it may have the unfortunate consequence, from the economic perspective, of lowering the incentive for people to produce goods and services to exchange and thereby reduce the sum total of the goods and services available in an economy. Economists note that Social Security taxes, most sales taxes, and lotteries take more from the poor than from the rich and that corporations as artificial persons pass their taxes on as a burden to consumers, owners, employees, and suppliers. So, to the extent that some economists favor redistribution, they do so also with the belief that economic wealth will be limited by acts of redistribution. Other arguments for redistribution, whether moral or political, fall outside the scope of the present discussion.

A discussion of economic rationales would be incomplete without a brief account of government failures. Government failure refers to situations in which governments act to deal with actual or alleged market failures, but instead cause decreases in allocative efficiency or equity. Economists attribute government failures to a variety of factors, including the limited capacity of governments to gather information and predict behavior, the political process favoring those who have political power, and implementation difficulties. From the 1930s to the 1960s, economics literature developed a wide variety of related analyses of market failures as discussed here that promoted government intervention into economic activities, with only a few economists systematically criticizing such interventions. The rationales for economic intervention had the benefits of simultaneously arguing for doing good and making economists and their work very important. Most mainstream economists appeared to be firmly committed to supporting governmental intervention in cases of market failure. Beginning in the 1960s and more so in the 1970s and 1980s, various economists produced theoretical and empirical work showing various explanations of government failure and systematic evidence of the costs of government failure. Since the 1990s, mainstream economists appear to acknowledge government failure—even if they only say that government intervention in market failure situations is not always successful. In effect, mainstream economists' enthusiasm for governmental corrective actions for market failures declined when they saw that the theoretical capacity to correct market failures was not always realized in practice. The concept of government failure also could be applied to nonprofit organizations as they provide similar goods.

Nonprofit organizations constitute a special situation relative to rationales for public organizations. Although many of the economic rationales are the same, nonprofit organizations must rely on voluntary payments rather than involuntary ones; most of their revenue comes from fees for services. For that reason, they often have to provide some other sort of benefit to individuals or companies beyond any collective benefit that they may produce, as explained by Mancur Olson in *The Logic of Collective Action.* Also, the existence of nonprofit organizations in the United States stems from governmental laws and regulations that grant them that status and confer benefits on them. Governments require that nonprofit organizations serve public purposes as a requirement for granting nonprofit status. In that sense, nonprofit organizations simply extend some government activities.

Aside from economic rationales for serving the public, nonprofit organizations create many of the advantages enjoyed by private for-profit organizations: continuity, limited legal liability, expertise, capacity for efficient operations, and focus. These advantages enable them to be effective instruments for human purposes.

Functions

When economists look at government, they see three functions. Following Richard Musgrave, a pioneer in the development of public finance economics, economists call these three functions allocation, distribution, and stabilization. Allocation refers to directing or applying resources to various uses, goods, or services. Distribution refers to imposing costs and giving benefits to various members of the public. Stabilization refers to regulating a whole economy in respect to growth, employment, and prices. (Stabilization is discussed as macroeconomic policy later in this chapter.) Economists view the functions as interrelated. However, they recommend analyzing and devising policies to deal with each function separately.

The allocation function concerns governments intervening in economic activities to produce different allocations from those that would result from a completely free market. Governments allocate resources by choosing what goods and services to provide and securing resources to provide those goods. When governments allocate resources, they also determine the relative shares of an economy controlled by governments and by the private sector.

Direct provision decisions are very clearly allocative. Government decisions affect allocation in a variety of ways. For example, when a government allocates resources to a particular good, the private sector may choose to reallocate resources formerly allocated to that good. For example, publicly funded fire departments replaced efforts by insurance companies to suppress fires. Economists describe this phenomenon as a "crowding-out effect."

The stated intent of many taxes and tax expenditure provisions is to encourage or discourage resource allocation toward or away from particular uses. Criminalization of certain activities and subsidies for certain activities are conceptually similar to taxes and tax expenditures for allocation as they raise or lower the perceived price of engaging in those activities. Government decisions work indirectly to affect allocation as they change prices, which are incentives or disincentives for certain behaviors or choices. Businesses, for example, may choose to operate near large governmental facilities; tax preparation services depend on government for their existence.

The distributive function concerns how governments affect the distribution of costs and benefits in society, which in turn affects allocative efficiency. When governments collect revenues, those revenues have differential impacts on members of the community from whom the revenues are collected. Likewise, many services have differential impacts on members of a community. Any particular revenue or expenditure measure will redistribute wealth or well-being from some people to others. In analyzing the distributive function, economists frequently examine the situation of people with differing incomes or wealth. Many revenue measures, such as lottery tickets, sales taxes, and Social Security taxes, redistribute wealth by taking more proportionally from poor people than rich people; other measures, such as federal personal income taxes, do just the opposite. Many expenditure measures redistribute

wealth by providing more proportionally to poor people than rich people—
for example, some income security and education services; some do the
opposite—for example, other income security and education services. Primary
and secondary public education and traditional welfare programs providing
assistance to poor people redistribute wealth to poor people; Social Security
redistributes wealth to the well-off because they live longer than poor people
to collect old-age benefits, and public higher education favors the well-off as
they are in a position to take advantage of educational opportunities. Efforts
to redistribute wealth may undercut the incentives that people have to engage
in productive economic activity, thereby lessening the sum total of wealth in
a community. Efforts to redistribute wealth can take many forms and have
different impacts on the overall wealth of a community. History is littered
with attempts to redistribute wealth that has gone off-track. Some years back,
a federal luxury tax on yachts cost a number of Americans their jobs in the
U.S. yacht-building industry. The tax increased the cost of new yachts, the
rich did not buy as many new yachts in the United States as they had previously, and instead they bought used yachts in the United States, new yachts
elsewhere, or did something else with their money.

Roles

Public organizations participate in economic activity in a variety of roles.
First of all, as providers, they make goods and services available. Second,
as producers, they directly create goods and services, and in doing so they
are also buyers by purchase or rental of the means of production, and they
may be sellers of what they produce. Third, as owners of assets, in addition to using assets in providing and producing, they also may be sellers,
lessors, or investors. Fourth, as providers, they may become debtors.
These roles, although they often intertwine, are discussed separately here.
Public organizations' economic roles, particularly those of governments,
affect everyone.

Because resources are always and everywhere scarce, public organizations
choose from available options in fulfilling their purposes. They choose to
make goods or services available (provide) or not. The reasons for choosing
a particular provision option include serving the public interest (even if for
only one group) in line with a public organization's purpose or mission, being
the best available alternative, and being supported by an organization's public
or supporters. Generally, being in the public interest is equivalent to one of
the economic rationales for action by public organizations. The reasons for
not choosing a particular provision option include: that the option is outside
the purposes or mission of the organization; that the option does not truly

serve the public interest; that the option is unlikely to succeed (government failure); and that resources are too scarce to allow that choice.

Public organizations provide in various ways. Production is the most obvious alternative, and many times production and provision are decided together. However, much of what public organizations provide is actually produced by individuals and organizations operating independently of the providing public organizations. Public organizations also provide through payments, the use of other incentives and disincentives, the creation and enforcement of rights and duties, the creation of privileges, administrative regulation, and exhortation. Production is discussed below, and the other provision options are discussed here. Providing through payments means that public organizations pay some other parties to be or to choose the direct producers of goods or services; those payments include all grant and other transfer payment funding. Some payments specify the goods or services paid for (e.g., medical care or highways), and some payments allow the recipient to choose the specific goods and services. Other incentives and disincentives include tax expenditures and subsidies on one hand and targeted taxes and civil penalties on the other hand. The creation and enforcement of rights and duties by governments allow people to choose certain kinds of behavior and require them to do certain things (e.g., jury duty). The creation of privileges (e.g., licenses for drivers and vehicles, taxi and cable television franchises, and honorific titles such as Poet Laureate of the United States) enables holders of those privileges to act in ways barred by other parties not granted those privileges. Public organizations, particularly governments, regulate in a variety of ways. Governments regulate by declaring certain acts criminal and prosecuting those who violate criminal laws. Governments also engage in two kinds of administrative regulation, economic and social, in which they create, communicate, and enforce rules through hearing cases, creating rules, or discretionary actions. Economic regulation concerns the regulation of entry, exit, price, and terms of service for particular industries where imperfect competition appears to be a problem. The scope of economic regulation has shrunk considerably from its high point when airlines, trucking, railroads, and telephone services were covered. Current examples include taxicabs in many cities and electrical power in most states. Social regulation concerns the regulation of activities or products (e.g., food, drugs, and automobiles) relative to broad social concerns such as health, safety, equity, and the environment. Finally, public organizations provide through exhorting others to behave in certain ways and not in other ways (e.g., "Don't drink and drive" and "Do unto others as you would have them do unto you").

Economists generally prefer that governments act through the manipulation of incentives and disincentives as represented by payments and other incentives and disincentives in the preceding discussion. However, economists also are cognizant of circumstances requiring governmental production.

Public organizations profoundly affect communities by providing goods and services, mostly public goods. Their provision determines the kinds of communities that exist and many specific facets of those communities. Public organizations are one source of differences among countries of the world and among state and local communities. Public organizations structure human activity by creating political, legal, physical, spiritual, and economic frameworks within which people live. Those frameworks simultaneously limit and enable ordered possibilities. For example, laws specify what is required, allowed, and prohibited. Oliver Wendell Holmes Jr. expressed the effects of governments on people succinctly when he said, "Taxes are what we pay for civilized society."

Public organizations use a variety of considerations to decide whether to produce goods and services as opposed to using another provision alternative. First, why or in what situations would a public organization choose to produce goods and services? Often, public organizations continue to produce what they have produced in the past. Public organizations, especially governments, may choose to produce in order to protect the public or because no other producer is available. Public organizations become the producers of last resort when no other alternative is available. Where the production of a good or service may be subject to abuse, governments may produce or only allow production by public organizations to protect the public. Examples include natural monopolies, regulation of behavior, national security activities, services in the political and legal systems, and the control of public monies. Alternative producers may be lacking because of capital requirements, apparent economic risk (e.g., for exploration and basic research), or liability concerns.

Second, why or in what situations would a public organization choose not to produce goods and services? The general answer is when the results are likely to be more efficient than having public organizations produce the goods or services. Where the goal is to change behavior, allowing the consuming parties to choose what to consume increases allocative efficiency as consumers pick products that they prefer (housing, medical care, food, or other products). Other producers may be more productively efficient (charging a lower unit cost for goods and services) thanks to their scale of operations, operational flexibility, expertise, and incentives for innovation. Examples may help here. Small local governments purchase police services from larger governments because of economies of scale. Private insurance companies process Medicare claims for the federal government because of their expertise and operational flexibility. Federal and state governments use competitive grants to foster innovation.

As producers, public organizations rent or buy what is necessary. In some cases, they rent land, buildings, and equipment from others. The choice of renting rather than buying occurs when public organizations desire flexibility, when they plan to use the items for a limited time period, and when renting provides financial or legal advantages. The financial advantages may arise because private parties are able to deduct the depreciation of assets from their tax liabilities, because other parties are able to dispose of assets in a more financially beneficial fashion, and because public organizations are unable to secure funding to purchase land, buildings, or equipment. Legal advantages occur when governments do not have the legal authority to borrow money to purchase assets; then, renting might be the only legal option for obtaining assets without having funding on hand. Even then, a rental contract, often called a lease-purchase agreement, may include an option to buy at a future time. The payment schedule in rental contracts with such options may be similar to a debt repayment schedule for a debt-financed purchase. Public organizations buy land, improvements to land, buildings, other forms of infrastructure, equipment, personnel services, other services, and supplies.

As buyers, public organizations deal with the same sorts of concerns as other buyers. However, they have special concerns. Their personnel often have to meet higher or more stringent standards than those applied to private parties. Some special personnel standards include a specific religious calling, a higher than average ability to exercise judgment in situations in which many lives may be at stake, capacity to fulfill responsibilities to the public, and loyalty to the employing public organization. Personnel standards may also include laws concerning required and prohibited conduct involving secrecy, ethics, following orders, and the treatment of prisoners. Similarly, public organizations, particularly governments, guard against persons trying to take advantage of public organizations through fraud, waste, or abuse. Because ownership incentives are exceedingly diffuse, special routines and procedures have been instituted to protect public organizations.

Monopsony is a special concern relatively unique to public organizations. Monopsony refers to a situation in which one purchaser is in a position to control the price of something because it is the only purchaser. When a number of purchasers work together or behave in a similar fashion, those situations may be equivalent. Monopsony poses problems when a purchaser or a group of purchasers relies on one producer. In such cases, a failure by the sole producer could be devastating to a public organization's capacity to provide. In monopsony situations, purchasers are tempted to push prices downward without considering the consequences. Getting into situations with only one producer is one consequence. Another consequence of downward price pressures is a decline in the quality of what is made available for sale. That consequence may be particularly pronounced in personnel services as many public sector jobs are unique in requiring trustworthiness. Bribery and corruption in many countries stem partially from the low salaries of public officials.

As sellers, public organizations have similar concerns as private parties as well as special concerns. Those special concerns include operating monopolies, balancing public and private benefits, and avoiding conflicts with organizational missions. When public organizations have monopoly or near-monopoly positions, they should guard against using that advantage to maximize revenue at the expense of consumers.

When selling goods and services, public organizations should balance public and private benefits when setting prices. When the benefits of publicly provided products are wholly private, prices should reflect the costs. When the benefits are primarily public, the price may be a small portion of the cost. Even when minimal, prices indicate that a product is an economic good. Prices ration products, reducing expenditures; provide some revenue; and generate information about public demand, helping budgetary decision-making. Two common problems with prices for public products are that they do not keep pace with price inflation and that those products become underpriced relative to their private economic value to private parties.

Public organizations should take care when selling to avoid conflicts with their fundamental mission. In the fourteenth to the mid-sixteenth century, the Roman Catholic Church experienced widespread and open corruption related to money and favoritism. Corrupt church officials bought or sold church offices (simony); appointed family members to church positions, including their own illegitimate children (nepotism); and simply took money for promises of divine grace (indulgences), which were believed to spare people some of the temporal punishments of purgatory, although church teachings indicated that divine grace could only be gained in cases in which people were truly repentant, had properly confessed, had been absolved of their sins, and had, in addition, donated money to the church. These practices conflicted with the mission of the Roman Catholic Church, causing internal disputes and the rise of competing churches that protested a variety of Catholic practices. Today, some critics argue that the marketing of state lotteries to the poor conflicts with those states' avowed intention of protecting consumers rather than taking advantage of them.

Public organizations possess many assets of tremendous financial value. They use many of those assets to provide and produce goods and services. Assets not used for providing and producing can be rented, sold, or invested. Physical assets may be rented or sold. For example, public organizations can choose to sell or rent land, natural resources, buildings, and equipment not used for public purposes. Recently, state and local governments have sold or leased operating toll roads, parking garages, water systems, and airports to private sector entities for financial gain. Many proposals have been made to privatize state lotteries (through sale or lease). Financial assets are held as money or in a form convertible to money. Financial assets are used to provide services through payments and production. Assets held as money may be invested to pay for previously incurred liabilities or to fund future provision. In the nineteenth century, physical assets were given away as incentives to encourage the development of railroads and to encourage land settlement in the American West. Public sector investments mostly are related to current year cash flows, to future pension or debt payments, and to accumulations of resources for future capital expenditures.

As debtors, public organizations commit their publics to repaying loans. Those commitments include loan guarantees that are really commitments to repay loans if the borrowing party cannot do so. Recent experience has shown that loan guarantees do lead to loan repayments in some cases. Public sector debt may cause an increase in the cost of debt for others in an economy by increasing demand. Also, loan guarantees lower the risk for lenders but decrease the relative availability and increase cost of debt for those attempting to borrow without a guarantee. The federal government is the only public sector organization large enough to affect debt markets regularly.

Macroeconomics

Macroeconomics concerns the behavior of whole economies, mostly national economies. Economists observe and theorize about whole economies. They focus particularly on levels and changes in levels of output, employment and unemployment, and prices. Ultimately, they hope to describe, explain, and predict those phenomena.

National governments attempt to stabilize or regulate their economies using macroeconomic policies. Macroeconomic policies can be divided into monetary and fiscal policies. Both kinds of policies affect economic behavior. Monetary policy concerns the quantity of money available in an economy. Fiscal (budget) policies concern the size of public budgets, the features of revenue and expenditure measures, and the difference between total revenues and total expenditures (surplus or deficit). A variety of economists and others argue for particular monetary and fiscal policies that they believe will solve economic problems, such as inadequate economic growth, high unemployment, or high price inflation.

We start with monetary policy. Money serves various purposes, takes different forms, and matters for a variety reasons. Money serves the three purposes of exchanging, measuring, and holding wealth. First, people exchange money for goods and services. U.S. currency, for example, shows the words, "This note is legal tender for all debts, public and private." Second, people measure the value of exchanges in terms of money units. Third, people store wealth from one time period to another in money. The multiple purposes of money mean that changes in one aspect of money may affect one or both of the other aspects.

Money takes various forms, which makes controlling it difficult. The narrowest definition of money is currency, coins, and checks and other demand deposit accounts. A wider definition includes accounts that are easily and quickly convertible to money (e.g., savings and money market fund accounts). An even wider definition includes deposits of money that become available at a later date. Beyond money itself, other forms of wealth and credit arrangements relate very closely to money. Other forms of wealth vary in how quickly and easily they may be converted to money. The value of other forms of wealth relative to money fluctuates, and attempts at quickly converting other forms of wealth to money might quickly lower their selling prices. Credit arrangements, loans, and credit cards facilitate exchanges as people can exchange a promise to pay for goods and services. However, credit arrangements neither store nor measure wealth.

Money matters because money supply changes affect an economy generally and specifically help and hurt distinct groups. Governments operate monetary policies to regulate the overall supply of money in their economies. They increase or decrease the amount of money. A money supply increasing faster than the amount of goods and services in an economy increases causes price inflation and a decrease in the value of each unit of money. Conversely, a money supply decreasing relative to the amount of goods and services in an economy causes price deflation and an increase in the value of each unit of money. As long as a money supply keeps pace with changes in the amount of goods and services in an economy, prices generally remain stable, despite prices of specific items varying for various reasons. However, when prices change in reaction to money supply changes (and, some economists say, expectations of changes), then people might react, especially if the changes are extreme. The array of effects exceeds our present space, but two possible changes are people trying to gain advantages and people acting based on how wealthy they feel. People can gain advantages in purchases and borrowing or lending money. Increasing prices encourage earlier purchases; decreasing prices encourage delays in purchases. Increases in the money supply help debtors and hurt creditors and people with fixed incomes because of the change in value of units of money. Conversely, decreases in the money supply help creditors and those on fixed incomes and hurt debtors. People tend to spend more when they feel wealthier. Money supply increases may be referred to as making money relatively more "cheap" or "loose"; decreases may be referred to as making money relatively more "dear," "expensive," or "tight."

Monetary policy historically has had two basic problems, with possibly a third problem added in the twentieth century. The first basic problem is simply ensuring an adequate amount of money for exchanging and storing wealth for an economy to function. Economists often refer to this problem as maintaining "liquidity" because money is the most available of all assets for deployment. Without money, people barter or are self-sufficient. In the past, commodity money—money based on items of intrinsic value, such as gold, spices, or horses—served the purposes of money but presented difficulties in portability, divisibility, storage, and quantity control. Modern money resolved these problems. Modern money is money because governments say it is and because people accept it.

The second basic problem for monetary policy is radical price changes caused by changes in the money supply. Radical price changes have occurred in many countries throughout the world over human history; they often cause great social and political upheaval as portions of a society become impoverished. The most well-know example of radical price changes being associated with upheaval was the hyperinflationary period starting in 1923 in Germany that lifted Adolf Hitler from obscurity to lead that country into World War II. Governments, in many cases, including some in recent years, caused radical price inflation when they created money to pay for their operations because they were unable to raise revenues any other way. The current best-known case is Zimbabwe, although several governments in Latin America and Eastern Europe also have experienced government-induced hyperinflation in the last three decades. Today, governments typically control money supplies to maintain relatively stable prices.

The possible third basic problem that emerged in the twentieth century was whether and how money supply changes could be used to improve economic conditions. This problem will be addressed below in the context of fiscal policy.

The U.S. Federal Reserve System (FRS), an independent quasi-public and quasi-private institution created under federal law in 1913, increases and decreases the money supply in three general ways: (1) by buying and selling federal debt; (2) by setting reserve requirements for commercial banks; and (3) by loaning money to commercial banks and other financial institutions. First, buying federal debt puts more money into the supply, and selling it pulls money from the money supply. Second, reserve requirements specify how much of each commercial bank's assets must be held as a reserve. When commercial banks loan money, more money is created because a loan to one party is deposited in one or more other banks that then have more money available to loan. Decreasing reserve requirements increases the money supply as commercial banks can loan more money; increasing reserve requirements decreases the money supply. Third, the availability of loans, the amounts, and the rates at which commercial banks and others can borrow from the FRS affect the money supply. When commercial banks have more money from loans and especially if the loans are at a more favorable rate than can be obtained on the open market, then commercial banks have more money to loan, which creates more money. In 2008, the FRS as the lender of last resort took extraordinary steps in loaning money to a variety of financial institutions because of concerns over liquidity.

Macroeconomics as a policy-oriented activity can be divided into the preclassical, classical, Keynesian, and post-Keynesian periods. Those recommending policies tend to focus on different problems and sets of circumstances during the different periods. Also, a common, alarmist misrepresentation of macroeconomic concerns is addressed here.

In the preclassical period—human history up to 1776—different people advanced a wide variety of macroeconomic theories related to economic well-being. For whole economies, those theories were more notable for failures than successes. For example, in the sixteen and seventeenth centuries when mercantilist economic theories held sway in ruling circles in Europe, governments attempted to acquire as much gold and silver as possible and to minimize purchases from foreign countries. Mercantilist theories contributed greatly to the motivation of European countries to develop colonies.

Classical economics can be seen as starting with Adam Smith's *Wealth of Nations* in 1776. Classical economists disagree on some points, but they tend to agree on key points. First, they argue that a level of economic output is determined by the amount of available labor and resources. Second, money is principally a medium of exchange and not in itself wealth. Third, the greatest possible level of output is achieved by allowing individuals and firms to make decisions on what to produce and to purchase (the "invisible hand" of the marketplace coordinating production and consumption through money prices). Fourth, the role of government is to provide essential public services that other entities cannot provide and to avoid causing unnecessary difficulties in the functioning of economies.

Economic growth was spectacular for countries that generally followed classical economic precepts, including the United States, even though those countries did not hesitate to deviate from those precepts in many specific cases. However, those countries' economic situations were not ideal. Despite periods of elevated levels of economic growth, those countries also experienced economic problems associated with an economic pattern called the business cycle. The business cycle involves an irregular cyclic pattern over time of rising and falling rates of output growth that appear as waves and troughs or peaks and valleys when represented graphically. Neither the changes in growth rates nor the time periods display regularity, but changes in levels of employment and prices tend to relate to the cyclical pattern. When growth rates are high, employment levels and price inflation tend to be high. When output grows at a lower rate or actually declines, employment levels tend to be lower and prices tend to be stable or falling. Classical economists were familiar with the business cycle but argued that the consequences of the business cycle were temporary, offset by the benefits of economic growth, and not something that could be improved by governmental intervention.

The Keynesian period emerged following the publication in 1936 of *The General Theory of Employment, Interest, and Money* by John Maynard Keynes, a British economist. A worldwide depression with declining economic output and extremely high unemployment contributed to policy-makers' interest in a new way of dealing with whole economies. Also, the brutality of the World War I undermined confidence in the widely held assumption of continuous progress. Keynes explicitly argued against classical economic precepts. First, he argued that actual output is determined by the aggregate (total) level of demand for goods and services, even though an economy's upper production limit depends on available resources and labor. Second, he argued that some people treat money as wealth and not merely as a medium of exchange. Third, he argued that the greatest possible level of output could be achieved by manipulating aggregate demand and the quantity of money to maximize an attainable growth rate. Fourth, he argued that government intervention in national economies was essential to smooth out the business cycle.

A key issue for Keynes was the tendency of some people to hoard money as wealth during economic downturns instead of either consuming goods and services or investing in productive enterprises. That hoarding meant aggregate demand was inadequate for achieving an optimal growth rate. He argued that the hoarding tendency explained the Great Depression of the 1930s. His solution to that economic situation was increasing aggregate demand by government action. Aggregate demand can be increased by increasing government spending, reducing government revenues, creating or increasing budget deficits, and increasing the money supply. Increasing the money supply had at least two purposes. First, the resulting price inflation provides people with incentives to consume and invest rather than to hoard money because increasing prices means a decreasing value for hoarded money. Second, price inflation alleviates the stickiness of labor prices by changing the apparent price of labor, which is expected to encourage people to work. Keynes and his followers predicted that his policies would counteract an economic downturn and result in more employment, more growth, and moderate price inflation.

The vast majority of economists came to agree with Keynes by the mid-1940s, although his work was open to different interpretations on many specific points. The general opinion of Keynesians was that economies could be fine-tuned to produce an optimal growth rate with high levels of employment and moderate price inflation. Although U.S. involvement in World War II increased aggregate demand and produced positive effects on the U.S. economy as predicted by Keynes, the first avowed Keynesian act by the U.S. government was the Employment Act of 1946. Lawmakers feared that high levels of unemployment would follow World War II, as had occurred after World War I. The bill that was the basis for the act was originally titled the Full Employment Act and included mandatory provisions for governmental action in response to specific levels of economic statistics. The act only mandated that the president should craft and recommend macroeconomic policies for full employment and price stability.

The aggregate demand–decreasing side of Keynesian economics does not garner much attention compared to the aggregate demand–increasing side. The aggregate demand–decreasing side calls for actions exactly opposite of those necessary to increase aggregate demand. Those actions, which would be applied when the growth rate and price inflation are overly high, are decreasing government spending, increasing government revenues, creating or increasing government surpluses, and decreasing the money supply. Keynesian economics calls for these actions when an economy is growing excessively in order to keep it from also rapidly declining. Although most economists were convinced of Keynes's correctness and despite the Employment Act of 1946, federal policy-makers did not move to implement Keynesian policies to any serious extent until the 1970s.

The post-Keynesian period constitutes a reemergence of classical doctrines, refinement of Keynesian doctrines, and the emergence of new doctrines. The conditions starting in the early 1970s that led from the Keynesian period to the post-Keynesian period were low levels of growth, high levels of unemployment, and high levels of price inflation, which came to be called "stagflation." Presidents Nixon, Ford, and Carter attempted various macroeconomic policies without apparent success. These conditions, especially high unemployment, caused the U.S. Congress to pass the Full Employment and Balanced Growth Act of 1978. That law, like the Employment Act of 1946, did not have any mechanisms for directly affecting employment. The then orthodox Keynesian economics was discredited by the end of the decade because of its failures in explaining that situation adequately and in providing curative policy measures. A very visible graphic representation of Keynesian policies, the Phillips curve, suggested that more price inflation could be traded for more employment. In the 1970s, employment levels did not appear to respond to price inflation, and price inflation became so high that further intentional price inflation was not politically palatable. Particularly discredited was the idea of fine-tuning an economy. Many economists, policy-makers, and members of the public looked for other macroeconomic theories. Economists subsequently developed new macroeconomic theories (many of which are not mentioned here), but two theories gained creditability among policy-makers and the public. Both of these views, supply-side economics and monetarism theories, have classical roots.

Supply-side economics is essentially a restatement of classical economics. Ronald Reagan popularized that economic viewpoint when he championed it in his successful 1980 presidential campaign. Supply-side economics starts by rejecting Keynes's doctrines and arguing that Keynesian policies waste resources, expand government unnecessarily, create unnecessary inflation, and reduce economic growth. Supply-side advocates drew inspiration from Jean-Baptiste Say, a French economist whose *Treatise on Political Economy or the Production, Distribution, and Consumption of Wealth* was published in 1803. His most famous pronouncement, called Say's Law, is "Supply creates demand." Say's explicit argument is that one must have something to trade before trading. In Say's view, the creation of products is the prerequisite for wealth. Keynes explicitly claimed to refute Say's Law in the process of arguing for manipulating aggregate levels of demand.

Supply-side proponents argue in favor of eliminating Keynesian policies and minimizing government actions that inhibit people from supplying goods and services. Keynesian policies to be avoided include manipulating the size of government budgets as a matter of economic policy-making, designing revenue and expenditure policies to affect aggregate demand, creating budget deficits or surpluses, and purposely creating price inflation. Supply-side economic proponents argue for using government only to carry out policies that other entities are unable to perform. Particular concerns of supply-side economics include tax policies and taking a cost-benefit perspective. The tax policies concern marginal personal income tax rates, capital gains taxes, corporate taxation, and the availability of tax shelters. According to supply-side proponents, high marginal personal income tax rates discourage supply for both investors and people supplying labor. For investors, lower post-tax returns make using their resources for consumption more attractive. For people supplying labor, high marginal income tax rates make using their time for leisure more attractive. Proponents argue that income taxes on capital gains (investment income) reduce the incentives to invest; some would prefer a zero rate of taxation on capital gains. They also argue that corporate and personal income taxation on capital gains constitutes double taxation of income (once to the corporation and once to the person) and that high corporate income taxes put the United States at a relative disadvantage to other countries for investments. Tax shelters, literally places to put investments to avoid income taxes, are said to inhibit supply by encouraging investors to avoid taxes for gain rather than to seek investments. Proponents suggest a cost-benefit perspective so that the appropriateness of governmental actions is judged based solely on the good results produced, not their effect on stimulating demand. During the 1970s, one argument for expanding and adding to federal grant programs was that they would alleviate the problem of too much federal revenues lowering economic demand. Supply-side proponents also suggest subjecting regulatory programs to review using cost-benefit analysis.

The monetarist viewpoint, particularly associated with the Nobel laureate Milton Friedman, focuses on monetary policy. Monetarists prescribe a steady relationship between the money supply and the sum of goods and services, which generally means a growing money supply. They proscribe manipulating the money supply in any other fashion and manipulating fiscal policy, whether demand or supply. They argue that other monetary and fiscal policy manipulations result in delayed and uncertain economic responses as economic participants adjust to price changes.

The supply-side and monetarist viewpoints tend to be reinforcing as both are drawn from the classical perspective and both oppose Keynesian economics. They generally agree on a neutral money supply policy in the sense of trying to keep prices steady. They diverge in that supply-side economics favors manipulating supply factors and more strongly stresses smaller government in contrast to monetarism.

In the post-Keynesian period, no economic viewpoint has dominated; policies have been based on various viewpoints. Monetary policy has been mostly monetarist, tax policies have been mildly more supply-side oriented than previously, and occasionally federal officials attempt to stimulate demand. Overall, macroeconomic theories have been more argued than implemented, with limited impacts on the U.S. economy.

The relatively limited impact of macroeconomic theory on the U.S. economic system can probably be attributed more to the political system than the persuasiveness of macroeconomic theories or the degree of consensus, or lack thereof, among economists. The political system makes policy changes of great consequence relatively difficult. Prior to Keynesian economics, the prevailing political and economic theories were reinforcing in avoiding systematic manipulation of the U.S. economy. The major exception was the creation of the Federal Reserve System, a national banking system, to provide for monetary flexibility to prevent periodic booms and busts driven by the inelasticity of the money supply. Political opposition and distrust of bankers factored into the two earlier eliminations of federally created national banks.

The conjunction of a major economic and political crisis in the Great Depression, a macroeconomic theory promising relief, American elites reacting to their own disillusionment stemming from World Wars I and II, and the Progressive Movement's preference for greater government did not lead to the U.S. Government adopting mandatory Keynesian policies in 1946. When passing the Full Employment Act of 1978, the U.S. Government followed the same pattern and only mandated presidential recommendations for macroeconomic policies. The post–World War II consensus in favor of Keynesian economics may have influenced some policy-makers to favor governmental expansion in economic downturns, but the other side of Keynesian economics was ignored. A variety of other causes of U.S. government expansion can be found, although the Keynesian arguments for increasing aggregate demand in times of economic downturns was well-known after World War II. Increasing revenues and wealth, worldwide military involvement, and the public's desire for more social programming contributed to a larger federal government. Supply-side economics may have contributed to slowing down expansion of the federal government through its justifications for cutting revenue measures and its counterarguments about stimulating aggregate levels of demand. Monetarist theory may have contributed to a steadier treatment of the money supply. All in all, the post-Keynesian period has been thoroughly unsatisfying for theoretical purists.

Why different people in the U.S. political system embrace a macroeconomic theory might better be explained by the political attractiveness of particular economic theories rather than their intrinsic merits or the evidence supporting them. Indeed, economic theories may more closely resemble fashionable taste rather than a correct apprehension of reality. Classical economics reinforces a limited government ethos. Keynesian economics provides an explanation for the Great Depression and a possible way out of such problems, but more generally it provides an additional rationale for people who favor a more active government or simply more governmental activity generally. Supply-side economics and monetarism provide rationales for limiting government activities. Keynes was very concerned about the social consequences of unemployment and saw his theory as a way of alleviating unemployment. Reagan was very concerned about the social consequences of overly large government and saw supply-side economics as a way of alleviating those problems. Without accusing anyone of duplicity, one can see why leaders might prefer economic theories that fit with their existing political preferences.

Monetarism's lack of widespread popular support probably stems from its neutrality on the size of government and toward different groups in society. Also, monetarism does not lend itself to politicians' self-portraits of taking heroic economic policy positions.

The alarmist representation of macroeconomics is a commonly expressed view in the Keynesian and post-Keynesian periods. According to the alarmists, the size of the federal deficit or the federal debt is so great that it will cause the U.S. economy catastrophic harm. In contrast, many other commentators argue that large federal deficits or a large federal debt can cause negative impacts on the U.S. economy but not to the point of catastrophe. The two views differ in their explanations. The alarmist explanation is approximately that the federal deficit or the federal debt is so big that it will crush us, and the more moderate explanations are that federal deficits and debt crowd out other useful applications of resources or that they increase income inequality. Recently, the director of the Congressional Budget Office argued in testimony before a congressional committee that the current pattern of federal deficits is "on an unsustainable path" of federal debt growing much faster than the U.S. economy. Although the CBO director's words were grim, they were not alarmist.

A deficit occurs when expenditures exceed revenues. Deficits can be funded through prior savings, current borrowing, or inflating the money supply. Federal deficits have been funded by borrowing, resulting in federal debt. Each succeeding fiscal year of deficit and borrowing increases an entity's debt. Historically, the federal government has borrowed heavily to fund wars and then has paid off its debt. Beginning in the mid-1960s, the federal government started running deficits in most years. Since that period, the alarmist viewpoint has been relatively prominent in public discourse.

The alarmist viewpoint is intuitively appealing on first glance. For example, federal debt exceeded $10 trillion in September 2008, and federal deficits in recent years and in the foreseeable future were in the $200 to $400 billion range. Events in late 2008 and 2009 created even more impressive numbers: a federal debt of $11.5 trillion, steadily rising by June of 2009 with a current-year budget deficit expected in the range of $1.6 to $1.8 trillion and subsequent projected fiscal year deficits ranging from $300 billion to $1.2 trillion over the next decade (with the OMB predicting lesser figures and the CBO predicting higher ones). Some argue, however, that the proponents of the alarmist view fail to properly measure and assess the significance of federal deficits and debt. Just as the size of something appears to vary when viewed through a microscope as compared to a telescope, federal deficits and federal debt do not loom so large when adequately measured and assessed.

Nonalarmists argue that alarmists fail to appreciate that perspective matters. In the case of federal deficits and debt, the appropriate comparisons to put annual deficits and cumulative debt into perspective are the national economy and historically equivalent situations, not individuals or families who are unable to borrow billions of dollars annually and owe trillions of dollars. In both cases, the deficits and the debt are not as large as they have been in the past, based on their relationship to the national economy, share of current budgets, or constant (inflation-adjusted) dollars. Lenders' greatest concern in lending is repayment. Lenders charge the federal government less for loans than they do other borrowers partially because they trust that they will be paid back. Collective opinion on that question is that the federal government will continue to repay lenders as it always has.

Both annual deficits and cumulative debt can be measured and calculated in various ways. For example, calling all the obligations of the federal government "debt," including pensions, Social Security, and other future payments, increases "debt" figures. Conversely, reasonable adjustments of debt for price inflation and the existence of countervailing assets can radically reduce or eliminate annual deficits and cumulative debt; assets far exceed debt.

In *The Debt and the Deficit*, Robert Heilbroner and Peter Bernstein show calculations for the annual federal budget deficit in Fiscal Year 1988 that start at $255 billion and end up at $3 billion. Their initial figure of $255 billion (gross deficit) is the increase in federal debt from the beginning to the end of that fiscal year. They initially adjust the deficit downward (subtract) $93 billion for federal debt purchased during that fiscal year by federal agencies, producing a net deficit of $162 billion. They next adjust the deficit downward $53 billion for state and local government surpluses that were fueled by federal grants, producing a national deficit of $109 billion. They next adjust the deficit downward $66 billion for the reduction in the value of outstanding federal debt due to inflation, producing an inflation-adjusted deficit of $43 billion. They finally adjust the deficit downward using a conservative estimate of $40 billion in capital expenditures with federal funds to account for those expenditures the same way that they are accounted for by businesses, producing an operating deficit of $3 billion. The final deficit amount does not appear as threatening as $255 billion.

Similarly, the federal debt of $11.5 trillion and rising in the summer of 2009 is less intimidating when it is adjusted and compared. As E.J. Mishan notes in *21 Popular Economic Fallacies*, the public debt is not a public burden. Federal debt held by federal agencies in June 2009 equaled $4.4 trillion, which meant that approximately $7.2 trillion was publicly held. If the publicly held federal debt was sufficiently important, federal officials could reduce or even eliminate it by paying it off. If all federal debt was paid off, only the foreign-held part of it could be thought of as a burden, as the domestically held part would involve payments within the United States. In June 2009, publicly held U.S. government debt could be divided into two parts. The part held by foreign and international entities was approximately

$3.3 trillion. The part held by domestic parties was approximately $4.9 trillion. The foreign-held debt amount does not appear crushingly large when compared to the net worth (assets minus liabilities) of U.S. households and nonprofit organizations (approximately $50 trillion), the annual gross domestic product (approximately $14 trillion), or even the estimated Fiscal Year 2010 federal budget (approximately $3 trillion). Thus, nonalarmists argue that the U.S. economy continued to grow after many years of large federal deficits and increasing federal debt. The United States has had large budget deficits without economic collapse for more than thirty years.

Conclusion

Economics provides useful perspectives for understanding choices in public budgeting. The concept of opportunity cost means that a choice of one course of action forecloses or prevents people from taking other actions. The economic rationales for action by public organizations clarify public purposes, facilitate coping with those concerns, and assist in separating public and personal benefits. Market failures suggest action by public organizations, and government failures suggest cautious consideration of proposals for public action. The economists' list of three functions of government budgets provides a framework for analyzing how public sector organizations affect others. The consideration of the roles of public organizations in economic activities highlights what economic choices public organizations must make and some of their potential results. The discussion here of macroeconomic concerns explains the various rationales commonly used in the macroeconomic arena. However, no macroeconomic theory available at the present time has adequate political support or predictability in results to be a reliable basis for macroeconomic policy-making. Economic thinking also shows that the alarmist macroeconomic viewpoint is simply misinformed.

Additional Reading and Resources

Print

Modern public finance owes its current shape to Richard A. Musgrave. The first citation is to his initial article, the second is his comprehensive theoretical text, and the third is a simpler treatment of public finance:

Musgrave, Richard A. "The Voluntary Exchange Theory of Political Economy." *Quarterly Journal of Economics* 53 (February 1939): 213–237.

Musgrave, Richard A. *The Theory of Public Finance: A Study in Political Economy.* New York: McGraw-Hill, 1959.

Musgrave, Richard A., and Peggy B. Musgrave. *Public Finance in Theory and Practice.* New York: McGraw-Hill, 1973.

Contemporary texts in the area of public finance cover many issues discussed here and other issues:

Fisher, Ronald. *State and Local Public Finance.* 3rd ed. Cincinnati, OH: South-Western College Publishing, 2006.

Hyman, David N. *Public Finance: A Contemporary Application of Theory to Policy with Economic Applications.* 5th ed. Cincinnati, OH: South-Western College Publishing, 2004.

Rosen, Harvey. *Public Finance.* 8th ed. New York: McGraw Hill/Irwin, 2008.

Stiglitz, Joseph E. *Economics of the Public Sector.* 3rd ed. New York: W.W. Norton, 2000.

One can find Keynesian economics expressed in any introductory economics text that covers macroeconomics, or one can read the original text, which is generally considered difficult to follow:

Keynes, John Maynard. *The General Theory of Employment, Interest, and Money.* London: Macmillan, 1936.

A macroeconomics text comparing Keynesian and classical economics:

Abel, Andrew B., and Ben S. Bernanke. *Macroeconomics.* 2nd ed. Reading, MA: Addison-Wesley, 1995.

Contemporary accounts of the fragmented state of macroeconomics:

Snowden, Brian, and Howard R. Vane. *Conversations with Leading Economists: Interpreting Modern Macroeconomics.* Northampton, MA: Edward Elgar, 1999.

Snowden, Brian, Howard R. Vane, and Peter Wynarczyk. *A Modern Guide to Macroeconomics: An Introduction to Competing Schools of Thought.* Brookfield, VT: Edward Elgar, 1994.

Critiques of Keynesian economics:

Hazlitt, Henry, ed. *The Critics of Keynesian Economics.* 2nd ed. New Rochelle, NY: Arlington House, 1977.

Economists discuss federal debt and deficits:

Heilbroner, Robert, and Peter Bernstein. *The Debt and the Deficit.* New York: W.W. Norton & Company, 1989.

Discusses the fallacy of the public debt as a public burden:

Mishan, E.J. *21 Popular Economic Fallacies.* New York: Praeger, 1970.

Dicusses why individuals act collectively:
Olson, Mancur. *The Logic of Collective Action: Public Goods and the Theory of Groups.* Cambridge, MA: Harvard University Press, 1965.

Internet

National Bureau of Economic Research
The search facility at the National Bureau of Economic Research website can turn up any conceivable kind of economic research at www.nber.org.

Congressional Budget Office
Statement of Douglas W. Elmendorf, "The Long-Term Budget Outlook," before the Committee on the Budget of the United States Senate at www.cbo. gov/doc.cfm?index=9958. CBO regularly produces "The Long-Term Budget Outlook," which is available from its home page at www.cbo.gov.

Macroeconomic-related statistical sources:
U.S. Department of Commerce, Bureau of Economic Analysis
U.S. Department of Commerce, Bureau of Economic Analysis has a number of National Income and Accounts Tables, including Gross Domestic Product, Table 1.1.5, at http://.bea.gov/national/nipaweb/TableView.asp?SelectedTabl e=5&FirstYear=2008&LastYear=2009&Freq=Qtr.

U.S. Department of Treasury, Bureau of Public Debt
U.S. Department of Treasury, Bureau of Public Debt publishes "The Debt to the Penny and Who Holds It" at www.treasurydirect.gov/NP/ BPDLogin?application=np and provides links to other public debt reports at www.treasurydirect.gov/govt/reports/pd/pd.htm.

U.S. Department of Treasury, Financial Management Service
The U.S. Department of Treasury, Financial Management Service publishes a monthly "Treasury Bulletin" that contains Table OFS-2, "Ownership of Federal Securities, Estimated Ownership of U.S. Treasury Securities," which contains information on who owns federal debt, which is available at www. fms.treas.gov/bulletin.

Federal Reserve System
The Federal Reserve System publishes the "Flow of Funds Accounts of the United States (Z.1)," which includes the net worth of households and nonprofit organizations along with a wealth of monetary-related information at www.federalreserve.gov/releases/z1/Current.

Index

About the Authors

John W. Swain has taught budgeting and budgeting-related courses for more than twenty-five years and has written books, published articles, and led training seminars on budgeting and related topics. He is the author (with B.J. Reed) of *Public Finance Administration* (1997) and is a past winner of the American Political Science Association's Leonard D. White Award for the best doctoral dissertation in public administration.

B.J. Reed serves as dean of the College of Public Affairs at the University of Nebraska at Omaha. He has published in numerous journals, including *Public Administration Review*, *American Review of Public Administration*, *International Journal of Public Administration*, and *Public Budgeting and Finance*. He is also the author of several books on economic development, strategic planning, financial administration, and intergovernmental management.